1977—
sades,

American way of war /
27.99

NO LONGER THE PROPERTY OF
LONGMONT PUBLIC LIBRARY

HOW WE
FIGHT

Also by Dominic Tierney

FDR and the Spanish Civil War

Failing to Win (with Dominic Johnson)

HOW WE FIGHT

CRUSADES, QUAGMIRES, AND THE AMERICAN WAY OF WAR

DOMINIC TIERNEY

Little, Brown and Company
New York   Boston   London

LONGMONT PUBLIC LIBRARY
LONGMONT, COLORADO

Copyright © 2010 by Dominic Tierney

All rights reserved. Except as permitted under the U.S. Copyright Act of
1976, no part of this publication may be reproduced,
distributed, or transmitted in any form or by any means, or stored in a
database or retrieval system, without the prior written permission
of the publisher.

Little, Brown and Company
Hachette Book Group
237 Park Avenue, New York, NY 10017
www.hachettebookgroup.com

First Edition: November 2010

Little, Brown and Company is a division of Hachette Book Group, Inc.
The Little, Brown name and logo are trademarks
of Hachette Book Group, Inc.

Library of Congress Cataloging-in-Publication Data
Tierney, Dominic.
    How we fight : crusades, quagmires, and the American way of war /
Dominic Tierney. — 1st ed.
        p. cm.
    Includes bibliographical references.
    ISBN 978-0-316-04515-5
    1. United States — History, Military.   2. War — Public opinion.
3. Public opinion — United States.   4. National characteristics,
American.   I. Title.
    E181.T54 2010
    355.00973 — dc22   2010016859

10 9 8 7 6 5 4 3 2 1

RRD-IN

Printed in the United States of America

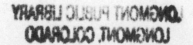

To Ben and Samantha, and to
Christian and Vuokko

CONTENTS

Can the U.S. use force—even go to war—for carefully defined national interests, or do we have to have a moral crusade or a galvanizing event like Pearl Harbor?

> Brent Scowcroft, National Security Advisor to President
> George H. W. Bush, December 1990[1]

I don't do quagmires.

> Donald Rumsfeld, July 2003[2]

HOW WE
FIGHT

CHAPTER I

Introduction

Unshakable resolve. The theme was a touchstone on the evening of September 11, 2001, as members of Congress gathered on the steps of the Capitol Building. The Republican Speaker of the House of Representatives, Dennis Hastert, announced that "Democrats and Republicans will stand shoulder to shoulder to fight this evil that's been perpetrated on this nation." The Democratic Senate majority leader, Tom Daschle, said that Congress "will speak with one voice to condemn these attacks, to comfort the victims and their families, to commit our full support to the effort to bring those responsible to justice."[1] A day that began in fear that the Capitol itself would be destroyed ended in a tableau of togetherness, as congressmen warmly embraced.

And then it started. A soft and calming sound at first: "Stand beside her and guide her." The television cameras pulled back, and the surprised anchors grew quiet. On the steps, the voices of men and women, blacks and whites, Democrats and Republicans, rose together in unison: "Through the night with a light from above." With fires still burning at the Pentagon just a few miles away, the song became huge: with pride, with tenacity, with sadness. "From the mountains, to the prairies, / To the oceans white with foam. / God bless America, / My home sweet home." It was a chorus that swept a nation, a truly *United* States of America, into a war to overthrow the Taliban regime in Afghanistan.

How things change. By 2010, many Americans saw the military campaign in Afghanistan as a futile endeavor. The layers of support for the war effort peeled away, one by one. Matthew Hoh, a State Department employee in Afghanistan, became the first senior official to resign in protest against the war. On September 10, 2009, he wrote that the families of Americans killed in action "must be reassured their dead have sacrificed for a purpose worthy of futures lost, love vanished, and promised dreams unkept. I have lost confidence such assurances can anymore be made."[2] Conservative commentator George Will argued that the United States must end its hopeless nation-building mission in Afghanistan "before more American valor...is squandered."[3]

In December 2009, President Barack Obama announced a new strategy in Afghanistan in a speech at West Point: "It's easy to forget that when this war began, we were united—bound together by the fresh memory of a horrific attack, and by the determination to defend our homeland and the values we hold dear. I refuse to accept the notion that we cannot summon that unity again."[4] Obama was right. Americans will summon that unity again—just not in regard to Afghanistan.

How had it come to this? Why did we shift from singing "God Bless America" to seeing America's blessed valor being squandered in a futile quagmire? Perhaps the mission in Afghanistan was simply a disastrous failure. But what if our experience of hope and disillusionment in the Afghan War reflected something deeper in the American mind and in American history? What if we are characteristically predisposed to revel in the overthrow of an evil regime and equally likely to see nation-building in Afghanistan as a grim and forbidding labor?

A Mirror on America

Sitting on the steps of the Lincoln Memorial in Washington, DC, and looking toward the Capitol, where members of Congress gathered that night to sing, we can see America's vision of how war is meant to be.

Behind us is a marble Abraham Lincoln, enthroned in his temple and flanked by the national hymns of the Gettysburg Address and his second inaugural address. Straight ahead lie the Reflecting Pool and the World War II Memorial. The shimmering water bridges America's two "good wars": the first to save the Union and free the slaves from 1861 to 1865, and the second to defeat fascism from 1941 to 1945. The fifty-six pillars and the giant arches of the World War II Memorial signify America's common purpose when the home front and the battle front united to crush evil. Anchoring the military vista, at the far end of the Mall, is a statue of Civil War general Ulysses S. Grant. On a platform of Vermont marble, Grant sits atop his horse, calm amid the fury of battle.

A triumphant tale unfolds before us, with World War II bookended by the Civil War titans, Lincoln and Grant. It's a panorama of glory and victory, a narrative of liberation through force of arms: freedom born; global freedom redeemed. This is what war ought to look like: decisive victory, regime change, and the transformation of the world—a magnificent crusade.

But if we broaden the view from the Lincoln Memorial, our peripheral vision reveals a less comfortable military narrative. Hidden away behind trees on the right-hand side is a memorial to the Korean War (1950–1953). This was no splendid crusade. There was no decisive victory. There was no regime change or transformation of the world. Instead, the United States fought its opponents to a draw. For Americans, it was a bleak ordeal and a profoundly confusing experience.

The raw immediacy of the Korean War Veterans Memorial is utterly different from the abstract triumphalism of the World War II Memorial. The depiction of the Korean War focuses on the human experience of battle. A group of nineteen men, cast in stainless steel, slog their way uphill, sorrowful and exhausted, burdened with baggage and shivering under ponchos from the elements. The bushes and granite strips signify the rough terrain and horrendous conditions. We asked these men to fight in this environment, and they did.

Meanwhile, concealed under trees to the left is a testament to America's tragedy in Vietnam from 1965 to 1973. This is what war ought *not* to look like. The United States spent years engaged in a futile nation-building effort in South Vietnam, trying to stabilize a weak government while battling a shadowy insurgency. With each step forward, Washington seemed to get further bogged down in the quagmire.

The Vietnam Veterans Memorial is a sunken black wall, inscribed with the names of the fallen. A knife cut into America's body exposes a dark wound. To read the names of the dead, you have to physically descend into the gloom. Facing the wall stand a group of U.S. soldiers, looking for something—perhaps their buddies, perhaps the meaning of this morass. The Vietnam Veterans Memorial does not commemorate the purpose of the war, but instead honors the sacrifice of the troops. There was no united home front to celebrate. In 1969, hundreds of thousands of demonstrators gathered on the Mall to protest against Vietnam in the largest antiwar rally in American history.

Hymns of Battle

For soldiers and civilians alike, war is often a traumatic experience. It is bound up with our very identity. As a result, war is a subject of overwhelming interest, which has prompted the spilling of almost as much ink as blood. How do we unlock the puzzle of American thinking about this most emotive and critical of subjects?

The key is to distinguish between two types of military conflict: *interstate war* (where we fight against other countries) versus *nation-building* (where we fight against insurgents). Inspired by idealism and vengeance, we view interstate wars like World War II as a glorious cause to overthrow tyrants. I call this the *crusade tradition*. These same cultural forces, however, mean that we see nation-building in places like Vietnam and Afghanistan as a wearying trial, in which American valor is squandered. Whether the stabilization operation is a success or a failure in reality, we usually perceive it as a grim labor. I call this the *quagmire tradition*.

In other words, Americans are addicted to regime change and allergic to nation-building. During the second presidential debate in 2000, George W. Bush said, "I don't think our troops ought to be used for what's called nation-building. I think our troops ought to be used to fight and win war. I think our troops ought to be used to help overthrow the dictator when it's in our best interests."[5] This sentiment is as American as apple pie.

The type of war that we are comfortable fighting is very narrow. The enemy must be a state and not an insurgency, and we need to march on the adversary's capital and topple the government. As soon as Washington deviates from this model, the glue binding together public support for the war effort starts to come unstuck. This insight explains why people back some conflicts but not others, how the United States fights, why Washington wins and loses, and how Americans remember and learn from war.

Many Americans view each conflict in history as a distinct and unique event, with no overarching sense of how these campaigns relate to our past and inform our future. But while America's wars don't repeat themselves, they do rhyme, producing a cadence in the nation's encounter with battle. Crusades like the Civil War, the world wars, and the Gulf War all follow a similar enthusiastic beat. Nation-building operations in Vietnam, Somalia, and Iraq hit the same weary notes.

If America's military experience is an epic song, each verse has a predictable rhythm. When the first shot is fired, the public rallies around the flag. Crusading enthusiasm sweeps the nation until the great dictator is overthrown. But once the United States begins nation-building in a conquered land, hope quickly turns to regret.

We saw this pattern play out in Iraq. In the spring of 2003, the public was confident and supportive as U.S. forces raced to Baghdad to eliminate Saddam Hussein's government. Then suddenly, the statue of Saddam fell, and Americans were in the midst of the greatest nation-building operation since Vietnam. As U.S. forces began fighting insurgents and overseeing elections, the entire tone of America's thinking about the war changed. By 2007, tens of thousands were protesting on the Mall against the intervention in Iraq.

This is a critical moment to reflect on the nation's experience of war. With fighting ongoing in Afghanistan and Iraq, Americans are trying to understand the new era of terrorism and counterinsurgency. The decisions that presidents make in the next few years may steer the course of U.S. foreign policy for generations.

The crusade and quagmire traditions have often served America well. The crusading instinct guided the United States to total victory in the colossal struggles of 1861 and 1941. Fears of a quagmire have sometimes deterred Americans from unwise interference in other countries' civil wars.

But the world is rapidly changing. The end of the Cold War and 9/11 caused sudden seismic shifts, while globalization produces constant dynamism. The primary threats we face arise not from great powers such as Nazi Germany or the Soviet Union, but from the interconnected issues of terrorism, rogue states, failed states, and weapons of mass destruction.

In this environment, we must pursue military campaigns that do not fall within our blinkered view of idealized war, but rather in our peripheral vision of uncomfortable conflict. Modern technology is so destructive that we may need to avoid crusades and fight limited interstate wars with restricted objectives that fall short of regime change. After all, we can't always march on the enemy's capital. And it's certain that the United States will have to engage in nation-building and counterinsurgency to stabilize failed and failing states. This is the face of modern war.

But limited interstate war and nation-building seem un-American and are politically very difficult. We prefer smashing dictators, not dealing with the messy consequences. In Iraq, we are paying a terrible price for these attitudes. The failure to plan for post-conflict reconstruction proved catastrophic as the country descended into a vortex of looting and violence.

Can we adapt to a changing world? For inspiration, Americans can look back through history. Our tendency to envision wars as either crusades or quagmires emerged at the time of the Civil War. Lost in popular memory is a very different military ethos that existed in the first years of the Republic.

The earliest Americans did not demand expansive crusades to crush enemy tyrants. Instead, they favored restricted campaigns against other countries. And the Founders also supported the military's involvement in nation-building, to develop the United States and open up the West to settlement. American soldiers dug canals and erected bridges. They built roads, dredged harbors, and explored and surveyed the land. They aided travelers heading west and offered relief to the destitute. The Founders created a multipurpose army designed for a wide range of challenges, and so should we.

This argument does not fit neatly into traditional categories. It's not liberal or conservative. It's not Democratic or Republican. It's not hawkish, dovish, neoconservative, or isolationist. Rather, at a time when we face new threats and are divided by extreme partisanship, we need to uncover the hidden assumptions that guide our thinking and generate a fresh perspective on the vital questions of war and peace.

Ways of War

When we refer to "Americans," we are describing a general tendency, not an absolute rule. The United States is an incredibly diverse society, which has changed in fundamental ways over time. In every conflict, there are exceptions to the crusade and quagmire traditions. During the Civil War, the northern Copperheads rejected a crusade to free the slaves and transform southern society. There have even been enthusiastic nation-builders in American history as well, like Adelbert Ames, governor of Mississippi, who fought for black rights during southern Reconstruction, and General David Petraeus, who helped to orchestrate a new counterinsurgency strategy in Iraq.

Given this variety of beliefs, can we talk about a single tradition in interstate wars (the crusade tradition) and another during nation-building missions (the quagmire tradition)? After all, Walter Russell Mead, in his excellent book *Special Providence,* identified four competing traditions that constantly push and pull American foreign policy in different directions: the Jeffersonian tradition, the Hamiltonian tradition, the Jacksonian tradition, and the Wilsonian tradition.[6] Similarly, in another superb work, Walter McDougall argued that there were actually eight traditions, running the gamut from exceptionalism to containment.[7]

There are benefits, however, in identifying a single dominant tradition in each type of military campaign. It means we can highlight what is most important. While Americans experience conflict in a multitude of ways, certain responses are more common than others. In every interstate war we have fought, there were people arguing for restraint and limited goals, but they were usually shouted down in the marketplace of ideas by a more numerous and vocal crusading block. And in every nation-building mission, there were true believers, but they grew increasingly lonely as the operation dragged on.

Identifying a prevailing tradition also makes prediction easier. It's hard to know which of McDougall's eight traditions or Mead's four traditions will emerge stronger at any one time. But the crusade and quagmire traditions offer a clear forecast about how Americans will respond to war, and the political pressures that will shape the decision-making environment for the president.[8]

This is an argument about America's "way of war," or our beliefs about military conflict, and how those beliefs shape policy. Russell Weigley popularized the term in his classic work *The American Way of War*.[9] Weigley argued that since the nineteenth century, the U.S. military has adopted a strategy of annihilation in wartime, aiming to win a crushing victory and completely overthrow the enemy. My claim that Americans favor transformational crusades in interstate war is broadly consistent with Weigley's thesis.

But whereas Weigley focused on attitudes in the military, strategic doctrine, and battlefield events, I take a very different approach by examining wider public beliefs and the cultural origins of our way of war. And whereas Americans confidently look to overthrow the adversary in interstate war, they rarely have the same enthusiasm when fighting insurgents.

In the following chapters, we will travel from Gettysburg to Manila Bay, from the bloody killing fields of France to the improvised explosive devices in Iraq today. But this book is not a comprehensive chronology of America's battles. Rather, it introduces the crusade and quagmire traditions, and then uses these sets of beliefs as tools to help us discover important patterns in the nation's experience of war. We will see the United States roused into a crusading fervor before falling into deep regret, only to be roused again. We will reflect on the ways that we remember war and how these memories take hold of us, how they awaken and limit our sense of the possible. Finally, we will turn to the founding generation and consider a very different vision of conflict.

The book draws on a wide range of literatures, on strategic culture, public opinion, psychology, idealism, and revenge. The sources include opinion polls, letters, poems, novels, memorials, newspapers, posters, photographs, songs, movies, *Star Trek*, and the engravings on Zippo lighters.

But it's not with a poll, or a letter, or a novel that we start. It's with a speech, the words of which are etched into the Lincoln Memorial where we sit.

CHAPTER 2

For Liberty and Vengeance: The Crusade Tradition

It began with a rhyme and a reference to history: "Fourscore and seven years ago." In a grave, repetitive cadence on November 19, 1863, Abraham Lincoln dedicated the cemetery at Gettysburg, Pennsylvania. At a time when speeches routinely ran for hours, Lincoln delivered just 272 words and retook his seat before many people realized he had finished speaking.

The Gettysburg Address symbolized the transformation of the American Civil War from a limited conflict for reunion into a great moral crusade for emancipation. With the Declaration of Independence, "our fathers brought forth on this continent a new nation, conceived in liberty, and dedicated to the proposition that all men are created equal." There would be no compromise peace with the South, and no return to the Union as it was, flawed by the original sin of human bondage: "This nation, under God, shall have a new birth of freedom."[1]

Lincoln's speech didn't just signal a radical shift in direction of the Civil War. It also set down a marker for an entirely new vision of war that would come to dominate the national consciousness:

the crusade tradition. Once battle commences, Americans believe that the United States should use all necessary force to attain majestic objectives, including regime change, thereby transforming the enemy in America's own image.

We are crusaders in only one kind of conflict: *interstate war*. This is a campaign in which U.S. ground forces fight against the official uniformed military of another country. There have been ten such conflicts since 1861: the American Civil War (1861–1865), the Spanish-American War (1898), World War I (1917–1918), World War II (1941–1945), the Korean War (1950–1953), the invasion of Grenada (1983), the invasion of Panama (1989), the Gulf War (1991), the first weeks of the Afghan War (2001), and the initial phase of the Iraq War (2003).[2]

On the eve of an interstate war, America doesn't usually resemble a nation of zealous crusaders. Quite the reverse: as conflict looms, the public is often deeply divided over the wisdom of fighting. But when the bugle sounds, Old Glory is unfurled, and the bullets start to fly, doubts suddenly vanish, as Americans don their crusading armor and favor this unique approach to war.

The crusade tradition has two elements. First, it captures American thinking about the proper *objectives* of war. In other words, what are we fighting for? The aim of interstate war is not to seize a few provinces, call it quits, and sign a peace treaty. Such limited wars, fought for modest goals short of regime change, are an alien concept to Americans. Like aristocracy or cricket, it's something Europeans do.

The fitting objectives of interstate war are different and altogether grander: to compel unconditional surrender, create a new democratic government, and transform the world. The pattern is striking. The U.S. public has supported the goal of regime change in every single interstate war since the Civil War.[3]

We often begin wars fighting defensively for the status quo, but soon a crusader wave swells up, and we end up battling for a new world order. Intoxicated by the whiff of grapeshot, doves sometimes turn into ardent hawks, pressing for expansive war aims with all the zeal of a convert. The conventional wisdom is that Americans are casualty phobic and seek to withdraw from battle at the sight of body bags.[4] But the death of U.S. troops in interstate war can strengthen the desire to fight for imposing objectives. An initial heady enthusiasm gives way to hardened political convictions and a steely determination to slug it out.

If the true objectives of interstate war are majestic, how are we to achieve these goals? The second element of the crusade tradition captures our preferences for the appropriate *strategies and tactics*. Put simply, Americans want to employ all necessary force to win. "If we are going to send even one more man to die," said John Wayne, "we ought to be in an all-out conflict."[5]

In peacetime, few countries have been as vocal as the United States in arguing for the need to protect civilians from the scourge of war. But once battle is joined, restraints on the use of force tend to fall away. More destructive weapons become acceptable. The list of legitimate targets is broadened. Noncombatants start to appear in the crosshairs. We prefer to use humane tactics as long as the enemy is not putting up much of a fight. But if resistance turns a campaign into a bloody slog, we will do whatever it takes to win.

German soldiers in World War II often executed civilians face-to-face. But U.S. troops tend to keep a healthy distance when killing noncombatants, whether they are destroying the crops of southern civilians in the Civil War but not sticking around to watch the subsequent deaths from malnutrition and disease, or obliterating German, Japanese, and North Korean cities from the heavens in World War II and the Korean War.

Despite such harsh wartime strategies, if the adversary surrenders and accepts its destiny of transformation, the United States is generous in victory, as, for example, with Germany and Japan after

World War II. These are not wars of annihilation. They are wars of Americanization.

Once peace breaks out, the crusader wave crashes, attention reverts to domestic affairs, and the public's interest in transforming the world abruptly washes away. Following years of intense preoccupation with brutal conflict, people try to blank out memories of the fighting entirely. Shortly after World War I ended, novelist Robert Herrick wrote, "It is as if the war had never been."[6]

Democracy in King Arthur's Court

Alexis de Tocqueville did not live to hear of Lincoln's Gettysburg Address, having passed away in 1859, on the eve of America's fratricidal slaughter. But the metamorphosis of the Civil War into a grand struggle might not have surprised the French writer and politician. Back in 1831, at the tender age of twenty-five, Tocqueville set out for the United States with his close friend Gustave de Beaumont. They brought with them a greatcoat, various hats, a leather trunk, two guns, an alarm clock, sketchbooks, and a flute—which they used to entertain their fellow passengers during the thirty-eight-day voyage across the Atlantic. After arriving in Newport, Rhode Island, the two men traveled more than seven thousand miles by horse, stagecoach, steamer, and canoe, from the cultivated East Coast cities to the wilderness of Michigan, meeting the sitting president (Andrew Jackson) and an ex-president (John Quincy Adams), all the while observing the progress of the young republic.

In his subsequent classic work, *Democracy in America,* Tocqueville predicted that Americans' usual love of peace could be transformed by conflict into a crusading zeal: "When war has lasted long enough finally to have wrenched every citizen from his peacetime activities...those very passions which made him attach so much value to peace will turn toward war." Military campaigning becomes "the great and only industry" as the country performs "marvelous feats."[7] It was hard to rouse the public to fight, but it was also challenging, once emotions were awakened, to get Americans to lay down the sword. "There are two things which will always be difficult for a democratic nation to do: beginning and ending a war."[8]

We can also illustrate the American way of war with a time-traveling munitions manufacturer from Hartford. In Mark Twain's 1889 novel, *A Connecticut Yankee in King Arthur's Court,* an American named Hank Morgan is transported to the age of Camelot in the sixth century AD. After various adventures, Morgan ends up battling an army of English knights. Naturally, he adopts a very American style of fighting.

For a start, the Connecticut Yankee isn't interested in a negotiated settlement—only in total victory. As he informs the knights, "We offer you this chance, and it is the last: throw down your arms; surrender unconditionally to the Republic."[9] Morgan aims to refashion medieval English society as a new America, with the introduction of telephones, newspapers, baseball, and even knights wearing soap advertisements. The Connecticut Yankee declares, "There is no longer a nobility, no longer a privileged class, no longer an Established Church; all men are become exactly equal; they are upon one common level, and religion is free."[10]

Despite being heavily outnumbered by the knights, Morgan employs his greater knowledge of science and technology to annihilate the adversary. In scenes of utter brutality, described by Twain with sardonic humor, Morgan retreats into one of Merlin's caves and surrounds his position with wire. When the knights climb through it, thousands of them are electrocuted. The rest are blown up with mines and mowed down with Gatling guns.

If this sounds vaguely familiar, swap Morgan for the U.S. military and replace the knights with the Japanese in World War II. In the 1945 Potsdam Declaration, the United States offered Tokyo a choice of destruction or unconditional surrender. When Japan refused these Morganite terms, large swaths of its military and civilian population suffered annihilation at the hands of American technological prowess.

Morgan's description of the aftermath of the war with the knights—"We could not count the dead, because they did not exist as individuals, but merely as homogeneous protoplasm, with alloys of iron and buttons"—sounds eerily like a reporter stalking through postapocalyptic Hiroshima or Nagasaki.[11] And just like medieval England, Japan was to be refashioned in America's image by promoting democracy, stock exchanges, and baseball. If Lincoln was a crusader president, then Tocqueville was a crusader prophet and Twain a crusader parodist.

The Exceptional Crusader

How unusual is this American vision of interstate war? Let's start with the targeting of civilians. Clearly, other nations have been far more murderous than the United States. Nazi Germany slaughtered close to ten million Soviet noncombatants during World War II. But since the nineteenth century, no country has engaged in the mass killing of civilians on as many separate occasions as the United States.[12]

Washington is also hardly unique in broadening its objectives in wartime. In World War I, for example, European leaders sometimes compensated for the horrifying slaughter in the trenches by offering their people more expansive visions of postwar gains. As the eternal sleepers mounted, so did the dreams.

But the belief that war should always end in a transformational outcome is extraordinary. When Americans think "interstate war," they think "unconditional surrender" and "regime change," but in modern history it's very unusual to insist that the enemy submit entirely to one's demands.

Consider the case of Britain. From the end of the 1500s through 1945, Britain twice battled alongside the United States, in World War I and World War II. Both of these allied campaigns ended in regime change. But during the same three and a half centuries, London fought more than a dozen wars without U.S. assistance, from the War of the Spanish Succession to the Crimean War. Not one of these conflicts resulted in unconditional surrender. Instead, Britain typically engaged in restricted campaigns, aiming to win colonial concessions in a negotiated peace.[13]

Or consider the example of China. In recent decades, China has fought a number of interstate wars for limited objectives, without much soul-searching. In 1962, China invaded disputed territory controlled by India, advanced a few dozen miles, gave India a bloody nose, and then withdrew. In 1979, China followed a similar model when it attacked Vietnam. Many Americans would find this type of military campaign hard to understand.

U.S. beliefs are also poles apart from those in Germany and Japan. These two countries have swung from one extreme to the other in the past eighty years, from the hyper-militarism of the 1930s to the pacifist trading paradises of today—the "axis of Eden." Germany remains uncertain about its past, espousing values of tolerance, not battlefield glory. In contrast to the festive World War II Memorial that recently opened on the Mall in Washington, DC, "the newest monuments in the German capital are dedicated to war's victims, not its heroes," historian James Sheehan writes.[14]

A similar situation exists in Japan. In World War II, more than two million Japanese soldiers died in a brutal campaign to build an East Asian empire. But since 1945, not a single Japanese soldier has died or killed an enemy combatant in wartime—or possibly even fired a shot in anger.[15] Both Germany and Japan remain nervous about using force, like two recovering alcoholics offered a glass of wine. There are few crusaders to be recruited in these lands.

Freeborn Sons of America

Why are we a crusader nation? Of course, American thinking in wartime often reflects the strategic environment and battlefield necessity. Military escalation can bring new goals into reach. Targeting civilians can weaken the enemy war machine. In conflicts like World War II, a clear and present danger may compel us to act in certain ways.

But our perceptions in wartime usually cannot be reduced to strategic logic. Americans favor the use of all necessary force to attain grand objectives, even in wars where U.S. national interests call for restraint. Revealingly, our allies often react to the same military situation with different preferences, suggesting that something unique to the United States is at work.[16]

To explain the crusade tradition, we must turn to U.S. culture and two powerful impulses lying in the American mind. The first is an idealistic sense of mission to spread our values. The second is a desire for retribution to punish evildoers. We fight for liberty and vengeance.

Idealism is the great bubbling torrent of American life, fed by the tributaries of liberalism and religion. Here liberalism doesn't mean we are left-wing; it means we believe in a set of principles rooted in the ideas of John Locke: democracy, limited government, republicanism, self-determination, the rule of law, equal opportunity, free enterprise, and free expression. From the earliest days of the colonists, material and social conditions in America favored the liberal creed, including the absence of a fixed aristocracy, plentiful land, and waves of new immigrants.

To be American is not to share a particular ethnicity, but to profess liberal ideas. The Declaration of Independence set out a promise of human rights and equality that many Americans assume is universally desired and that serves to unleash the potential of the human spirit. Contemplating war with Britain in 1812, Andrew Jackson proclaimed, "*Who are we? and for what are we going to fight? . . . We are the free born sons of america; the citizens of the only repub-lick now existing in the world; and the only people on Earth who possess rights, liberties, and property which [they] dare call their own.*"[17]

We like to think of ourselves as open-minded and eclectic, and in many ways we are. But not when it comes to the founding ideals of the nation. Indeed, Tocqueville wrote that he knew "of no country where there is generally less independence of thought and real freedom of debate than in America. . . . The majority has staked out a formidable fence around thought. Inside those limits a writer is free but woe betide him if he dares to stray beyond them."[18]

For sure, we argue, sometimes violently, over the meaning of liberal principles and how to promote them. And these tenets have been periodically challenged by other ideas, such as racism. But even here, over the long haul, the liberal creed has eroded support for slavery, segregation, and racial discrimination. Liberalism is stronger in the United States than in any other country, and remarkably few Americans question its basic assumptions. As Alexander Hamilton once noted, these principles are inscribed in the heavens by the hand of God.[19] We all agree that the celestial con-stellations should guide our national voyage, even while we vigor-ously debate the precise images formed by the stellar lights.

The Russians have lived through a dark history of tsarism and communism, in the shadow of Rasputin and the gulag. The Ger-mans have known kaisers and führers, blood and iron, Reichs and cattle cars. The French have enjoyed perhaps the most colorful expe-rience of all, witnessing governments of every ism and schism: Jaco-binism, Bonapartism, monarchism, socialism, arch-conservatism, and republicanism. But for two centuries in the United States, liberalism has been the only game in town. We were spared the foreign occupation or radical social revolution that might have challenged the liberal hegemony. As Louis Hartz wrote, "It is a remarkable force: this fixed, dogmatic liberalism....It is the secret root from which have sprung many of the most puzzling of American cultural phenomena."[20]

Are Americans truly ideological in the sense that the Soviet and Chinese Communists were ideological? Of course not— Americans are much *more* ideological. In other words, liberalism is more deeply rooted and more universally accepted in the United States than communism was in the Soviet Union or China. The leadership in Moscow and Beijing tried to impose a Communist ideology on top of a preexisting nationalist identity. During the 1980s and 1990s, it proved relatively easy for the Soviets and Chinese to discard communism and embrace the free market. But America's ideology *is* its identity and would be incredibly difficult to cast off.

Humor reveals a great deal about a country. In the USSR, jokes were one of the few ways to express one's true feelings about the Communist system—a tiny act of subversion and revolt. A popular joke went like this: How do we know that Adam and Eve are Russian? Because only Russians can run about naked, with merely an apple between them, lacking even a roof over their heads, and nevertheless claim to be in paradise. Such dark and ironic stories lampooned the absurdity of Communist ideology. But Americans rarely make jokes about the founding ideals of our nation. We take our liberal principles extremely seriously—so seriously, in fact, that many of us don't even realize we are ideologues. Perhaps Locke's greatest trick was to convince Americans that liberalism is not an ideology at all, but the natural order of things.

The second tributary of American idealism is religion. Reverend James Marcus King declared in 1898, "By historic origin and precedent, by principles of legislative action, by the character of our fundamental institutions, by judicial decisions and by the genius of our civilization, we are a Christian Nation."[21] An essential part of America's self-identity is the redeemer society, bestowed by a sacred covenant to save the world. This tradition reaches back to the early Puritans, who saw themselves as spiritual warriors in an ancient battle between good and evil (the saints and Satan), described in the apocalyptic prophecies of Saint John in the book of Revelation. The Puritans believed that they were the instruments of God—the elect—who had been blessed with an errand into the wilderness: to build the New Israel.[22] Since then, America's religious experience has been incredibly varied. The mainline Protestant churches have become inclusive, moderate, and unpopular. Their members are now safe, legal, and rare. Meanwhile, modern Evangelicalism has enjoyed explosive growth, extending its tent to cover around one-third of all Americans.

Religion plays a much greater role in the lives of Americans than in those of Europeans. (In this regard, Americans are closer to Latin Americans or Africans.) Indeed, according to one view, the United States "is the *only* religious rich nation in the world."[23] Tocqueville thought that one of the signs of conformist thinking in the United States—where "the majority has staked out a formidable fence around thought"—was the lack of any public discussion of atheism.[24] We live in a country where 48 percent of the public would not vote for a qualified nominee of *their own party* for president if that nominee also happened to be an atheist.[25]

The fusion of liberalism and religion—the secular and the sacred—has produced a potent idealistic cocktail. Indeed, as Tocqueville wrote, "Americans so completely identify the spirit of Christianity with freedom in their minds that it is almost impossible to get them to conceive the one without the other."[26]

How do we leap from idealism to a sense of mission in wartime? Of course, liberal principles and religious faith are sometimes used to oppose war and argue against escalation. In the Sermon on the Mount, Jesus told us to love our enemies, implying a presumption against war. But once we start fighting against another country, American idealism tends to ratchet up the military objectives by encouraging a missionary impulse to spread our values. To understand the temptation, open your wallet and take out a one-dollar bill. On one side, you'll find an image of the Great Seal of the United States. There's a pyramid, with the eye of providence watching approvingly over our endeavors, the date 1776 (in Roman numerals), and the phrase *novus ordo seclorum*. This doesn't mean "new secular age" or "new world order" (as is often believed), but "new order of the ages." It's a reference to the beginning of the American era and the inauguration of a global revolution against tyrants and monarchs.

The worldwide transformation would be a blessing for Americans and non-Americans alike. We often contend that the spread of liberal ideals, including democracy, will advance U.S. interests. While tyrants are unreliable and aggressive, democracies are trustworthy and don't go to war with each other. In the words of political scientist Tony Smith, "The most consistent tradition in American foreign policy... has been the belief that the nation's security is best protected by the expansion of democracy worldwide."[27]

The *novus ordo seclorum,* however, didn't require war. The United States could build the New Israel and act as a guiding star inspiring others to overthrow tyranny on their own. Indeed, in peacetime the public's desire to export American ideals is usually held in check. Americans consistently rank "promoting the spread of democracy" as one of the lowest foreign policy priorities, behind more immediate concerns like protecting jobs.[28]

The first bullet in wartime ignites a spark that lights America's missionary torch. The outbreak of battle simplifies the lines between good and evil and imbues Americans with a sense of faith in the potential of military power. What were just fantastical dreams in the recesses of the American mind are suddenly within reach. No longer will the United States extend its ideals simply by shining example. Now it can forcibly expand the domain of democracy and reform the international system so that war is renounced forever. The United States must pursue its purpose-driven life.

Many countries have seen themselves as a force for good in the world. A few states have even been ideological crusaders. During the revolutionary and Napoleonic wars, 1792–1815, France was committed to spreading its values at the point of the bayonet. The wartime policies of Nazi Germany from 1939 to 1945 also had an ideological tone—albeit one very different from that of the United States. But no people have been quite as consistently certain as the Americans about the unique mission they must perform. France's and Germany's ideological warfare was just a passing phase, while the United States has spent its entire adult life as a crusader.

The mystic chords of memory strengthen America's missionary impulse in wartime. Our national story is one of liberating foreign peoples, including both the oppressed and the oppressors. It's an epic saga in which two events stand out: the Civil War and World War II. In both conflicts, the United States employed all necessary force to spread its values and transform its enemies—a model for how crusading wars ought to be fought.

Most countries that have endured a civil war, such as Russia or Spain, remember it as unremittingly bleak. But for all the suffering involved, the American Civil War is imbued in our popular memory with glory and heroism—the great cause that freed the slaves and saved the Union.

Similarly, for Europeans, World War II was the most traumatic event on the continent since the Black Death, and they have tried to turn the page on this era ever since. But Americans don't want to turn the page on World War II. It's the first and most glorious chapter in the United States' rise to global leadership. Instead, we wonder whether we're living up to the standards of the greatest generation in protecting America and advancing its sacred values.[29]

How can such an idealistic society as the United States end up targeting civilians? When enemy resistance is light, our liberal and religious principles promote humane warfare and the avoidance of civilian casualties. But if wars turn into costly struggles, idealism can actually encourage us to kill noncombatants.

Protecting and advancing our sacred values justify almost any act. We should not shy away from a hard war when the prize is emancipation. Furthermore, the liberal creed of equal rights means that Americans rate the lives of their soldiers very highly, rather than seeing them as an expendable resource. Horrified by the losses of war and sensitive to public opinion, presidents can take the gloves off in a bid to win as quickly as possible. Qualms about targeting civilians melt away as we try to end the slaughter. The major barrier stopping the United States from destroying women and children in wartime is not our moral inhibitions, but the enemy's failure to offer sufficient resistance.[30]

American Wrath

The American crusader sows the seeds of liberty with one hand and carries an avenging sword in the other. Americans also fight zealously to punish those who violate our core values. Wrath is not something one talks about in polite company. After all, we usually associate morality with compassion, forgiveness, and humanitarianism. But the desire for vengeance based on moral outrage is a potent motivator for action.

When justice is the objective, material costs and benefits can go out the window. Consider that half of death penalty supporters in the United States would still back capital punishment even if it *increased* the murder rate.[31] Indeed, retribution can easily become all-consuming. The mountain of corpses at the end of *Hamlet* resembles a theatricide. In Euripides' ancient Greek play *Medea,* the title character even murders her own children to hurt her husband, Jason: "I love the pain, so thou shalt laugh no more."[32] The principle of "an eye for an eye" in the book of Exodus was designed to curb excessive retaliation: you are allowed to take *only* one eye for one eye.

The desire for revenge is heightened in men. In one study published in *Nature,* players competed in an economic game. Several of the players were secretly confederates, who were in on the experiment and deliberately behaved selfishly. Afterward, when female players watched the nefarious confederates receive electric shocks, MRI scans showed activity in parts of the brain associated with empathy. When men observed the scoundrels suffer, different parts of the brain lit up — those associated with reward.[33]

Why do people have this trait of wrath? It's probably rooted in human nature. The yearning for vengeance against moral transgressors may have evolved thousands of years ago, when people lived in small communities as hunter-gatherers. If there's no 911 to call, one of the most effective ways to deter attacks or theft is to threaten massive retaliation. And to make these threats credible, you have to punish even minor offenses. Therefore, the retributive instinct may have evolved as a means of deterring crime, encouraging cooperation, and allowing society to function smoothly.[34]

Aspects of American culture may reinforce the sense of wrath. Compared to other advanced democracies, Americans are unusually retributive — at least in terms of crime and punishment. The United States has the highest incarceration rate in the world. If its 2.3 million prisoners were gathered together as a state, it would have a larger population than New Mexico and would qualify for five votes in the Electoral College. The United States also employs the death penalty far more often than other advanced democracies.

In addition, Americans are tolerant of the use of extreme force to defend oneself and one's family and property.[35]

Why is this? First, Americans tend to believe that there are absolute guidelines for good and evil, while Europeans, Canadians, and Japanese are more likely to say that morality depends on circumstances.[36] Clear ethical standards mean clear violations of those standards, making vengeance easier to justify.

Second, Americans are more likely than Europeans or Asians to blame criminal behavior on an individual's character rather than the environment. The belief that each person has a lawful or unlawful disposition means that the social setting cannot "excuse" bad behavior and retribution is acceptable.[37]

Third, wrath may be stoked by certain strains of Protestant fundamentalism and Evangelicalism, which can espouse a black-and-white and punitive vision of the world. Americans, for example, are much more likely than the French or Germans to believe in the devil and hell.[38]

Fourth, scholars have pointed to a uniquely southern "culture of honor" to explain the retributive streak in American society. People in the South tend to favor the death penalty, approve of violence to protect property and lives, and support police who shoot to kill.[39]

The desire for revenge may be especially strong in international politics because we cannot call 911. One of the themes in *Medea* is that if you deny someone a legal avenue to gain justice, they will take matters into their own hands. In international politics, there is no sheriff; retribution is up to us.

Sometimes vengeance will be focused narrowly against a hostile tyrant. But if the adversary's behavior is deliberate and morally outrageous, the target of retribution can broaden to include the entire enemy military and civilian population, as with the Japanese in World War II.

Wrath further explains why we are so attracted to grand objectives in wartime. Regime change is a moral punishment against an evildoer. Retribution can also justify the death of civilians as collateral damage. After all, three-quarters of those who support the death penalty would still favor its use even if 1 percent of those sentenced to die were completely innocent.[40] We must pay any price for justice, and so must a demonized enemy, including its civilians.

Crusading Variations

America's crusading Bible is composed of Old Testament wrath and a New Testament mission to spread the good news. Both elements promote expansive war aims, such as unconditional surrender and regime change. A redemptive campaign will castigate transgressors and deliver a new birth of freedom. And as the fighting grows more costly, we naturally heighten the objectives. The payoff in the punishment of evildoers and the advancement of our ideals should be proportionate to the investment of blood and treasure.

The crusade tradition is a general tendency among Americans, not a universal impulse. In wartime, there is always variation in attitudes. At one end of the scale is the crusading vanguard, which is most committed to grand objectives and the use of all necessary force, and which typically includes whites, men, evangelical Protestants, and U.S.-born Americans. At the other end of the scale are the dissenters, who question the wisdom of fighting a crusade; this group often includes blacks, women, Catholics, and foreign-born Americans. There are no ironclad rules here, however, and the coalitions sometimes shift. Unsurprisingly, in the Civil War blacks were among the leading advocates of radical military objectives, including emancipation.

In wartime, most Americans don't make complex calculations based on abstract liberal and religious ideals. Instead, many Americans spend the war years focused on survival, either on the battlefield or on the home front. Radio technician Herbert Miner was on the *Indianapolis* when a Japanese submarine sank it in July 1945. Miner spent four days in the water and described his thinking during that time: "I could readily picture myself sitting out on the back porch drinking great quantities of ice-cold beer, and I vowed that I would live to realize my ambitions, earthly as they were."[41]

The crusade tradition remains a very powerful dynamic in American society. Usually, the president, influenced by a personal sense of idealism and wrath, buys into the tradition and supports all necessary force and escalating objectives. After all, the president is also an American. If the chief executive resists the crusade tradition and favors limited goals, he will face pressure from elites, media, or the mass public to ratchet up the war effort. In every interstate war since the Civil War, the crusaders were more prevalent and vocal than the dissenters. For even among the least-informed Americans, liberalism and religion lurk in the background, shaping perceptions. Terms such as "chosen people" are rarely heard anymore, but the sense of exceptionalism and the belief in individual rights are woven into our inherited customs and produce a reflexive crusading instinct in wartime.

The Wisdom of the Crusader

Does the crusade tradition have a positive or a negative effect? America's overall foreign policy record compares favorably with that of any other recent great power, like Britain, Germany, Japan, or the Soviet Union.[42] Looking at conflict specifically, we can note that the United States has never lost an interstate war. Not only that, but America ended many of its crusades, such as the two world wars, more powerful than when it began. It seems odd to criticize the traditions of a people with this kind of performance.

Idealism and wrath generate such fervor and commitment in wartime that the United States can unleash hell, compelling its enemies to submit to its will. In titanic struggles like the Civil War and World War II, the crusade tradition helped Americans keep their eyes on the prize of ultimate victory. In dealing with such extreme threats, a crusade is precisely what is needed. Only a decisive victory will permanently end the danger and create a just and lasting peace.

Meanwhile, idealism is the vitalizing source of much of what is most attractive about the United States, including its optimism and moral courage. The ideals we strive for in wartime, such as emancipation, often represent a profound good. The belief in spreading representative government helped synchronize U.S. goals with one of the great forces of the twentieth century: democratization.

Even vengeance may have some utility, by deterring transgressors. Which country would want to repeat Japan's experience in World War II? Resisting the United States can lead to the destruction of everything one is fighting for—as Robert E. Lee discovered. If retribution is proportionate, it can promote justice. After all, the murderous tyrant should not live a life of contentment.

But there is also a dark side to the crusade tradition. Our addiction to regime change represents a powerful escalatory force. Since the Civil War, all presidents have faced political challenges when waging limited interstate wars involving restricted objectives and a fine-tuned application of firepower. It's also difficult for any American leader to cut U.S. losses by scaling down the fighting in the middle of a war or by negotiating with an adversary. How can he make a deal with the devil?

Crusading campaigns can be highly destructive, risking exhaustion and military overstretch. Former State Department official George Kennan thought that the United States was like a "prehistoric monster," which was slow to be provoked but once aggravated "lays about him with such blind determination that he not only destroys his adversary but largely wrecks his native habitat."[43] And since U.S. objectives tend to grow more expansive during the fighting, the consequences of war are very hard to predict in advance. If a driver straps his foot to the accelerator, where will the car end up?

The desire to lash out and punish transgressors can be disastrous, provoking misdirected and costly conflicts that undermine U.S. interests. There is a reason, after all, why wrath is one of the seven deadly sins. Retribution isn't always as sweet as we hoped. As Charlotte Brontë wrote in *Jane Eyre,* "Something of vengeance I had tasted for the first time. An aromatic wine it seemed, on swallowing, warm and racy; its after-flavor, metallic and corroding, gave me a sensation as if I had been poisoned."[44]

We sometimes forget that military campaigns are not an end in themselves, but a means to an end: achieving specific political objectives. The primary purpose of war is not to punish evil, but to establish the conditions that will prevent future conflict. Extravagant war aims should be pursued only when they are strictly necessary.

The crusade tradition is imbued with moralism, but it can produce immoral outcomes. Just war theory stretches back to Plato and Saint Thomas Aquinas and tries to establish ground rules for an ethical conflict. Two of the key principles are that a war must have a *just cause* (to correct a grave evil) and that the use of force ought to be *proportionate* (minimal force should be employed, with care taken to avoid collateral damage, and the peace terms demanded of the adversary should be reasonable). But once Americans believe that a war has a just cause, they don't want minimal force and limited objectives—they want all necessary force and maximum war aims. The mission is not to restore the prewar status quo, but to change the world.

The crusade tradition is especially dangerous today. In an era of economic interdependence, daisy cutter bombs, and weaponized anthrax, war has never been more complex, unpredictable, and potentially destructive. The United States must be flexible about using force across the whole spectrum of military scenarios, sometimes aiming for limited objectives and other times for far-reaching goals.

We may need to moderate our beliefs about how wars should be fought and ended. A boxer who considers only a first-round knockout to be an acceptable victory will have a difficult and frustrating career in the ring—especially as conditions and opponents change over time. The same holds true for a country that sees the surrender ceremony in Tokyo Bay in 1945 not as a great exception, but as a model for how interstate war ought to conclude.

American society is not always a crusading society. There is another tradition that drives us. At times our confidence and zeal fade away, replaced by suspicion and regret. To illustrate this very different experience of war, let's turn to a mission that was *not* accomplished.

CHAPTER 3

Through a Glass, Darkly: The Quagmire Tradition

The great adventure in nation-building began under a Republican president. The torch of liberty was supposed to light
the darkness, spread the values of democracy and human
rights, and reveal a country made anew in America's own image.
But U.S. troops ended up warily policing a hostile population. In a
society awash with weapons, disaffected insurgents began a systematic campaign of terrorism. As hopes were dashed, the American will to continue the mission was steadily eroded. Within a few
years, the U.S. public, and especially Democrats, saw the mission as
a failure and supported a withdrawal of forces.

No, this is not Iraq. It was Reconstruction in the southern states
after the American Civil War ended in 1865. The parallels are no
coincidence. Reconstruction and Iraq are the first and the latest
examples of what I call the quagmire tradition—or Americans'
deep distaste for nation-building missions and our tendency to
judge them as failures.

The Skeptical American

There are two major uses of force involving U.S. ground troops. One is *interstate war,* where we fight against another country's military, which I discussed in chapter 2. The other is *nation-building,* or interventions within another country to create a stable and usually democratic government or to defeat insurgents. Interstate war is about destroying an enemy state. Nation-building is about constructing a friendly state.

What do Americans think about nation-building? Common images include sand trap, swamp, quicksand, morass, sinkhole, bottomless pit, or "the Big Muddy," Pete Seeger's allusion to Vietnam. These metaphors all suggest a messy operation in which the objectives are vague, withdrawal is difficult, and each stride forward only gets the United States further entrenched.

The most popular image is quagmire, meaning "land with a soft yielding surface."[1] In 1900, Mark Twain described the U.S. intervention in the Philippines as "a quagmire from which each fresh step renders the difficulty of extrication immensely greater."[2] In 1965, journalist David Halberstam published *The Making of a Quagmire,* depicting Vietnam as a swamp from which the United States could not free itself.[3] Three decades later, in 1993, the *New York Times* warned against sending U.S. ground troops to the Balkans, where they would face "a Bosnian quagmire."[4] Senator John McCain feared the repercussions of intervening in Haiti in 1994: "What happens to our credibility if we find ourselves in a quagmire?"[5] The Republican House Whip, Tom DeLay, had similar feelings about the deployment of U.S. troops to Kosovo in 1999, calling it "a big dangerous quagmire."[6] In 2004, former president Jimmy Carter criticized the situation in Iraq: "We've reached a point in Iraq that it's become a quagmire."[7] In January 2009, *New York Times* columnist Bob Herbert titled one of his pieces "The

Afghan Quagmire," depicting a war that "long ago turned into a quagmire."[8]

I call the American response to nation-building the quagmire tradition. Put simply, we just don't like it. Opinion polls consistently show that the public is much more comfortable with the idea of battling an enemy state than with using force to combat insurgents or build democracy inside another country.[9] The U.S. military also is traditionally skeptical about nation-building, viewing this activity as a distraction from its core task of fighting interstate wars. General Colin Powell commented in 1993, "We have a value system and a culture system within the armed forces of the United States. We have this mission: to fight and win the nation's wars. That's what we do.... We're warriors."[10]

When the United States undertakes nation-building, Americans almost always perceive the outcome as a failure. Since the nineteenth century, the United States has launched an incredibly diverse range of interventions in the former Confederacy, the Philippines, Mexico, Nicaragua, Russia, Germany, Japan, Italy, Austria, South Korea, Vietnam, Somalia, Bosnia, Kosovo, Afghanistan, and Iraq, along with multiple operations in Cuba, Panama, Haiti, the Dominican Republic, and Lebanon. These missions have covered everything from peacekeeping to imperialism, from counterinsurgency to humanitarian intervention. They have varied in every possible dimension: from climate and geographical location to the cost in dollars and lives, from the strategic aims to the duration.

But they have had one striking feature in common: remarkably, of all these nation-building operations, only those in the former World War II Axis countries have been consistently seen as a success. Most of the rest have been viewed as disastrous quagmires. Over time, perceptions of failure erode support for a mission, encourage withdrawal, and make us wary about future interventions. Indeed, the reason we dislike nation-building in principle is because we don't think it works.[11]

There is a cycle of American nation-building, with a series of distinct stages:

1. The United States emerges victorious in interstate war, begins reconstructing conquered territory, and, in a confident mood, looks for additional countries to stabilize.
2. Hope quickly fades into frustration and disappointment, and there is widespread relief when U.S. forces eventually withdraw.
3. We swear never to undertake nation-building again and often feel guilty about our actions.
4. Sooner or later, the United States wins on the battlefield, and we return to stage 1.

This cycle, with its brief moment of hope followed by disillusionment, has played out half a dozen times since the Civil War, from the regret over southern Reconstruction in the 1870s to the gloom about nation-building in Afghanistan and Iraq today.

Good Wars and Bad Wars

In the American mind, nation-building and interstate war are polar opposites. War against insurgents is hell; a campaign against another country is a hell of a war.

Interstate war is like a football match. The two sets of players line up in their respective jerseys. The front lines move forward and back based on each team's skill and strength. One side scores by making it to the end zone. The team with the most points wins. Interstate war, like football, is a great American pastime, as long as we play to win.

But nation-building is a different ball game altogether. This time, the opponents aren't wearing jerseys at all. They mingle with the crowd, and we can't tell a player from a spectator. We move the football and score a touchdown, but we don't get any points. Someone changed the rules.

Consider some of the striking differences in how we perceive and experience these two types of conflicts.

Interstate war is a "good war"; nation-building is a "bad war."

Interstate war unifies the public; nation-building divides public opinion.

Interstate war is usually seen as a victory; nation-building is usually seen as a defeat.

Interstate war inspires popular tunes like "The Battle Hymn of the Republic"; nation-building produces few if any stirring anthems.[12]

Interstate war unearths a legion of heroes, like Grant, Jackson, Pershing, MacArthur, Patton, and Schwarzkopf; nation-building generates almost no heroes.

In interstate war, when U.S. soldiers die, it's the price of victory; in nation-building, it means we're "knee deep in the Big Muddy."[13]

In interstate war, battlefield defeat can spur a redoubling of efforts; in nation-building, it produces calls for withdrawal.

In interstate war, when the enemy kills civilians, as the Nazis did, it proves the righteousness of our cause; in nation-building, if insurgents commit atrocities, as in Iraq, Washington is blamed and it signals that we're losing.

In interstate war, if U.S. soldiers kill noncombatants, it's collateral damage; in nation-building, it's a war crime, testifying to the immorality of the conflict.[14]

The Dash for Khartoum

Does everyone end up feeling blue about nation-building, or is this skepticism uniquely American? There are certainly plenty of examples of other countries growing weary of foreign interventions. The French public, for instance, became disillusioned with France's savage war of peace fighting against insurgents in Algeria in the 1950s.

But there are also some important national differences. For centuries, Europeans saw colonial nation-building as heroic and glorious. The British public devoured novels like G. A. Henty's *The Dash for Khartoum: A Tale of the Nile Expedition* (1891) and *With Clive in India, or The Beginnings of an Empire* (1884), while the graduates of Oxford and Cambridge flocked to become imperial administrators. But today's Ivy League graduates would rather head to Wall Street than run Afghanistan.

Europeans, Japanese, Australians, and Canadians remain more at ease with nation-building than Americans. In 2002, 72 percent of Europeans approved of using force to "help bring peace in a region where there is civil war," compared to only 48 percent of Americans.[15] In 2000–2001, about seven times as many troops from European Union countries were engaged in UN peacekeeping as were soldiers from the United States.[16]

Since World War II, many Europeans, Japanese, Australians, and Canadians have come to see their military not as warriors in the American sense, but rather as well-armed police, with a primary role of peacekeeping and humanitarian duties. Americans fear that if they nation-build too much, their soldiers will end up as social workers. By contrast, Germans don't want their troops doing anything but social work. In Afghanistan, German forces stick to reconstruction activities in the relatively tranquil north of the country, marching in the opposite direction of the sound of guns.

Similarly, the Japanese are comfortable using force outside their borders only if it's a peaceful nation-building mission. In the 1990s, three-quarters of the Japanese saw their peacekeeping operations in Cambodia and Mozambique as successful.[17]

In 1999, Australians enthusiastically supported the intervention to stabilize East Timor. At a time when Republicans in the U.S. Congress were harshly rebuking President Bill Clinton's nation-building missions in Haiti, Bosnia, and Kosovo, not a single politician in the Australian House of Representatives criticized the decision to send troops to East Timor.[18]

Canadians were asked in 1995 for their country's greatest contribution to the world. The top choice was, surprisingly, *not* hockey but peacekeeping (39 percent), followed by foreign aid (13 percent).[19] Is there a single American who would make the same selection? The Peacekeeping Monument in Ottawa, dedicated in 1992, celebrates the more than 110,000 Canadians who have served in peacekeeping operations. Needless to say, there is nothing like it in the United States.

Admittedly, there isn't much love among our allies for nation-building in Afghanistan. But then, of course, it was the United States that was attacked on 9/11, not Europe or Canada. How committed would Americans be to counterinsurgency efforts in Afghanistan if 9/11 had happened in Germany or Australia? Furthermore, although it's true that our allies become nervous when nation-building turns violent, they are at least comfortable with peaceful stabilization operations. Americans dislike nation-building across the board.

Meanwhile, developing countries often have a higher tolerance than the United States for casualties in peacekeeping missions. One reason is money: UN compensation for these operations (more than $1,000 a month per peacekeeper) provides a profit motive to stay the course. The deaths of eighteen American soldiers in the infamous "Black Hawk Down" battle in Somalia in 1993 led Washington to leave the country. But when Pakistan lost twenty-four soldiers in a single day in Somalia, it did not withdraw.

Myths and Realities

Why do U.S. nation-building missions end in tears? There's a very simple explanation for the quagmire tradition: these interventions are depressing because in reality they always fail. Washington certainly makes its share of nation-building mistakes. The U.S. military, for example, has traditionally resisted adapting itself to stabilization missions, preferring to plan for reruns of World War II. Incredibly, the 1976 army training manual didn't even mention counterinsurgency—even though the United States had just lost more than fifty thousand men battling insurgents for eight years in Vietnam.[20] As if saying the name of the guerrilla bogeyman might summon it again.

In nation-building missions, Washington has sometimes put too great an emphasis on firepower and destroying rebels, rather than on the key objective, which is providing security to the population and winning over insurgents. Partly because of these errors, there have been several debacles. Vietnam, of course, stands alone. But nation-building in Iraq has also proved to be very costly because of disastrous—and avoidable—mistakes made in the first months of the occupation.[21]

Washington, however, doesn't always fail. After the American Civil War ended, southern Reconstruction broke the chains of slavery and transformed the lives of blacks. Despite its many flaws, the U.S. occupation of the Philippines from 1898 to 1946 helped turn the archipelago into one of the freest, best educated, and most prosperous countries in Southeast Asia.

The missions in post–World War II Germany, Japan, Italy, Austria, and South Korea were notable successes. In 1958, U.S. troops averted a dangerous crisis in Lebanon. The intervention in Somalia in 1992–1994 saved 100,000 lives. The peacekeeping operations in Bosnia and Kosovo in the 1990s stabilized the war-torn Balkans. If

Iraq went to hell between 2003 and 2007, it also came back, partly as the result of a new counterinsurgency campaign orchestrated by General David Petraeus and Secretary of Defense Robert Gates.

Nation-building operations are not always costly. In Lebanon, there was only one battlefield fatality, and in six of these campaigns (Germany, Japan, Italy, Austria, Bosnia, and Kosovo), U.S. deaths were zero. In Somalia, there were forty-three American fatalities, or one for every 2,500 Somali lives saved. The eighteen Americans killed in Mogadishu in 1993 generated incredible press coverage and national soul-searching. But the same number of U.S. service members die through accidents and suicides every week, while producing almost no media and public attention.[22]

We often think of rebels as invincible—guerrillas in the mist, striking anywhere without warning—like Mao's famous image of the insurgent fish swimming in the sea of the broader population. But historically, most rebellions fail. Indeed, the militias in "ethnic conflicts" sometimes turn out to be composed largely of drunken and sadistic bullies who are quite capable of slaughtering unarmed civilians but run away when confronted with a show of force.[23]

Insurgencies can be quelled with tried-and-true strategies, including building up capable indigenous forces, gathering intelligence, upholding the rule of law, using minimal force, isolating the insurgents from the broader population, and co-opting more moderate rebel elements. The United States overcame a wave of Ku Klux Klan violence during southern Reconstruction and later defeated insurgents in the Philippines, Haiti, the Dominican Republic, and, *perhaps,* Iraq.

Good Guys and Bad Guys

Nation-building ends in tears, not because of consistent failure but because of our allergy to stabilization operations. But why is this?

And in particular, what happens to the crusader's zeal to fight for vengeance and liberty?

In interstate war, wrath motivates Americans to battle for grand objectives using all necessary force. We might expect exactly the same dynamic in nation-building operations. After all, insurgents sometimes commit terrible atrocities: killing our troops, defiling their corpses, and torturing and murdering civilians. As expected, soldiers on the front lines in counterinsurgency wars are often retributive. One U.S. private recalled that his unit went to the village of My Lai in Vietnam in 1968 "in a mood to get even."[24]

But for the American public back home, the urge to retaliate fades dramatically in nation-building missions. Wrath is spurred by a black-and-white, good-versus-evil view of a conflict. Interstate war provides exactly the kind of clear ethical lines that promote retribution. It's our country against their country, our military against their military, and our heroic leader against their diabolical tyrant. Now it's time for payback.

In nation-building, however, the ethical lines become blurred and confusing, taking the wind out of the retributive sails. Civil wars can seem to be driven by complex ancient hatreds with all groups guilty of atrocities. The population we are protecting may be ungrateful or actively hostile, making it difficult to perceive the campaign as morally black-and-white. The enemy may be hard to identify and track down. We end up asking a question that we never ponder in interstate war: who are the good guys and the bad guys?

The tempering of retribution in nation-building is probably a good thing. If the American people were driven to exact revenge against the Iraqi insurgents or the Iraqi people, this would only worsen the conflict. But the absence of wrath also helps to explain why our will to continue these missions is soon running on empty.

Alien to American Sentiment

What about the other source of crusading fuel—our sense of mission? The perception of interstate war as a quest to spread our liberal and religious ideals encourages Americans to broaden the military objectives and seek regime change. Imparting the blessings of liberty seems like a good idea when we're engaged in the *negative* part of the equation—removing a tyrant and the barriers that prevent freedom from flourishing. But once we knuckle down and start the *positive* work of reconstructing foreign societies— overseeing elections and policing ethnic conflicts—the mission becomes frustrating, and accomplishments seem elusive. Suddenly, our ideals may no longer motivate us. Instead, they can have the opposite effect, actually sapping our desire to continue. John Locke gets us in, and John Locke gets us out.

The objectives of nation-building are explicitly political: promoting democracy and stability. Here idealism encourages Americans to set a very high bar for success. Before handing out the laurels of victory, we want the target country to live up to our sacred principles of freedom, representative rule, and good government. Indeed, we're only certain that an intervention worked if the country ends up looking as stable and free as the United States.

Perceptions of success in nation-building may hinge, therefore, not on anything the United States does or fails to do, but on the condition of the target country before we arrive. Americans saw the interventions in Germany and Japan after World War II in a positive light because those countries soon resembled our prosperous democracy. But Germany and Japan were already advanced industrial societies before American troops appeared, and they had a relatively short distance to travel to look like the United States.

By contrast, impoverished societies like Somalia and Afghanistan, racked by war and ethnic divisions, have absolutely no chance of living up to our ideals or looking like America. Interventions in these countries, therefore, are virtually certain to be seen as quagmires. Once Washington owns a country like Afghanistan, with all of its problems, Americans are struck by the chasm that exists between the principles they hold dear and what they see in front of them: corruption, social division, and electoral fraud.

In other words, in interstate war, we *fight for our ideals*. The righteousness of the cause excuses a multitude of sins, such as killing civilians. But in nation-building, we are running the government, and now we have to *live up to our ideals*. Unsurprisingly, we usually fall short.

Idealism not only raises the bar for success; it also makes people expect too much too soon. Americans often assume that U.S.-style democracy is a universally desired form of government, held back by the obstruction of tyranny. Therefore, elections in the target country will be a panacea, unleashing freedom's fury, solving all major ills, and creating a mirror image of the United States.

But American liberal democracy is the result of a distinctive Anglo-American political tradition stretching back centuries. It's not a product that can be quickly exported like Iowa corn. The best the United States can do is to steer within the waters of the local culture — although this can still produce significant positive effects.

We set a high bar for success in nation-building and adopt unrealistic expectations in part because we have only a vague idea of what life is like in many other countries. Foreign films represent less than 1 percent of the U.S. movie market, and books and news from abroad have a similarly tough time reaching a wide American audience.[25] This lack of information may help to explain why the missionary impulse is attractive in the midst of interstate war, when democratization is an abstract idea, but it becomes wearisome when we're suddenly confronted by the complexities of spreading our ideals in an alien society we don't understand.

Since we know little about target countries like Haiti or Afghanistan, we look to elites to help us judge the results. U.S. leaders often encourage harsh evaluations of their own interventions through idealistic rhetoric and promises of rapid success. Presidents rarely diminish public expectations with realistic language or qualify their fellow citizens' belief in the universal attraction of American values. They talk of hope, dreams, freedom, and democracy, rather than blood, toil, tears, and sweat. The irony is that presidents use grandiose rhetoric to mobilize support because they realize Americans don't like nation-building. But this aversion is based on the belief that interventions fail, and exaggerated promises at the start of a mission only heighten later disillusionment.

How should we judge the success of nation-building? The issue is not whether U.S. ideals have been fully achieved, because this is often mission impossible. True success depends on whether there's been a reasonable degree of progress since U.S. forces arrived. And here we need to keep expectations firmly in check when considering failed states suffering from ethnic conflict, famine, or corruption. We should also consider the likely outcome if we had *not* acted. An intervention can have a positive effect if it significantly improves the lives of people in the target country, even if that country never comes close to resembling the United States.

The problem is that most of us can't remember what the condition of a country was before we arrived—for example, the Taliban era in Afghanistan. So we compare the situation today with a more immediate reference point: our idealistic assumptions about what a stable and democratic country ought to look like.

Americans also grow gloomy because nation-building seems to violate particular U.S. ideals. One of our most cherished principles is *anti-imperialism*, or the belief that colonial rule is incompatible with freedom, equality, and self-determination. Unlike Europeans, we have rarely taken pride in governing foreign territories. Our country, after all, was born as a result of a revolt against the

British Empire. President William McKinley thought that imperialism was "foreign to the temper and genius of this free and generous people," and therefore "alien to American sentiment, thought and purpose."[26]

In America's earliest nation-building missions in the former Confederacy and the Philippines, it was often conservatives who railed against the interventions as a dangerous form of imperialism. But over time, the critique of nation-building as empire became associated with the left. Howard Zinn and Noam Chomsky are the latest in a long line of leftists to view operations in places like Vietnam, Kosovo, and Iraq as sinister attempts to exploit and dominate, orchestrated by corporate interests.[27]

Most U.S. nation-building missions, however, bear little resemblance to classic European imperialism, in the sense of permanent colonial rule of territory. U.S. interventions usually aim to promote self-determination by facilitating elections. They have increasingly been multilateral, with UN approval and troop contributions from allies. And far from wanting to annex territory, the United States is typically eager to leave as quickly as possible.

Nation-building, therefore, cannot count on a friendly audience on the left. But neither can it rely on the backing of the political right. Interventions can breach a second ideal cherished by Americans in general and conservatives in particular—*limited government*. Our liberal ideals promote the belief that people should make their own way in life, free from state meddling. Nation-building can look like a conservative nightmare. We use big government to shape foreign societies, with wasteful expenditures, massive social engineering, and welfarism. Our fearsome warriors spend their time giving handouts to foreigners.

Consider that Americans often viscerally dislike foreign aid and see it as a complete waste of money. People vastly exaggerate the cost of development assistance, believing that we spend 15 to 20 percent of the federal budget on foreign aid, compared to the real figure, which is less than 1 percent. Studies show that even when Americans are told the truth, they still want to slash these payments.[28]

Defense Secretary Donald Rumsfeld argued in a February 2003 speech titled "Beyond Nation Building" that the United States should avoid lengthy operations like those in the Balkans. Such missions created a dangerous "culture of dependence," which made it difficult for Kosovo Albanians to stand on their own two feet.[29] He could have been talking about welfare mothers.

If the left's depiction of nation-building as imperialism is often inaccurate, the right's critique of nation-building as welfare is also misplaced. Where there are systematic barriers against democracy or economic opportunity, such as endemic corruption or ethnic strife, free markets will not function effectively, and people cannot simply stand on their own two feet.

Nation-building suffers from a pincer movement by both liberals and conservatives. If the United States is too self-interested, it's accused of imperialism. If Washington's too altruistic, it's blamed for turning foreign policy into social work. Indeed, left-wing and right-wing critics can end up sounding quite similar: local people should determine their own fate, free from big empire or big government. What chance does a mission like Kosovo have when Noam Chomsky and Donald Rumsfeld team up to attack it?

In interstate war, our national story—especially the Civil War and World War II—reinforces the idea that we should fight for grand objectives using all necessary force. But in nation-building, America's historical memory further encourages gloom and doom. Each nation-building "debacle," real or imagined, strengthens the notion that we always fail at this line of work. For instance, the shadow of Vietnam fell like a shroud over later interventions, from Somalia to Afghanistan.

In other countries, these ideals and memories don't have the same effect. It's hard to see nation-building by the Australians,

Canadians, Japanese, and Europeans as imperialism, given how weak they are. In any case, talk of empire may prompt Europeans to recall the glory days, rather than engage in self-criticism. As welfare societies, these countries are also less sensitive to the idea of big government nation-building: war is welfarism by other means. And having avoided any recent Vietnam-style conflict, the Canadians, Japanese, and Europeans are unlikely to see the Vietcong hiding in places such as Bosnia.

Meanwhile, idealism isn't a problem when developing states engage in peacekeeping missions. Pakistan doesn't expect its troops suddenly to transform the target society into a Western-style democracy. Neither are Pakistanis agonized if the situation on the ground fails to live up to John Locke's sacred principles.[30]

The Nation-Builders

The quagmire tradition is a general tendency, not an ironclad law. In every nation-building mission, there are Americans who remain optimistic and supportive. Men like Adelbert Ames, governor of Mississippi, championed efforts to build a multiracial democracy in the South after the Civil War. More recently, officials such as General David Petraeus have encouraged a shift in the U.S. military toward prioritizing counterinsurgency. The 2007 *U.S. Army / Marine Corps Counterinsurgency Field Manual*, written in part by Petraeus, states that U.S. soldiers are now expected to be "nation builders as well as warriors."[31]

The quagmire tradition is like a magnet drawing Americans toward a gloomy appraisal, but other forces can oppose or facilitate the pull. In the case of Afghanistan, for instance, the close connection to 9/11 meant that Americans initially resisted seeing the mission as a failure.

But while the quagmire tradition can be challenged, it can

rarely be denied. The president may personally conclude that a mission is a quagmire and favor withdrawal. Alternatively, the president may remain a true believer, but elite, media, and public criticism will limit his or her room to maneuver and create growing pressure for a pullout. In the 1870s, Adelbert Ames was overthrown in Mississippi as Washington renounced nation-building in the South. Public confidence about the mission in Afghanistan held up for a while against the backdrop of 9/11, but optimism is now eroding. In recent years, Petraeus and others have tried to reorient the military toward post-conflict stabilization, but they have had their work cut out for them, because broader American society has long seen U.S. soldiers as warriors, not nation-builders.

A Healthy Skepticism?

Is the American aversion to nation-building healthy? Skepticism could, after all, reflect a wise and prudent approach to the use of force. Stabilization missions can prove to be incredibly expensive (the Iraq War alone will cost upward of a trillion dollars), and they risk overstretch for the U.S. military. For all of America's good intentions, nation-building can provoke a nationalistic response by the target population against the foreign invader. What seem to be universal values to us may look like imperialism to others. How would we feel if foreign peacekeepers who didn't speak our language began reconstructing our society?

But the quagmire tradition can be extremely dangerous for U.S. interests. At best, it leaves Americans blind to the positive impact that nation-building can have. At worst, it's a kind of self-fulfilling prophecy, where the public and elites become skeptical about the progress of an intervention and less enthusiastic about investing the resources necessary to win. In interstate war, we have, if anything, too much appetite for battle. But in nation-building, we have no stomach for the fight.

In stabilization missions, a significant and long-term commitment of troops and money usually promotes positive results. James Dobbins and colleagues found that the more U.S. soldiers there are on the ground, the fewer casualties there are, with undermanned operations being most at risk of attack. Furthermore, a minimum of five years is required to produce an enduring democratic transition: "While staying long does not guarantee success, leaving early ensures failure."[32]

But our allergy to nation-building makes it difficult for Washington to display the necessary resolve. Back in the 1870s, for example, the false belief that Reconstruction was a grievous debacle led to the end of nation-building, decades of apartheid in the South, and very real failure. A century later, the mission in Somalia saved tens of thousands of lives, but perceptions of failure prompted President Clinton to withdraw U.S. forces, undermining the gains from the operation. After we left, the country became a base for Islamic extremists and pirates.

The quagmire tradition gifts our enemies with a playbook for defeating the United States. It's the modern-day equivalent of discovering in a clover field, as one Union soldier did in 1862, an envelope containing three cigars and Robert E. Lee's strategic plans, which helped northern forces blunt the Confederate assault at Antietam.

Since we judge success based on American ideals, almost any violence on the ground automatically signifies failure for the United States. This makes the insurgents' task quite easy: all they need to do is create mayhem. If the rebels can kill a few American soldiers, this can be especially effective in undermining public support. The Somali warlord Mohamed Aideed told U.S. special envoy to Somalia Robert Oakley, "We have studied Vietnam and Lebanon and know how to get rid of Americans, by killing them so that public opinion will put an end to things."[33]

The quagmire tradition also skews our memory of the past, so that we learn the wrong lessons. When the United States was perceived as having failed in Somalia in 1993, Washington was reluctant to repeat this supposed error by intervening the following year to stop the genocide in Rwanda, where close to a million people were slaughtered.[34]

The quagmire tradition is a problem for Democrats and Republicans, liberals and conservatives. Americans are skeptical about missions that liberals champion, like the protection of civil rights during southern Reconstruction and the humanitarian intervention in Somalia. But Americans also grow weary of operations that conservatives promote, such as fighting communism in Vietnam and terrorism in Iraq. The gloom is equal opportunity.

All of this leaves the United States ill equipped to deal with the future of war. The Department of Defense's 2006 *Quadrennial Defense Review* claims that "irregular warfare has emerged as the dominant form of warfare confronting the United States."[35] We live in an era in which the primary security challenges arise from rogue states, failed states, terrorism, and drug trafficking. These challenges will undoubtedly lead the United States down the path of nation-building. Otherwise, we may remove a threat, whether it is Al Qaeda in Afghanistan or ethnic fighting in the Balkans — only to see it reemerge. After all, we can't just plant the flag, declare victory, and walk away from the ruins.

Yin and Yang

The crusade and quagmire traditions are two threads woven together in the American way of war. No other country has the same combination of zeal for majestic aims in interstate war and disdain for nation-building. How, then, do the traditions fit together?

The most striking observation is how different they are. For every American who has died while nation-building, more than one hundred Americans have been killed in interstate war.[36] Yet we spurn relatively peaceful stabilization missions and glory in bloody campaigns against other countries.

Indeed, there is an almost schizophrenic contrast between the confidence of the crusade and the gloom of the quagmire. Interstate war is like rolling a boulder downhill, with the stone gaining momentum and threatening to lurch out of control. Nation-building is more like pushing a boulder uphill: a wearying Sisyphean labor.

But the traditions also reinforce each other, because the zeal for regime change leads the United States into nation-building. Under the so-called Pottery Barn rule of "You break it, you own it," the United States has little choice but to stabilize the lands it conquers.[37] This helps to explain why Americans keep engaging in an activity they so deeply dislike. Indeed, interstate war can make nation-builders out of the most unlikely of presidents. Franklin Roosevelt and George W. Bush both came to power eschewing nation-building, but both ended their time in office with grand visions of remolding foreign societies, in the former Axis states and in Afghanistan and Iraq, respectively.

Of course, our support for regime change and our distaste for stability operations make for a combination of attitudes uniquely designed to breed frustration. We like breaking it; we don't like owning it.

The story of how we fight begins not with the American Revolution, but with the Civil War, the first of America's crusades. In each of the next six chapters, we contrast a glorious interstate war with a wearying nation-building mission, seeing crusade followed by quagmire followed by crusade: the Civil War and Reconstruction; the Spanish-American War and colonialism in the Philippines;

World War I and interventions in Latin America; World War II and Vietnam; the Gulf War and Somalia; and the overthrow of the Afghan and Iraqi regimes and efforts to stabilize both countries. In the final chapter, we turn to the era before the Civil War and explore the Founding Fathers' very different image of war, as an inspiration to rethink the crusade and quagmire traditions.

As we begin the tale of America's experience of war in a southern prison in 1863, the crusading spirit is high, and the woes of nation-building are still years in the future.

CHAPTER 4

Birth of a Nation

In 1863, in Libby Prison in Richmond, Virginia, Confederate jailers delivered terrible news to the Union prisoners of war: the North had been crushed at the battle of Gettysburg. The prisoners grew despondent, until a black servant brought them food, and told them the truth about the outcome. An Ohio chaplain began to sing, "Mine eyes have seen the glory of the coming of the Lord," and soon all the prisoners joined in.[1]

The song was "The Battle Hymn of the Republic," written by Julia Ward Howe in November 1861. After visiting troops near Washington, DC, Howe composed the lyrics in the gray light of morning. The words just appeared to her, and she scribbled them down with "an old stump of a pen" while barely looking at the paper. The *Atlantic Monthly* paid Howe five dollars for what Mark Twain later called "the most beautiful and the most sublime battle hymn the world has ever known."[2]

Howe's words are a righteous warrior's cry. The "terrible swift sword" of the Union cause was God's cause and the fulfillment of the apocalyptic prophecies of Revelation, where evil is destroyed by wrath. Emancipation was Christ's work: "As he died to make men holy, let us die to make men free."[3] The song became an anthem of the northern cause, reprinted a million times and sung on a thousand marches.

Its success attests to the transformation of the Civil War into a great crusade from 1861 to 1865. Over time, the Union war aim became the utter conquest of the Confederacy and the destruction of its social system, based on slavery. Meanwhile, in the South, only total independence was acceptable. "God knows how reluctantly we accepted the issue," wrote Union general William T. Sherman in 1864, but "the Northern Races though slow to anger, once aroused are more terrible than the more inflammable of the South."[4]

It was right here, amid the minié balls, bayonets, and stockades of the Civil War, that the crusade tradition was born: the preference in interstate war for using all necessary force to achieve grand objectives and recast the enemy's society along American lines. Although northerners would have balked at the label, the Civil War was a de facto interstate war. In other words, the Union was effectively fighting against another state—one that created its own constitution, raised armies, issued currency, and was underpinned by a sense of nationalism.[5] "The Battle Hymn of the Republic" would endure as America's crusading anthem long after the guns fell silent in 1865.

Rally 'Round the Flag, Boys

By the 1850s, the northern free states and the southern slave states were like two great tectonic plates buckling against each other. One of the central causes of the fissure was slavery and whether this peculiar institution would be allowed to expand into the western territories. Sometimes there was surface calm, even as the tectonic plates grated below. But the convulsions grew steadily louder and more frequent. A virtual civil war broke out in Kansas between proslavery and antislavery factions. In 1857, the Supreme Court issued its notorious decision in the *Dred Scott* case, ruling that slavery must be allowed in the territories. A new northern antislavery party called the Republicans emerged. Finally, after President Abraham Lincoln's election on the Republican ticket in 1860, passion strained the bonds of affection beyond repair, and seven southern states seceded from the Union (soon joined by four more). The great pressure was suddenly released, and the country was torn apart by an unprecedented and cataclysmic force.

In the run-up to the Civil War, northerners who championed a violent struggle to free the slaves were considered lunatics and terrorists. Lincoln detested slavery, but when he ran for president, destroying the institution seemed like an impossible dream. Slavery was no growth that could be cut out of the nation's body with a few sweeps of the legislative knife. It was a cancer that had invaded America's most vital organs, forming the basis of the southern economy and society. How could it possibly be excised without the patient's death? Lincoln's goal in 1860 was containment: preventing slavery's advancement, while leaving the abolitionist cure for future generations.

After the Confederacy was formed, Lincoln still hoped that peace would prevail. Secession, he thought, was just a bluff. The silent majority of southern Unionists would soon restrain the gang of radical hotheads. Some in the North were even willing to accept southern independence. In the spring of 1861, religious publications like the *Independent* held a consistent line: "Let them go!"[6] As long as the guns were silent, so was the crusader's trumpet.

The whistling train of the first southern shell fired on Fort Sumter, South Carolina, on April 12, 1861, was a shot heard throughout the North. People were immediately overpowered by feelings of patriotism and righteousness. The drug of war was wonderful, arousing a kind of intoxicating madness. Ralph Waldo Emerson had devoted his life to philosophy, poetry, and a "religion of peace." But in the face of "a sentiment mightier than logic, wide as light, strong as gravity," Emerson committed himself to the struggle and took up the religion of war.[7]

Americans rallied around the flag—literally. For the first time in history, Old Glory flew freely from churches, homes, and storefronts. Lincoln's secretary, John Hay, noted how everyone followed the same beat: "The coldest conservatives sprang forward to the front and the wildest radicals kept time with the new music."[8] Lincoln's call for 75,000 militiamen was met with enthusiastic support, and 640,000 men volunteered by the end of the year. States competed to send the most soldiers, in the quickest time, to Washington. Ohio's governor was asked to provide thirteen regiments—he begged to dispatch twenty.[9]

But what was the objective? Lincoln initially outlined limited war aims: to restore federal authority and suppress the rebellion, while avoiding what he called a "remorseless revolutionary struggle."[10] As the fighting progressed, however, northern opinion shifted in favor of a zealous campaign to refashion the Confederacy by emancipating the slaves. The crusader wave rose in fits and starts, and there were times when the desire to transform the South seemed to recede. But Confederate resistance and Union loss produced a progressively sharper vision of the war.

In 1861, the commander of U.S. forces, Winfield Scott, proposed that the North slowly strangle the Confederacy with a naval blockade, while building up large Union armies, which would steadily advance into the South in the so-called Anaconda Plan. But rather than constrict southern air passages, northerners wanted to go for the jugular. The cry rang out, "To Richmond!" and a Union army hastily marched south into Virginia to confront the Confederates near a river called Bull Run.

The Union commander at the battle was Irvin McDowell, a man who drank no alcohol but ate voraciously. His Confederate counterpart was P. G. T. Beauregard, a romantic and dashing figure of French Louisiana heritage who was often compared to Napoleon. The generals led troops dressed in widely varying uniforms of blue, gray, and bright red.

But the soldiers were green almost to a man. The raw recruits who lined up on that hot July day found the fog of war to be doubly impenetrable. Plans went awry and confusion reigned as the two armies blundered around the battlefield. Soldiers left the lines to rest and find food, blocked each other's advance, and mistook friends for enemies and enemies for friends.

Dozens of Washington notables traveled to witness the battle. Some were voyeurs, observing the carnage while enjoying picnic lunches. Most had a reason to be there. One abolitionist congressman from Illinois came just to watch but succumbed to war fever, grabbed a gun, and joined the fray. Another man had two sons in the Union army. One of the boys broke from the battle to have lunch with his father, then was killed shortly after reentering the fight.[11]

William T. Sherman was at Bull Run, as were James Longstreet and a man named Thomas Jackson. Most people never find out if great events would stir unknown depths in their character. But Jackson, formerly an uninspiring teacher, discovered hidden talents in the crucible of war. When southern troops held their ground under northern assault, a general reportedly said that Jackson was "standing like a stone wall." There are doubts about whether the line was intended as praise or criticism, but the legend of "Stonewall" Jackson was born. Confederate reinforcements arrived on the scene, and southern troops counterattacked with the rebel yell. The Union army fled back toward Washington, accompanied by the city's elite, escaping in their carriages.

By later standards, the slaughter was light. Around eight hundred men were killed—just a taste of death, a flavor of the ten thousand battles and skirmishes to come. But the loss at Bull Run was a shocking result for northerners, who expected the war to be over by the time the leaves turned brown. Walt Whitman described "a horrible march of twenty miles" before the Union troops returned to the capital "baffled, humiliated, panic-struck. Where are the vaunts, and the proud boasts with which you went forth?... Well, there isn't a band playing—and there isn't a flag but clings ashamed and lank to its staff. The sun rises, but shines not."[12]

In his poem "The March into Virginia," Herman Melville wrote, "All wars are boyish, and are fought by boys, / The champions and enthusiasts of the state." The Union soldiers "gaily go to fight, / Chatting left and laughing right," but finally "perish, enlightened by the volleyed glare."[13]

The bloodshed at Bull Run and elsewhere forged northern opinion into a tougher and more resilient product. The initial heady enthusiasm was commuted into a grim commitment to slug it out and a desire to escalate both objectives and tactics. Historian James McPherson examined the letters and diaries of hundreds of Union soldiers and found that during the first eighteen months of fighting, almost three soldiers in ten saw emancipation as a central goal of the war.[14] But as a member of the Third Wisconsin remarked, "The rebellion is abolitionizing the whole army."[15] A soldier from Illinois concluded, "There is a mighty revolution a going on in the minds of men on the niger [sic] question."[16] In 1863, a poll of the fairly representative Fifteen Iowa regiment found that half the men supported emancipation, a quarter were opposed, and a quarter had no opinion.[17] Joseph Allan Frank and Barbara Duteau studied eight hundred soldiers in the Wisconsin militia and discovered that by 1863, the men wanted to crush the South's ability to resist by freeing the slaves.[18]

Millions of Americans dissented from the great crusade. Some had more prosaic concerns than transforming the South. One Union soldier found out that his wife had been seen with another man and wrote her a curt letter: "I was glad to hear from you and that you were pretty well but I suppose that beau of yours that you picked up on the picnic fanned you so much that you caught cold....He better look out I know how to shoot."[19] Others grew weary of the endless fighting. The 161,000 men who failed to report when drafted were not committed crusaders. Neither were the estimated 280,000 Union soldiers who deserted—at rates that increased in the second half of the Civil War.[20]

Northern "Peace Democrats"—Copperheads to their ene-mies—resisted emancipation and sought an immediate end to the war. The Illinois legislature railed against the conversion of the struggle into a "crusade for the sudden, unconditional and violent liberation of 3,000,000...slaves"—and this, of course, was Lincoln's home state.[21] Opposition to emancipation, the enlistment of blacks into the Union army, and the draft sometimes turned violent. Resentment against the "nigger war" sparked an orgy of bloodshed in New York City in July 1863 and a pogrom against blacks.

If the Copperheads were at one end of the spectrum, the cru-sading vanguard was at the other. These were the true believers, including among their ranks prewar abolitionists, intellectuals, African Americans, native-born Americans, professionals, skilled workers, and much of the Protestant clergy, especially Methodists. The vanguard was the first to see the war as a noble cause and slavery as the enemy. It had its own institution, the Republican Party, to champion a more energetic war effort, emancipation, and the enlistment of black troops—whose heroism under fire would challenge northern racist assumptions and bring blacks into focus as *men*.

The vanguard played a critical role in the Union army. In the Wisconsin militia, about 17 percent of the troops were highly articulate and politically motivated. One of these soldiers, a gun-ner, wrote in 1863, "By the success of our arms, slavery is doomed. Out of this dreadful war our nation will come cleansed and puri-fied, with not a slave in the land."[22] This core group encouraged and educated the other soldiers. They discussed issues around the campfire. They read newspaper articles aloud. They were a bridge connecting the Republican Party and the fighting men.

Lincoln concluded that only total victory and emancipation would save the Union. The president labored to hold together the northern coalition in a kind of national "team of rivals" and to build broad support for a "strategy of unconditional surrender."[23] He appealed to conservatives by highlighting the overarching aim of reunion, as well as his willingness to consider schemes like the colonization of blacks abroad. At the same time, however, he impressed on the vanguard the radical effects of the war. On September 22, 1862, Lincoln issued the preliminary Emancipation Proclamation, but even this document was cautious in tone and applied only if the war continued into 1863.

The apparent moderation masked an essential truth: the Civil War was now a crusade for freedom. Former slave Frederick Douglass said of the proclamation, "I hail it as the doom of Slavery in all the States.... We are *all* liberated by this proclamation."[24] One escaped slave, Samuel Cabble, joined the Union army and wrote to his wife in Missouri: "i would like to no if you are still in slavery if you are it will not be long before we shall have crushed the system that now opreses you.... great is the outpouring of the colored people that is now rallying with the hearts of lions against that very curse that has separated you and me."[25] From dawn's early light on New Year's Day 1863, when Union soldiers marched into Confederate land, they brought freedom in their wake.

The North was willing to fight a hard war to bring about the doom of the South. At first, Lincoln and his generals resisted seizing or destroying civilian property. Students at West Point were taught a code of military principles that stressed the protection of innocent noncombatants. In 1861, William T. Sherman criticized the depredations of Union troops in Virginia: "My only hope now is that a common sense of decency may be infused into this soldiery to respect life and property."[26]

But over time, the northern population and its leaders lost their inhibitions, as the Civil War slid closer toward total war. Lincoln concluded in 1862 that the great cause could not be prosecuted with "elder-stalk squirts charged with rose-water."[27] He was not alone. In 1863, the men of the Wisconsin militia wanted "to fight the war more ruthlessly and press the issue with more tenacity and vigor."[28]

In the final years of the Civil War, Union forces deliberately targeted southern noncombatants. Civilians were not directly slaughtered; rather, they were stripped of the means to live, with towns, farms, barns, and mills all torched. McPherson has estimated that fifty thousand southern civilians died in the Civil War from violence, disease, or starvation.[29] In November 1864, Union general William T. Sherman gave orders for Atlanta to be evacuated and burned. Sherman then sent sixty thousand veteran soldiers marching to Savannah and the sea. These men were a different species than the amateur enthusiasts of Bull Run. They knew how to march, fight, and forage. Sherman's army cut a swath of devastation through Georgia and the Carolinas, living off the land and razing what it could not consume. The men destroyed hundreds of miles of railroads and seized thousands of cattle and millions of pounds of corn and fodder.

By the November 1864 presidential election, the Union war effort had evolved into a ferocious crusade involving all necessary force, the targeting of civilians, and maximum war aims. Lincoln ran on a platform calling for emancipation to be written into the Constitution and won by the largest margin of any president since Andrew Jackson (receiving nearly 80 percent of the soldier vote). With the Confederacy crumbling in early 1865, the president set out his peace terms. There would be no compromise on slavery, and all southern forces had to disband. The Confederates recognized the proposal for what it was—a demand for unconditional surrender.[30]

Independence or Extermination

The northern crusade in the Civil War smashed headlong into a counterpart crusade in the South. The Confederacy fought its own campaign for maximum objectives. The citizens of Richmond—living in a city that was tightly linked to the northern economy and close to the fissure where the tectonic plates met—were initially wary of secession. But the moment the shooting began at Fort Sumter, there was a surge of support for independence. Crowds, illuminated by torches, filled the streets, urging disunion.[31] Few doubted that the Confederacy would win. As a southern arithmetic text asked, "If one Confederate soldier can whip 7 Yankees, how many soldiers can whip 49 Yankees?"

Yet these ratios proved inaccurate, and the cost of war was terrible in the Confederacy. By 1865, half the white men of military age were either dead or maimed. Given these hardships, southerners displayed an astounding commitment to the cause. There were class and economic divisions in the South, and strongholds of Unionism. But a higher percentage of southern whites supported secession from the United States in the 1860s than backed secession from the British Empire in the 1770s.[32] Over time, the war aim of complete independence became more strongly entrenched. Confederate president Jefferson Davis presented his terms for peace in 1864: "We are fighting for independence and that, or extermination, we will have."[33]

Confederates also put aside "elder-stalk squirts" and targeted civilians when they had the chance. In Missouri, the sustained brother-against-brother guerrilla warfare was exceptionally brutal on both sides, featuring desperadoes and psychopaths like William Quantrill, William T. "Bloody Bill" Anderson, and Jesse James. In 1863, Quantrill and his men attacked the Unionist stronghold of Lawrence, Kansas, and killed 150 men—all they could find.

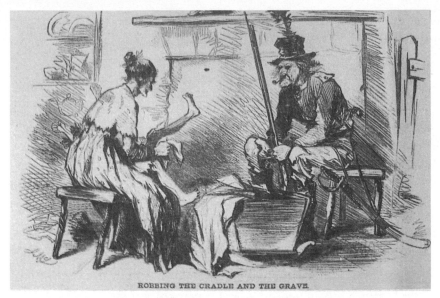

ROBBING THE CRADLE AND THE GRAVE.

In this northern cartoon published in Harper's Weekly *in 1864, a southern woman sends her aging father and infant son to the army: "Jeff Davis had better take little Pete along too. You'd both be jest the age for two soldiers." The purpose was to ridicule the Confederacy, but the cartoon implicitly recognized the incredible commitment of the southern war effort.*

In a sense, the two crusading nations were mirror images. As Frank and Duteau noted, "By 1863 neither army would have accepted limited war aims."[34] In both North and South, women identified strongly with the cause, and they were active as nurses, factory workers, and advocates for temperance, improved sanitation, and, in the North, abolition. Several hundred women disguised themselves as men and fought for the Union and the Confederacy.[35] Northerners and southerners even sang from the same songbook. The Union anthem "Battle Cry of Freedom" included these lines: "Down with the traitor, up with the star; / While we rally 'round the flag, boys, rally once again." In the South, the song had different lyrics: "Down with the eagle, up with the cross; / We'll rally 'round the bonnie flag, we'll rally once again."[36]

Fighting for the Last, Best Hope

Why did Americans perceive the Civil War in this zealous manner? Part of the explanation is cool strategic thinking. Many northerners were convinced to support emancipation because it would deprive the South of a key labor source, facilitate reunion, and shorten the conflict.[37]

But perceptions of the Civil War were not primarily driven by an objective military logic. Northern opinion was split over the crusade for emancipation, and this division closely mirrored underlying partisan, religious, and racial cleavages. Although emancipation was in part a tactical device to force reunion, the meaning of "the Union" broadened during the war to include not just a geographical area, but also the idea of liberty—a community where individual rights were respected. The war was fought to save the Union and also to make the Union worth saving.[38]

The northern public perceived the conflict as a mission to protect and spread their liberal and religious ideals. Lincoln sometimes talked in public as if he was an arch-pragmatist, as if freeing the slaves was a chess move to end the rebellion. Yet his thinking was imbued with American idealism, as he sought to save a form of government "whose leading object is to elevate the condition of men."[39] By passing through the purifying fire, the nation would be born again on true principles. On December 1, 1862, Lincoln announced in his annual message to Congress, "We shall nobly save or meanly lose the last, best hope of earth."[40]

Many northerners concluded that the entire American project, and perhaps even global freedom, were endangered by a rapacious slave power. In McPherson's sample of more than one thousand Civil War soldiers, he found that about two-thirds of the men offered patriotic reasons for fighting, while 40 percent discussed

Abraham Lincoln photographed in April 1865, four days before his assassination

the war using complex ideological arguments about individual rights and democracy.[41]

One private from Massachusetts wrote home to his wife, "I do feel that the liberty of the world is placed in our hands to defend."[42] The war would preserve the United States, in the words of a thirty-five-year-old sergeant from Indiana, as "the beacon light of liberty & freedom to the human race."[43] Senator Charles Sumner argued that "in ending slavery here we open its gates all over the world, and let the oppressed go free."[44]

An Ohio soldier named Ebenezer Hannaford was wounded in the neck and spent a year recuperating in a hospital. Hannaford's injuries were so serious that he almost lost his life. "It was there that

Death drew near and bent over my pillow," he wrote, "so close that I could feel his icy breath upon my cheek, while in mute, ghastly silence we looked steadfastly each in the other's face for weeks together." Despite all this, when his fellow patients sang "The Battle Cry of Freedom," Hannaford felt "the grand infinitude of principle—of Right, and Truth, and Justice—that was underlying the whole fierce struggle, and had made our Cause one that it was, oh! how noble a thing to have fought and suffered for, and, if need be, yet to die for!"[45]

Northerners hated the institution of slavery more than they loved the slaves. Even Lincoln didn't see blacks and whites as intellectual equals and never envisaged social integration of the races. Reverend Moses Smith told a white congregation about the reality of race relations in the North: "This being a 'nigger' in society, and 'a nigger' at the communion table is probably the most heartless and unrelenting slavery beneath the skies. It may not shackle the body, but it crushes the mind and kills the heart."[46] The one group that consistently fought for black rights as American citizens were the blacks themselves. Corporal John Payne wrote in 1864, "Liberty is what I am struggling for; and what pulse does not beat high at the very mention of the name?"[47]

Some northerners struggled to reconcile the war with their religious faith. "Read all of Christ's teaching," remarked one lieutenant colonel in the Fifty-seventh Indiana, "and then tell me whether *one engaged in maiming and butchering men*—men made in the express image of God himself—*can be saved* under the Gospel."[48]

But more often, religion hardened the will of soldiers, who came to see the struggle as a holy war, with Christ and his armies arrayed against "the Beast." The Civil War was preceded by a great revival of religion from 1800 to 1850, with a surge in evangelical Protestantism and millennial ideas of building a thousand-year era of peace and prosperity. History was progressing rapidly toward the kingdom of God, with America at its cutting edge. The Civil War was both a punishment for America's sins and a cleansing stage on the path to perfecting the Union and the world. According to abolitionist Thomas Wentworth Higginson, not since the days of Oliver Cromwell were there soldiers "in whom the religious element held such a place."[49]

At first, many northern clerics argued for restraint and Christian reconciliation. But this view evolved into a perception of the struggle as an irrepressible conflict between God and Satan. Historian Peter Parish has shown that the northern Protestant clergy overwhelmingly backed the war, providing a "providential interpretation," which "helped the wider public to manage the transition from a limited war to save the Union into a monumental struggle for loftier and more far-reaching goals."[50] One Pennsylvanian wrote, "Every day I have a more religious feeling, that this war is a crusade for the good of mankind."[51] Oliver Wendell Holmes, who fought in the Civil War and later became a Supreme Court justice, saw the Union war effort as "the Christian crusade of the 19th Century."[52]

Liberal and religious idealism countenanced no concessions to a treacherous slavocracy. As one Vermont soldier put it, "As well might Jehovah compromise with Satan and give him back part of Heaven."[53] A New York captain noted, "If we lose in this war, the country is lost and if we win it is saved. There is no middle ground."[54] Montgomery C. Meigs, the Union quartermaster general, wrote to his son, "No peace in compromise with the South is possible for our industrious educated democratic people. Death or victory is the...necessity of our cause and I do not less doubt the ultimate victory though God for our sins leads us to it through seas of blood."[55] Meanwhile, the northern churches were notably silent on the issue of civilian deaths. The inflictions of war were terrible but were excused by a righteous cause.[56]

As the fatalities mounted, Americans demanded a greater payoff in the advancement of the nation's principles. Lincoln remarked at

Gettysburg, "From these honored dead we take increased devotion to that cause.... we here highly resolve that these dead shall not have died in vain."[57] One soldier argued that only a grand crusade could justify the "wondrous price of lives, misery, agony & desolation" resulting from this terrible war.[58]

The Confederates didn't cede an inch of liberal or religious idealism to the North. Given their inferior material power, it was impossible for southerners to remake the North in their own image; instead, they fought to protect their ideals. One soldier offered his "whole heart to the cause of the Confederacy because I believe that the perpetuity of republican principles on this Continent depends upon our success."[59] Southern whites believed that emancipation would make them little more than slaves before a tyrannical alliance of northern Republicans and freed blacks. Among the most popular songs was "The Bonnie Blue Flag": "We are a band of brothers, natives of the soil, / Fighting for our property we gained by honest toil; / But when our rights were threatened the cry rose near and far: / Hurrah for the Bonnie Blue Flag that bears a single star."[60]

As they abandoned the ship of state, the Confederates clung to the American Revolution like a life raft. They saw themselves as the true guardians of the values of George Washington, who featured prominently on the Confederate Seal. The South had maintained the sacred Revolutionary promise, while the North had broken with the ideals of 1776. Ella Thomas, a Georgian, said, "They are attempting to deprive us of that glorious liberty for which our Fathers fought and bled and shall we tamely submit to this? Never!"[61]

Religion was the glue that bound the South together, even as Union armies tore the nascent nation apart. The Confederate constitution, unlike the U.S. Constitution, explicitly invoked God. President Davis announced in his first annual message to Congress,

"We feel that our cause is just and holy."[62] Clerical voices provided an essential moral and theological justification for secession and war: Satan's spell had turned the North into a nation of marauding aggressors. There could be no compromise on the righteous struggle. As one private in the Ninth Tennessee put it, "We will fight them until Dooms Day or have our independence."[63]

Unionists and Confederates alike perceived themselves as bastions of virtue and piety, saw the dead as martyrs, and sanctified the war with fast days. Both sides viewed victory as evidence of God's favor and defeat as a cathartic event—a signal to purge one's sins. And both engaged in a theological arms race. In 1864, when the North feared it was being out-Christianized, it put its money where its mouth was by stamping the phrase "In God We Trust" on its coins.

Vengeance Will Be Our Motto

Lincoln warned against retribution—"Let us judge not, that we be not judged"—but the desire for revenge for past crimes was a powerful motivator on both sides to escalate the means and ends of the war.[64] The crusading anthem "The Battle Hymn of the Republic" captured the duality of the northern crusade: the missionary idealism and the righteous punishment. Union soldiers marched to spread freedom, but they also unleashed the "terrible swift sword" of vengeance. When Union soldiers killed, they had no moral guilt, for they were the tools of God.

One Union officer remarked that even among educated and Christian communities, "wild and ferocious passions...[are]... aroused and kindled by...war and injustice, and become more cruel and destructive than any that live in the breasts of savage and barbarous nations."[65] An Ohio captain noted among his fellow soldiers "this passion...this desire for revenge....Hate rankled in their breasts."[66] As a Unionist from East Tennessee put it, "[We] will have an eye for eye and toth for toth."[67]

Only the complete destruction of the slave society would provide sufficient retribution for the South's crimes. An Illinois sergeant wrote, "I want to fight the rest of my life if necessary before we recognize them as anything but Rebels and traitors who must be humbled."[68] A major in the Thirty-first Wisconsin commented, "Truly may it be said that the South are reaping a most fearful retribution for the sin of cecession [sic] and rebellion."[69] Frederick Douglass noted, "Liberty came to the freedmen...not in mercy but in wrath."[70]

Punishing a demonized adversary could justify almost any act. After bloody battles against the Confederates at Shiloh and elsewhere, Sherman concluded that the southern zealots must reap what they had sown. "War is cruelty, and you cannot refine it," he wrote to the mayor and city council of Atlanta on September 12, 1864, "and those who brought war into our country deserve all the curses and maledictions a people can pour out."[71] He also noted, "The whole army is burning with an insatiable desire to wreak vengeance upon South Carolina."[72]

The yearning for retribution was even more powerful among Confederates. After all, the war, along with its crimes and hardships, had taken place mainly on rebel soil. One Missouri Confederate promised to recapture the state, and then "*vengeance* will be our motto."[73] A sergeant from Georgia heading north into Pennsylvania sought retaliation for the destruction of southern property: "Take horses; burn houses; and commit every depredation possible upon the men of the North."[74] After battle, some Confederates took pleasure from the sight of dead and bloated Union corpses. It was "doing my soul good," one remarked.[75] A young southern officer was comforted by the number of northern soldiers he had personally dispatched: "If they should kill me today and I had but time for one thought before I died, it would be that my account with them was more than even."[76]

Mourning in America

After the fighting ended in 1865, by the standards of most civil wars, the victors were generous. The North executed only one Confederate official, Henry Wirz, who was held responsible for the desperate conditions under which Union POWs were held at Andersonville Prison in Georgia. Even Jefferson Davis was released from prison in 1867, despite being completely unrepentant. In 1884, after two decades of reflection on the carnage of war, Davis declared before the Mississippi legislature, "If it were to do over again, I would again do just as I did in 1861."[77]

With the conclusion of hostilities, the crusader wave crashed. The northern press didn't dwell on issues of peace, but instead "moved on to mundane events, as if the war had never taken place."[78] But by the 1870s the nation's amnesia abated, and interest in the war exploded, with the appearance of thousands of books and articles about the campaign.

The Civil War became widely perceived as a noble cause, and memories were steadily purified. The war for reunion and emancipation was so blindingly wondrous that Americans did not need to ask the tough questions about why it was originally fought, the divisions on the home front, and the means employed to achieve victory. For the North, the struggle was "a consciously undertaken crusade so full of righteousness that there is enough overplus stored in Heaven, like the deeds of the saints, to take care of all small failings and oversights of the descendants of the crusaders."[79]

Meanwhile, the southern "lost cause" was later powerfully evoked in films like *The Birth of a Nation* (1915) and *Gone with the Wind* (1939). As the spirit of sectional reconciliation took wings, many northerners granted the South a moral victory for its valor, and Robert E. Lee was widely admired across the country.

The campaign became enveloped in a thick fog of heroism and glory, and the harsh reality was lost or blurred. There were the 620,000 dead—the same number that would be killed in all of America's other wars from the Revolution through Korea combined. There were the half a million deserters. There were the dead bodies with their thumbs gnawed off in a desperate bid to counter the pain of wounds. There was the disease, which killed twice as many soldiers as combat. There were the 30,000 amputations and the great mountains of rotting appendages, hacked off from dawn to dusk. One Union soldier who lost both forearms became a doorkeeper at the House of Representatives, wearing artificial limbs. He was a vivid reminder to legislators of the terrible price of even the purest crusade.[80]

Southern Reconstruction

Alonzo Ransier was born a free black man in Charleston, South Carolina, in 1834, and worked as a shipping house clerk. After the Civil War ended, when the North began the Reconstruction of the southern states, Ransier became a prominent black leader and an advocate of compulsory education. He was elected to the U.S. House of Representatives, where he clashed memorably in 1874 with Virginia Democrat John Harris.

"And I say there is not one gentleman upon this floor," declared Harris, "who can honestly say he really believes that the colored man is created his equal."

"I can," remarked Ransier.

"Of course, you can," Harris replied, "but I am speak-

ing to the white men of the House....The fact exists...
born in our ancestors...that the colored man was inferior
to the white."

"I deny that," interrupted Ransier, much to Harris's
annoyance.

"Sit down; I am talking to white men; I am talking to
gentlemen!" Harris admonished.

Ransier served one term but failed to gain renomination. Then,
following the collapse of southern Reconstruction and the resurgence of white supremacist government, he tragically ended his
days working as a street cleaner in Charleston until his death in
1882.[81]

Richard Gleaves was another southern black leader. During
Reconstruction, he became lieutenant governor of South Carolina.
After racists overthrew the state government, Gleaves was reduced
to waiting tables at the Jefferson Club in Washington, DC. The
depressing fate of such talented men symbolized the country's
retreat from Reconstruction and its abandonment of America's
blacks.

If war is the continuation of politics by other means, then peace
is the continuation of war by other means. The struggle between
competing northern and southern visions of the United States did
not end in 1865, but instead persisted in new forms. At Lincoln's
death, the baton of Reconstruction was passed to Vice President
Andrew Johnson, a former slave owner and ardent Unionist from
Tennessee, who had been placed on the Republican ticket in 1864
to broaden its appeal. Johnson promptly appeased the former Confederates by welcoming them back to Congress and recognizing
the South's "black codes," the new system of neo-slavery that
starkly limited black freedom.

Most northerners had little love for blacks, but given the

sacrifice of four years of war, they were warier still about a resurgent conservative South. In Shakespeare's play, Hamlet laments the speed with which his father's death was followed by his mother's betrothal: "The funeral baked meats, did coldly furnish forth the marriage tables." Similarly, in the South, just a few months after Lincoln's funeral, rebels like former vice president of the Confederacy Alexander Stephens were celebrating their imminent return to Congress.

Republicans saw southern blacks as a counterweight to the conservative revival. The protection of black civil rights, including voting rights, would defend the Union, prevent the restoration of the old order, build a Republican Party base in the former Confederacy, and, for the more enlightened, uphold America's promise that all men are created equal.

Reconstruction was America's first nation-building mission, beginning during the Johnson administration and continuing through the two terms of Ulysses S. Grant. In its arc of hope and disillusionment, the mission established a template for America's experience of nation-building that would be repeated time and again through Iraq and beyond.

In 1867, the Republican Congress placed the southern states under military rule. Federal troops acted like modern-day peacekeepers, maintaining order, setting up new governments, monitoring elections, and overseeing the welfare of blacks. The new state governments and their representatives were recognized only when they accepted the Fourteenth and Fifteenth Amendments to the Constitution, guaranteeing the civil rights and suffrage of blacks. Much of the South was now governed by a loose Republican Party alliance of "carpetbaggers" (the 20,000 to 50,000 northerners who had headed south), "scalawags" (the one-fifth of southern whites who backed the Reconstruction regimes), and freed slaves.

Almost Nauseating

Reconstruction was soon viewed in the North as a quagmire, with no end in sight. Southern Republican governments were perceived as corrupt and bumbling, while the carpetbaggers were seen as charlatans who had packed their few belongings in a carpetbag and headed south to exploit the exhausted Dixie. In four years, the Civil War had produced a galaxy of stars, like Lee, Grant, and Jackson, who would become legends for the ages. Reconstruction also produced brave champions like Adelbert Ames of Mississippi, who fought for black rights. But such figures went almost completely unrecognized; not a single popular hero emerged from the decade-long mission.

Support for Reconstruction steadily eroded. In 1871, the *New York Times* commented that the "mere mention of [Reconstruction] is almost nauseating."[82] The *Nation* said that as an experiment in government, Reconstruction had "totally failed."[83] And as the *Mobile (Alabama) Register* put it, "The North have come to their senses. The negro has disgraced and ruined the party which pushed him forward, and the oscillating pendulum of public opinion is now swinging over to the side of the Southern white man."[84]

It was no surprise that Democrats were sharp critics of Reconstruction, having opposed the federal intervention to protect black civil rights from the start. More striking was the legion of Republicans who had originally championed southern Reconstruction but then turned against the mission with extraordinary gusto.

Journalist James S. Pike was seen as a credible source on the nation-building efforts in the South precisely because of his long-established antislavery and radical Republican credentials. Therefore, when Pike utterly denounced Reconstruction, his words resonated with northerners. Pike's 1874 book, *The Prostrate State: South Carolina*

Under Negro Government, concluded that "the civilized and educated white race was under foot, prostrate and powerless, and the black barbarian reigned in its stead."[85]

In the early 1870s, the Liberal Republican movement broke away from the Republican Party, campaigning in favor of civil service reform, low taxes, and free trade. One of the most prominent Liberal Republicans was the German American Carl Schurz, who had arrived in the United States in 1852 in the wake of the failed 1848 revolution in Prussia. A skilled orator with long hair and a wild look, Schurz was "a wonderful land pirate," in the words of Lincoln's secretary, John Hay.[86] Schurz initially joined the crusading vanguard against slavery as a division commander in the Civil War and became a vigorous proponent of Reconstruction. But he ended up condemning "that system of wholesale robbery and misrule prevailing in the South."[87] Another Liberal Republican believed that the carpetbaggers were "clouds of vampires, lighting upon and sucking the blood of the body politic."[88] And these, remember, were *Republicans.*

Criticism of the nation-building mission reached a crescendo after 1874, with the *Chicago Inter-Ocean* finding "overwhelming public sentiment *at the North* adverse to the protection of life at the South by the use of the Federal authority."[89] The 1874 midterm elections were, in part, a referendum on Reconstruction, and the outcome was a soaring victory for the anti-Reconstruction Democrats. "We are busted, squelched, scooped!" one Republican newspaper wrote.[90] The *Observer* of London noted the change in mood since the Civil War: "People who risked their lives and property for a cause which they believed to be holy so long as it was struggling, now talk dubiously and hesitatingly of the results of emancipation."[91]

A New Birth of Freedom

Rarely have perceptions of a U.S. military operation been so skewed. The Reconstruction regimes certainly made their fair share of mistakes, and corruption was real. But overall, far from being a failure, Reconstruction was a historic experiment in inter-racial democracy that transformed the lives of black citizens. The mission didn't self-destruct; it was forcibly overthrown in a violent counterrevolution, while northerners looked the other way.

Any judgment of southern Reconstruction must begin by rec-ognizing the exceptional difficulty of this nation-building opera-tion. Southern cities were in ruins. In Charleston, South Carolina, desolation reigned, with thoroughfares overgrown with grass and buildings reduced to haunting wrecks by shells and fire. Much of the southern population was hungry, destitute, and illiterate, weak-ened by rickets and hookworm. Conservative whites were embit-tered and motivated by an ideology of racial supremacy. Former slaves stepped blinking into the bright sunlight of freedom, with little or no training as citizens and voters.

"Given the daunting problems faced by the Reconstruction governments," wrote historian Eric Foner, "their accomplishments were indeed remarkable."[92] For a brief period after 1867, there was a new birth of freedom, as blacks voted, served on juries, and held high office. Alonzo Ransier was one of fourteen blacks elected to the House of Representatives, while two blacks served in the U.S. Senate.[93] White Democrats were in no position to complain about the inexperience or ineffectiveness of these men. The South's best and brightest had led the region into a catastrophic war in 1861.

Hospitals, schools, and universities were established through-out the South. Thousands of northern teachers, three-quarters of them women, flocked to teach the freedmen. In 1860, Florida, Mississippi, and Georgia collectively educated in public schools not 18 *percent* of blacks, but a total of 18 *individual* free blacks. By 1876, almost two-fifths of the black children in the former slave states were enrolled in school. During Reconstruction, about one-quarter of southern blacks became landowners, and black income rose from 23 percent of white income in 1857 to 52 percent in 1880.[94]

What about the much-vaunted corruption of the southern Republican regimes? Levels of corruption were roughly in line with those in the South before the Civil War, as well as those in the North at the time. Indeed, the extent of fraud and bribery in the former Confederacy was dwarfed by the tens of millions of dollars lost in New York's infamous Tweed Ring scandal of the early 1870s. Most carpetbaggers weren't crooked despots, but philan-thropists, entrepreneurs, investors, and idealists—desperately needed by a region short on human and monetary capital.[95]

The Bloody Shirt

Given these impressive successes, why did Americans view Recon-struction as a failed experiment, so utterly at odds with the glorious Civil War? It's tempting to see a very simple explanation: racism. After all, blacks were largely shunned in the North, and in 1868 only eight northern states allowed black suffrage. But racism isn't the whole story. If it were, there would not have been a significant push for civil rights. To understand why the northern public per-ceived Reconstruction as a futile quagmire, we need to look at what happened to the vitalizing forces that had fueled the crusad-ing impulse in the Civil War: wrath and mission.

The desire for revenge inspired Americans to fight for maxi-mum war aims in the Civil War. By the mid-1870s, however, northern wrath—and therefore northern willpower—was a rap-idly ebbing force. Unlike the Civil War, which was characterized by stark ethical divides, the nation-building mission in the South didn't resemble a struggle between good and evil. The carpetbagger regimes were widely vilified, and there was growing sympathy for southern whites.

What about the sense of idealism that had transformed the Civil War into a righteous crusade? Now that the North began the practical work of remaking the South in its own image, liberal and religious principles, ironically enough, encouraged weariness and regret.

For one thing, northern idealists sometimes held impracticable expectations about the speed and magnitude of change they would bring to the South—guaranteeing disillusionment. Americans needed a realistic appreciation of how much commitment and patience was required. Instead, Republicans often envisioned the postwar South as being primed for an economic takeoff. It had the natural resources, a fine climate for agriculture, and well-trained farmers. Now that the chains of slavery had been removed and legal rights bestowed on the freedmen, liberty and prosperity would suddenly blossom like a thousand flowers.[96]

Radical Republican senator Richard Yates said, "The ballot will finish the negro question; it will settle everything connected with this question.... We need no vast expenditures, we need no standing army.... Sir, the ballot is the freedman's Moses."[97] The *Washington Chronicle* concluded, "In November of 1863 we had a theory of liberty, a hope of equality, a dream of justice to all men. In May of 1869 that theory is a fact, that hope is fulfilled, that dream is a reality."[98] Mission accomplished!

American idealism also dramatically raised the bar for success. The laurels of victory would be bestowed only if the South were somehow transformed into a replica of northern democracy and stability. For instance, Liberal Republicans were extremely moralistic reformers, seeing themselves as the virtuous protectors of the sacred principles of the Republic. With Reconstruction's flaws highlighted in the glare of national attention, the mission inevitably fell short of those ideals and was condemned. Carl Schurz concluded that the Deep South would never rise to the level of stable republican government and that, therefore, further federal intervention was pointless.[99] As the *Mobile Register* put it, "The North have found that they could not make a silk purse out of a sow's ear, and have cast Sambo overboard."[100]

Northern idealism, with its unrealistic expectations and high bar for success, gifted the southern extremists with a surefire ticket to victory. Constant instability and violence in the South would not only terrify and intimidate the local black population, but it would also ultimately wear down northern patience.

White supremacists formed the Ku Klux Klan in Tennessee in 1866. This ghoulish menagerie of dragons and hydras quickly spread across the region. Wearing long flowing robes and hoods, sometimes supplemented by animal skins and women's dresses, the Klan whipped blacks into line, burned down schoolhouses, and killed more than one thousand people in Louisiana alone in 1868 — most of them black.[101]

The U.S. military proved effective at counterinsurgency when the will was present. In 1871, Congress passed the Ku Klux Klan Act, which expanded federal powers to tackle southern terrorism. Hundreds of suspected Klansmen were indicted across the South, and a mixture of punishment and clemency meant that within a year, the Klan was no longer a significant force in southern politics. The 1872 elections were the fairest in the South until 1968.

Southern extremists gave up the Halloween costumes and reorganized as rifle clubs and White Leagues, with uniforms and military drills. Now a person could see the face of the man who killed him or her. The violence became more systematic and focused, and the strongholds of Republican rule in the South were soon under siege.[102]

In 1873, Colfax, Louisiana, was a small town of scattered build-

ings on the banks of the Red River, surrounded by cotton plantations. On Easter Sunday, it was the scene of the single bloodiest act
of terrorism and racial violence during Reconstruction. The outcome of the 1872 elections in Louisiana was disputed, and rival
claimants arose for the governorship and local positions across the
state. Freedmen mobilized in Colfax to protect the Republican
Party government and began collecting weapons and digging
trenches. Fearing black rule, and with lurid rumors of a plot to capture white women and raise a new race, white supremacists formed
their own militia.

Around 150 whites attacked the town on Easter Sunday. When
the outgunned blacks took cover in the town's courthouse, the
white supremacists forced an old black prisoner to set fire to the
building. To escape being burned alive, the blacks inside surrendered, initiating, as one witness described it, "a savage and hellish
butchery." Men were killed where they stood or knelt in supplica-
tion. Later, black prisoners were taken out and shot, the sound
resembling, as one witness put it, "popcorn in a skillet."[103] That
night, visitors to Colfax found the courthouse in flames and a terrible smell of burning flesh. In the shifting light cast by lanterns, they
discovered a town littered with as many as one hundred corpses.

The massacre subsequently became a source of great pride for
the local community. In 1921, a marble obelisk was erected in the
Colfax cemetery by white townsfolk in honor of the heroes "Who
fell in the Colfax Riot fighting for White Supremacy."[104] Today
the cemetery is filled entirely with the bodies of whites. In death,
the races are equal but separate.

In the short run, the Colfax Massacre heightened the desire of
some northerners to punish southern extremists. But outrage was
quickly replaced by exhaustion and terrorism fatigue. A chasm
opened up between northern ideals and the reality of the South.
People grew weary of the torturous news of murders, racial
division, and government incapacity. Instead, they wanted to hear

exciting tales of battles against the Apaches and Sioux, the construction of the transcontinental railroad, and gold strikes in places like Deadwood, South Dakota, where "Wild Bill" Hickok met his maker at a poker table, holding aces and eights, the "dead man's hand."

In 1875, President Grant complained that "the whole public are tired out with these annual, autumnal outbreaks in the South."[105] Adelbert Ames also recognized the changing mood: "The political death of the Negro will forever release the nation from the weariness from such 'political outbreaks.' "[106] One Republican felt that northerners were sick of "this worn out cry of 'Southern outrages'!!! Hard times & heavy taxes make them wish the 'nigger,' 'everlasting nigger,' were in —— or Africa."[107]

Welfarism and Imperialism

The Reconstruction project also suffered in northern eyes because it violated the ideal of limited government. The "free labor" ideology of the North defined freedom as each man's right to compete and struggle against others in a socially and economically fluid society. The *negative* task of removing the slave system and the barriers to individual enterprise was consistent with this ideology. As one former colonel remarked in 1874, "We have done our whole duty when we have established and enforced, in favor of the freedmen, *equality of right under the law.*"[108]

But *positive* intervention to aid the former slaves raised the specter of special favors and welfare for blacks who were too lazy to work. Government should not step into the marketplace to raise one group over the other. The *New York Evening Post* thought that the South should "get out of the federal nursery, stand upon its feet and take care of itself."[109] The *Chicago Tribune* wondered, "Is it not time for the colored race to stop playing baby?"[110]

Even radical Republicans shied away from redistributing land from the southern plantation owners to the former slaves. This might have anchored a transformation of the region, but it breached the sacred tenets of free labor and property rights. It was better for blacks to build up their landholdings slowly through the sweat of their brow.[111]

In an era of labor violence in the United States, worsened by the disastrous economic depression of 1873, and with fears of radicalism stoked by the Paris Commune of 1871, many northerners began to see blacks as un-American socialists. Republican newspapers like *Harper's Weekly* increasingly depicted blacks as radicals who demanded government expansion, endless handouts, confiscation of wealth, and proletarian revolution.[112]

A Pennsylvania election poster from 1866 illustrates the view of southern Reconstruction as a form of welfare for blacks.

Liberal Republicans believed that once blacks had the vote, everything else would fall into place as the free market worked its magic. When things didn't work out this way, rather than question the underlying ideology, Liberal Republicans condemned blacks for being unable to compete with whites due to their inherent inferiority. This naive belief in the free market—that blacks should "get out of the federal nursery"—ignored the fact that systematic terrorism subverted democratic rule and made a mockery of a level playing field.

Reconstruction contravened another American liberal ideal—anti-imperialism, or the belief that foreign occupation is incompatible with democracy. The nation-building mission in the South raised fears of standing armies, military rule, tyranny, an end to states' rights, and empire. John Dean Caton, former chief justice of the Illinois Supreme Court, condemned President Grant's efforts to repress the Ku Klux Klan: "This is the very essence of despotic power. The Czar of Russia can possess no more unrestrained power over the meanest of his subjects."[113]

Reconstruction was repeatedly compared to the Roman Empire. Grant, after all, was a military man, and critics were quick to spot the gleam of the bayonet and the impending end of democracy. The *Cincinnati Commercial* ran the headline "Long Live Caesar!"[114] Liberal Republican Roeliff Brinkerhoff saw Grant's actions as "continuous steps in the old beaten track of despotism.... The shadow of the man on horseback is not far off."[115] Lawyer and poet William Cullen Bryant feared that forcing black suffrage on the South would mean "the republic converted into an empire."[116]

The *New York Tribune* had been a supporter of Reconstruction, but it changed its tune by 1877: "I have no sort of faith in a local government which can only be propped up by foreign bayonets. If negro suffrage means that as a permanency then negro suffrage is a failure."[117] As whites reasserted their power, the *Tribune* glowed with pride: "The South was so long a conquered province, ruled by the Attorney-General's quill and held in place with the bayonets of the army, that it is hard to realize that it is free at last."[118]

Fears of despotic federal rule and a new Roman Empire were exaggerated to the point of absurdity. Outside of Texas (where much of the U.S. military guarded the border with Mexico), there were only 6,000 troops in the entire South in 1869. By 1872, this number had been cut to 3,400. Adelbert Ames summarized the forces available to impose a tyrannical imperial rule in Mississippi: "Three hundred and twenty two men, including the regimental band, non-commissioned staff, clerks and orderlies &c. &c. are all I have with which to force a state to vote against its will!"[119]

The southern counterrevolutionaries knew exactly which buttons to press in the northern psyche. By constantly highlighting the themes of corruption and local rule, by raising the twin specters of welfarism and imperialism, by employing just enough violence to ensure constant turmoil without provoking federal intervention, the enemies of Reconstruction cultivated a gloomy northern prognosis that aided the fall of Richard Gleaves, Alonzo Ransier, and the other black leaders from grace to a more appropriate station in life.

Redemption

When Maurice Jasper, the last surviving slave of George Washington, died in 1872, the *New National Era* claimed that Jasper had lived to see the "second revolution."[120] But like many revolutions, Reconstruction produced a powerful reaction.

In 1875, the nation began to celebrate its centennial with endless fireworks, parades, speeches, and images of liberty and unity. The North also chose this moment to abandon southern blacks. In its first incarnation, the quagmire tradition had a disastrous effect by eroding the country's commitment to fulfill the promise of emancipation. Perceptions of Reconstruction as a failure proved to be a self-fulfilling prophecy, diminishing northern will and facilitating a racist counterrevolution and the end of nation-building.

Conservatives called the process "redemption," implying a new birth and requiring a blood sacrifice—by blacks. Appeals to racial identity, threats, and economic pressure peeled the scalawags away from the Reconstruction coalition, until southern blacks and their carpetbagger allies stood alone. Torchlit parades intimidated and overawed, while massacres signaled the price of resistance, as the strongholds of Republican rule were surrounded and destroyed.

After the disputed presidential election of 1876, with northern interest in civil rights fading rapidly, a backroom deal put Republican Rutherford B. Hayes in the White House in return for an agreement to end Reconstruction.[121] As the South descended into an era of apartheid, the great African American writer W. E. B. DuBois concluded: "The slave went free; stood a brief moment in the sun; then moved back again toward slavery."[122] Blacks voting, blacks serving on juries, black senators in Congress: all of it was soon gone with the wind.

Profiles in Courage

It was critical for the white supremacist project that southern Reconstruction be remembered—*reimagined*—as an unmitigated disaster. The mantra of failure and Washington's bungling attempt to force "Negro rule" on the South was endlessly repeated in newspapers, novels, historical accounts, and films like D. W. Griffith's *The Birth of a Nation*.

Even John F. Kennedy got in on the act. His Pulitzer Prize–winning book *Profiles in Courage,* published in 1956, included among its adulatory portraits the Mississippi white supremacist L. Q. C. Lamar. In a chapter of unintended historical fiction,

Kennedy argued that Mississippi had suffered terribly from the misgovernment of carpetbagger rule.[123] At least Kennedy had second thoughts. After witnessing white violence against blacks in Mississippi in 1962, the president remarked, "It makes me wonder whether everything I learned about the evils of Reconstruction is really true."[124]

The skeptical view of Reconstruction became so widely accepted that people acted as if it was reality. The nation-building mission was a warning from history that solidified southern white opposition to a weakening of segregation and rationalized northern indifference to the fate of blacks. Inspired by false memories, America turned its back on the better angels of its nature until a new generation of civil rights leaders emerged after World War II.

Two Clocks

During Reconstruction, two clocks were ticking, and the fate of the intervention hinged on which ran out first. The first clock counted down to the moment when progress in education and economic development strengthened blacks and their allies sufficiently that they could protect the revolution in the South. The longer the Republican regimes survived, the more likely the transformation would endure, as southern whites adapted to the new order. The second clock counted down to the moment when northern will and commitment ended. The problem was that the first clock would take a decade or more before it ran out, while the second clock was liable to run out at any time.

Furthermore, the first clock was started too late. Under Andrew Johnson's leadership, the North missed what is known as the "golden hour" of nation-building: the moment following regime change when radical reform is easiest—or least difficult. The period after Appomattox was the moment to create enduring change in the South, with land reform, sustained enforcement of civil rights, and a broadening of the Reconstruction coalition to divide the planter elite from the southern whites who had never owned slaves.

Even here, there were no guarantees of ultimate success. Racial identity could not simply be wished away. Land reform would have left small black landholders to struggle in a tough era for southern family farms. But we might have avoided a lost century of black civil rights.

The Civil War was the good war: a heroic and glorious struggle for emancipation and Union. The United States employed decisive force to achieve imposing objectives. Crusade begat crusade. One side's harsh rhetoric and refusal to offer concessions hardened the stance of its adversary. What chance was there of a compromise peace when both sets of combatants were American?

Reconstruction was the bad war: a grim and depressing quagmire without progress, without moral clarity, and without heroes. The northern public was destined to grow weary of the operation and seek to withdraw federal troops.

Perceptions of the Civil War and Reconstruction were fundamentally connected. As part of the process of reconciliation, the South accepted the northern victory in the Civil War, and the North saw Reconstruction as the campaign that the South won— and deserved to win. Thus both sides could shake hands over the grave of black liberty.

To be truly united, however, North and South required a common crusade, and in 1898 a suitable adversary arose in the shape of the crumbling Spanish Empire.

CHAPTER 5

Heel of Achilles

M r. Dooley may be the only Irish barkeeper whose philosophical musings have been read out in cabinet meetings.
A fictional creation of Finley Peter Dunne and first published in the *Chicago Evening Post* in 1893, Mr. Dooley quickly
became a nationwide phenomenon. In 1898, the barkeeper reflected
on the Spanish-American War, which began when the United
States launched a military campaign to free the island of Cuba from
Spanish rule.

Mr. Dooley at first envisaged a limited campaign: "Whin I
wint into it, I thought all I'd have to do was to set up here behind
th' bar with a good tin-cint see-gar in me teeth, an' toss dinnymite
bombs into th' hated city iv Havana." But gazing at Madrid's larger
empire, Mr. Dooley's horizons soon broadened: "Look at me now.
Th' war is still goin' on; an' ivry night, whin I'm countin' up the
cash, I'm askin' mesilf will I annex Cubia or lave it to the Cubians?
Will I take Porther Ricky or put it by? An' what shud I do with the
Ph'lippeens?"[1]

As in the Civil War, a crusading spirit overtook the nation in
1898, and U.S. objectives became increasingly majestic over time. A
conflict that began with the goal of regime change in Cuba ended

with the annexation of Puerto Rico, Guam, and the Philippines. The United States went to sleep a republic and woke up an empire.

Cuba Libre

A *grito,* or cry for freedom, rang out in February 1895 in the village of Baire, Cuba, heralding a revolt against Spanish rule. Hardly anyone noticed. It was just the latest in a long line of risings for *Cuba Libre.* But the cry set in motion a train of events that spiraled in unforeseen fashion and ultimately led U.S. forces to build an empire of liberty nine thousand miles away from Cuba in the distant archipelago of the Philippines.

Since Spain posed no clear and present danger to the United States in 1898, historians have had to dig deeper for the causes of the Spanish-American War, unearthing a cornucopia of explanations, from commercial lust to strategic interests, from idealism to social Darwinism, from gender identity to the psychic crisis of the 1890s. Many historians point to exaggerated reports of Spanish atrocities against the Cuban people in the hawkish "yellow press," named after the Yellow Kid, a comic strip character in the *New York World* who was colored with bright yellow ink. The *World* captured the complexity of sociopolitical conditions in Cuba in its inimitable style: "blood on the roadsides, blood in the fields, blood on the doorsteps, blood, blood, blood!"[2]

But the truth about Spanish atrocities didn't need exaggerating to shock the conscience of Americans. To crush the Cuban rebellion, the Spanish resorted to a brutal "reconcentration" policy that forcibly moved the population into prison camps, where 100,000 to 300,000 civilians died. Senator Redfield Proctor believed that reports of Spanish abuses were embellished, but a trip to Cuba changed his mind: "All my conceptions of wrong that could be inflicted on people falls short of this reality."[3]

"There may be an explosion any day in Cuba," wrote Senator Henry Cabot Lodge on January 31, 1898, which would "settle a great many things." Two weeks later, on February 15, the prophecy turned out to be literally true, when the battleship USS *Maine* blew up and sank in Havana harbor. Despite a lack of clear evidence, most people held the Spanish responsible.[4]

Americans were probably more hawkish on the eve of the Spanish-American War than before any other interstate war in history. Calls for a military campaign against Madrid grew intense, as people rallied around patriotic symbols and songs: "Theater audiences cheered, stamped, and wept at the playing of the Star-Spangled Banner."[5] The *New York World* conducted a poll on the Cuban question among "representative men of every occupation" across the country. The finding was "No More Delay"—it was time for war.[6] Journalist Henry Watterson claimed that the United States would march into battle "with a fervor, with a power, with a unanimity that would make it invincible if it were repelling not only the encroachments of Spain but the assaults of every monarch in Europe."[7] The French ambassador felt that a "sort of bellicose fury has seized the American nation."[8]

Almost every historian notes the popular clamor for war, but there were exceptions to this sentiment. Much of the business community was wary about fighting, as were many Catholic leaders, Quakers, and Unitarians. Major newspapers in Florida, for instance, were antiwar, and one study of opinion in Columbus, Ohio, found that hawkish fervor was more in evidence among activists than among the mass public.[9]

President William McKinley was personally hesitant about war, but he ultimately concluded that the United States had a duty to resolve a humanitarian crisis "right at our door."[10] To resist the growing public and congressional demand for military action would have been politically risky. In April 1898, with presidential backing, Congress passed a war resolution to end Spanish rule in

William McKinley

Cuba. But it was clear from the start that the United States did not trust the Cuban rebels and would seek to manage the process of Cuban independence under paternalistic U.S. tutelage.

On New Year's Day 1898, U.S. commodore George Dewey boarded the flagship *Olympia* in a Japanese city that would become infamous in a later crusade: Nagasaki. After Dewey's fleet docked in Hong Kong, one British officer worried that the American sailors would meet their match against Spain: "A fine set of fellows, but unhappily we shall never see them again."[11]

He had no need to worry. Following Sun Tzu's adage that victorious soldiers prevail first and then seek out the enemy, Dewey claimed that the campaign against Spain "was won in Hong Kong harbor."[12] As war drew near, Dewey carefully overhauled his war-

94

ships and drilled his crews. On May 1, Dewey led the fleet to Manila Bay, in the Philippines, while a band on deck played the hit tune of the war: "There'll Be a Hot Time in the Old Town Tonight."

His adversary was Admiral Don Patricio Montojo, who commanded an obsolete and outgunned Spanish fleet. Revealing his lack of confidence, Montojo placed his ships in shallow waters so that survivors could swim to safety. In a seven-hour battle, U.S. warships sailed back and forth, firing barrage after barrage that reduced their Spanish counterparts to skeletal wrecks burning in funereal pyres. The Spanish lost their entire fleet without killing a single American sailor.

A second Spanish fleet left Santiago de Cuba to engage the U.S. Navy. Within a few hours, it was also destroyed—although this time one American was killed. The last Spanish ship to sink was the *Cristóbal Colón,* or *Christopher Columbus,* symbolizing the end of Spain's empire in the Americas.

Among the U.S. troops that landed in southern Cuba was Theodore Roosevelt. He gave up his job as assistant secretary of the navy to help organize and join the First United States Volunteer Cavalry, or the Rough Riders, and his military exploits catapulted him to national fame. The Rough Riders were celebrated as a great melting pot of Harvard quarterbacks, cowboys, Pawnee Scouts, and bartenders. Edward Marshall noted in an 1899 history of the war that "officers ceased to be surprised when they found that an Arizona bronco buster had chosen as his bunkie some Eastern college man."[13] What the cowboys and aristocrats had in common was that they knew how to ride and shoot.

Roosevelt declared, "This is going to be a short war....I am going to get everything I can out of it."[14] He famously led the Rough Riders up the San Juan Heights, exalting in the charge, the moment, the deliverance—even as men fell all around him. Roosevelt's 1899 book on the campaign, *The Rough Riders,* focused so much on the protagonist that Mr. Dooley suggested a new title for the work: *Alone in Cuba*.[15]

After some stern resistance, Spanish forces in Cuba capitulated on July 16. The island of Guam was captured by a single U.S. naval boat, which sailed into the harbor and fired a couple of desultory shells at the Spanish fort. The Spaniards sailed out to greet the Americans, apologizing for not being able to return the salute, whereupon they were told they were under attack. The fall of Manila on August 14 brought the fighting to a close. With U.S. forces occupying Cuba, Puerto Rico, Guam, and the Philippines, an armistice was signed and peace negotiations began.

The Greatest Extreme Imaginable

Unlike in the Civil War, in 1898 Washington had no need to target civilians. After all, within just four months, the United States annihilated two Spanish fleets and won a convincing victory on the ground. Instead, Americans showed their crusading mettle with an escalation of war aims.

At first, the public supported a limited campaign to end the Spanish regime in Cuba and, as they saw it, free the Cuban people. McKinley proposed to "secure in the island the establishment of a stable government."[16] There is little evidence of any desire to wage a grander struggle. Dewey's attack on Manila was not part of a scheme to dominate East Asia, but rather an attempt to strike Spain where it was vulnerable, in order to bring the fighting to a rapid end.

Shortly after Dewey's victory, a straw poll of congressmen by the *St. Louis Republic* found only a single vote in favor of annexation of the Philippines. William Randolph Hearst's *San Francisco Examiner* led the cry for war but depicted the archipelago as a poison pill: "a source of corruption and weakness to Spain," and likely the United States, too, if it stayed there.[17] Piero Gleijeses examined forty-one major U.S. newspapers, as well as debates in Washington, and found that essentially "no one in the press, in Congress, or in the White House, even hinted before the outbreak of the war that the United States should acquire any part of the Philippines."[18] Mr. Dooley noted, "Tis not more thin two months since ye larned whether they were islands or canned goods."[19]

As the fighting with Spain progressed, Americans broadened the scale of their ambitions. Beliefs about the wisdom of colonizing the Philippines changed dramatically, and by the fall of 1898, a majority had emerged in favor of annexing and "uplifting" the islands. On August 4, *Public Opinion* claimed that twenty-eight major daily newspapers backed annexation, and others were falling into line. By September, the *Literary Digest* reported that support for taking the Philippines was running at three-to-one among publications.[20] McKinley went on a speaking tour of the Midwest in the fall and floated the idea of annexation as a trial balloon, while his aides carefully recorded the response of the crowds. McKinley concluded that "an overwhelming majority" of the American people favored colonizing the islands.[21]

At the forefront of the campaign for maximum goals were Protestants and Republicans: a reunion of the crusading vanguard from the Civil War. There was also a significant lobby against annexation of the Philippines, including the Anti-Imperialist League, labor figures worried about competition from Filipino workers, eastern Liberal Republicans disaffected by government corruption, and many southern Democrats. Although the Anti-Imperialist League had some illustrious supporters, it failed to win over most Americans. Former president Grover Cleveland opposed annexation but found that "the ears of our people are closed to reason."[22]

McKinley's war aims evolved in tandem with the nation's

changing preferences. In April 1898, he sought the removal of Spanish influence from Cuba. In June, he suggested that Washington could take a naval base in the Philippines. By August, he thought that the United States might annex one Philippine island. Finally, in October, the president decided to seize the entire archipelago.[23]

The Treaty of Paris was signed with Spain in December 1898, ending Spanish rule over Cuba and ceding Puerto Rico, Guam, and the Philippines to the United States in exchange for $20 million.[24] The treaty was approved in the Senate on February 6, 1899. Just forty hours before the final vote, fighting broke out in Manila between U.S. forces and rebels battling for Philippine independence—a harbinger of the far less enjoyable war to come.

America's final objectives in 1898 were truly imposing. After all, what more could the United States have demanded? It was physically impossible for Washington to force regime change in Madrid: an Iberian D-Day was beyond the capabilities of even this rising power. Spain condemned "the greatest extreme imaginable in the claims of the United States," as it was stripped of its imperial vestments and left to cling to a few last remnants in North Africa.[25]

With the annexation of the Philippines, the United States departed from its traditional policy of appropriating only territory that was sparsely populated and, with the exception of Alaska and Hawaii, geographically contiguous. The United States was now master of seven thousand islands, with a population of seven million, an ocean away. No one thought that the Philippines would become a state in the Union. In a diplomatic dance, the two antagonists swapped roles. Spain's long career as a colonial power was all but over, while America's brief tenure as an imperial state had just begun.

In the Name of Liberty

Can the expansion of U.S. objectives be explained simply by strategic logic? Perhaps the United States was just another great power, taking advantage of Dewey's triumph in Manila Bay to enlarge its territory. After all, the Philippines offered naval bases close to the shimmering El Dorado that was the Chinese market. And McKinley was certainly worried about the strategic consequences if the islands fell into the hands of the British, French, Germans, or Japanese. Senator John C. Spooner argued for annexation on precisely these strategic grounds. Americans, he thought, must put their ideals of self-government to one side and be practical for a moment. Other nations were selfish, and Americans must "look to their own interests and the interests of their own people."[26]

But it's striking how rare this kind of narrowly strategic argument was in the debate over U.S. war aims. Most supporters of occupying the Philippines claimed that both American ideals and national interests were served by annexation. Captain Alfred T. Mahan expounded the gospel of naval strength and expansionism from his influential perch as president of the Naval War College. But Mahan's arguments were fused with idealism. He was a devout Protestant who believed that the United States had a sacred mission to perform. Americans were only roused to act, he felt, "by the sense of wrong done, or right to be vindicated."[27]

Others argued that *only* U.S. ideals were promoted by occupation, and it was the task of Americans to altruistically sacrifice their blood and treasure to help the backward Filipinos. "Woe to any nation," the *Churchman* wrote, "called to guide a weaker people's future which hesitates for fear its own interests will be entangled and its own future imperiled by the discharge of an unmistakable duty."[28]

It's not easy to explain U.S. behavior in 1898 in terms of traditional national interests. The war against Spain was not a necessary war. American security was not endangered. And even the cheerleaders of expansion soon concluded that the Philippines offered zero strategic benefit—indeed, *less* than zero, as the islands were highly vulnerable.

The desire to spread liberal and religious ideals propelled Americans toward grand war aims in the Spanish-American War. The campaign pitted the highest form of government ever devised against the home of the Inquisition and the conquistador: a backward, cruel, and Catholic land. McKinley concluded that annexation of the Philippines was consistent with America's destiny, its duty, and its mission: "Territory sometimes comes to us when we go to war in a holy cause, and whenever it does the banner of liberty will float over it and bring, I trust, blessings and benefits to all the people."[29]

Republican senator Orville Platt declared, "I believe the same force was behind our army at Santiago and our ships in Manila Bay that was behind the landing of the Pilgrims on Plymouth Rock. I believe that we have been chosen to carry on and to carry forward this great work of uplifting humanity on earth.... We propose to proclaim liberty and justice and the protection of life and human rights wherever the flag of the United States is planted. Who denies that? Who will haul down those principles?"[30] As for doubts about whether the Declaration of Independence should restrain Americans from annexation, pro-imperialist Albert Beveridge claimed that the text was applicable only to "people capable of self government," which obviously didn't stretch to "Malay children of barbarism."[31]

Religion spurred Americans to perceive the occupation of the Philippines as a sacred mission. Protestantism was the faith of a large majority of Americans in 1898, and the dominant Protestant interpretation of the war was a battle between good and evil, liberty and tyranny, true Christianity and backward Romanism. "We may conclude," one historian wrote, "that the great preponderance of vocal religious sentiment, in the summer and fall of 1898, was in favor of retaining the Philippines and the other Spanish islands which had yielded to American arms."[32] Reverend L. B. Hartman depicted the United States as the "handmaid of Providence," adding that "our Republic...has been created and ordained to do a specific work, to serve the cause of freedom, humanity and civilization."[33]

McKinley was a pious Methodist, whose mother had maintained a Methodist church in Niles, Ohio. As a devout man in an era of profound evangelical sentiment, the president sincerely believed that occupying the Philippines was an integral part of God's plan. McKinley considered it "a holy cause" to propel "the banner of liberty" across the Pacific.[34]

The president reportedly told a group of visiting missionaries how he decided on annexation: "I didn't want the Philippines, and when they came to us, as a gift from the gods, I did not know what to do with them." Night after night, he thought through his options and fell on his knees in prayer. Finally, McKinley reached his verdict: "There was nothing left for us to do but to take them all, and to educate the Filipinos, and uplift and civilize and Christianize them, and by God's grace do the very best we could by them, as our fellow-men for whom Christ also died." The next day, McKinley sent for a cartographer and told him to put the archipelago "on the map of the United States."[35]

When Americans needed a guide for fighting a missionary campaign against Spain, they had only to look back to the last crusade — the Civil War. By 1898, people had forgotten the death, disease, and amputations. Newspaper stories, books, and a thousand parades by veterans in the Grand Army of the Republic conjured up the image of a heroic contest between blue and gray. "The past always looks better than it was," noted Mr. Dooley. "It's only pleasant because it isn't here."[36]

These memories legitimized war and expansion. The postmaster general commented that "the hand of Providence has been in this work as distinctly as the hand of Providence was in the war of the Revolution, or in that great war of 1861."[37] Bishop C. H. Fowler delivered a sermon that highlighted the three great missionary events since Calvary: the conversion of Saint Paul, the attack on Fort Sumter, and the destruction of the *Maine*. Sumter "made the Anglo-Saxon race fit to be used in the world's evangelization," while the *Maine* "set us about our job, namely the deliverance and salvation of the nations."[38] New lyrics were written for "The Battle Hymn of the Republic," with the words now reading, "Let us furl again Old Glory in the name of Liberty."[39]

Majestic war aims would show that the Americans of 1898 were worthy inheritors of freedom's banner. For decades, Civil War veterans were seen as a great generation, and they naturally became the standard against which the men of 1898 judged themselves. Theodore Roosevelt felt that U.S. society had lost its edge, surrendering to materialism and sloth. An idealistic crusading experience akin to the Civil War was needed to restore the virile spirit of the men of '65.[40]

The new crusade would bind up the wounds of the old. McKinley commented that "North and South have mingled their best blood in a common cause and today rejoice in a common victory."[41] Former Confederate officer Joe Wheeler led the sons of Civil War veterans in Cuba. When the Spanish fled the battlefield of Las Guásimas, Wheeler had flashbacks to the 1860s, declaring to his troops, "We've got the Yankees on the run!"[42]

Critics of expansion also appealed to American ideals. Republican Carl Schurz thought that annexation of the Philippines would "turn that war which was so solemnly commended to the favor of mankind as a generous war of liberation and humanity into a victory for conquest and self-aggrandizement."[43] The United States was aping the very colonialism that Americans had originally rebelled against. One professor at Yale argued that Spain had defeated the United States because we had become like them.[44]

But the expansionists claimed that U.S. imperialism was a very different animal than the European species: a benevolent and self-sacrificial variant. The profound American sense of mission in 1898, inspired by liberalism, religion, and historical memory, explains why Americans could honestly see the annexation of the Philippines as the liberation of the territory. It would set Filipinos free—to be tutored in the ways of American-style government. The thoughts of the locals themselves were a secondary consideration.

Wrath also fueled the outbreak of war with Spain and the escalation of U.S. objectives. In 1898, Americans were outraged by a series of Spanish transgressions: the campaign of atrocities in Cuba; the apparently unprovoked attack on the *Maine,* which killed more than 260 U.S. sailors; and a private letter from the Spanish minister in Washington deriding McKinley as a cheap politician, which was stolen and published in the *New York Journal.*

Of all these crimes, the destruction of the *Maine* packed the greatest emotional punch. "It cannot be denied," wrote Alexander K. McClure and Charles Morris in 1901, "that this unparalleled outrage intensified the war fever in the United States, and thousands were eager for the opportunity to punish Spanish cruelty and treachery."[45] Dozens of songs about the supposed attack quickly appeared, such as "My Sweetheart Went Down with the *Maine.*" At least ten of these tunes were titled "Remember the *Maine,*" with one including these lyrics: "From North and South and East and West / From city, farm, and plain / Loud comes a cry will never rest / For vengeance unto Spain."[46]

George Hamner was one of the last three surviving Rough Riders, dying in 1973, just shy of one hundred years of age. Before the Spanish-American War, he trained as a soldier in San Antonio, Texas, where he wrote to his future wife, "So you think the war could have been averted, eh? How about the 'Maine,' dear? Do you think it would have been upholding the honor of the nation to let such an act of treachery go unpunished? I am fighting, or going to fight, to avenge the 'Maine.' And 'Remember the Maine!' is our war cry!"[47]

American idealism and wrath ensured that a negotiated settlement based on a limited victory was off the table. Any hint of giving the Philippines back to Madrid raised a firestorm of protest at home, as stories emerged of barbarous Spanish rule on the islands. The U.S. negotiators bargaining over the treaty with Spain suggested a compromise deal to divide the Philippine territory, but McKinley was unyielding: "Do we not owe an obligation to the people of the Philippines which will not permit us to return them to the sovereignty of Spain?" The president was willing to make concessions on commercial aspects of the treaty, but not on "questions of duty and humanity."[48]

Neither could the United States hand the archipelago over to another colonial oppressor like Britain and wash its hands. Idealism also forbade Washington from annexing choice pieces of the Philippines and leaving it as a rump state. Territory touched by the crusader's sword had to be freed from Spanish rule and placed under American control. Beveridge said, "We can not retreat from any soil where Providence has unfurled our banner."[49]

Splendid Little War

At the time, the Spanish-American War was viewed as a triumphant event and a noble crusade. It united, if briefly, a divided society, heralded the arrival of a new great power, and turned military heroes like Theodore Roosevelt and George Dewey into national celebrities. Dewey, a veteran of America's first crusade, the Civil War, and a champion of its second, the Spanish-American War, became a prophet of the nation's third crusade when he told a reporter, "Our next war will be with Germany."[50] McKinley was widely applauded as a tough war president almost on a par with

Lincoln.[51] Here the crusading tale had room for only one hero: the United States. The Cubans were written out of the story. Indeed, the customary name for the conflict, the Spanish-American War, is a little like calling the American War of Independence the "Anglo-French War."

It's surprising, however, how quickly the conflict slipped from popular memory. We recall Roosevelt's Rough Riders but little else. U.S. diplomat John Hay labeled it a "splendid little war."[52] But perhaps it was too little and insufficiently splendid. Spain did not, after all, offer much resistance. A letter to the *New York Times* in February 1898 remarked that if the United States must fight a war, "let it be a contest with a power equal to our own, and one which it will be an honor to meet in respectable combat, rather than an effervescent and quixotic race, whom it would be no credit to ourselves to thrash."[53]

After burning bright, the Spanish-American War was soon eclipsed by the Civil War and the world wars. It began to seem like a mercurial and whimsical adventure. Dimming recollections remained entirely rosy, however, while the dark side of the war was forgotten. Around 350 Americans died in battle, but several thousand were killed by disease—much of it caused by scandalous conditions in the army training camps in Florida and elsewhere. Not for the first time, typhoid proved to be one of the soldiers' most dangerous enemies.

A Savage War of Peace

Rudyard Kipling was born in Bombay, in British-ruled India, in 1865. Three decades later, in 1899, he published his poem "The White Man's Burden" in *McClure's* magazine. It was subtitled "The United States and the Philippine Islands" and was widely read as a brazen exhortation to empire: "Go bind your sons to exile / To serve your captives' need." Theodore Roosevelt judged the effort by the future British poet laureate as "poor poetry" but "good sense from the expansionist standpoint."[54]

"The White Man's Burden," however, is hardly a ringing endorsement of empire. Kipling wrote that an imperial United States was destined to fight "savage wars of peace," in which many of its colonists would die. Americans would try to end famine and sickness, but the end result would "bring all your hopes to nought." Finally, after "the thankless years" of nation-building, what is the end result? "The blame of those ye better, / The hate of those ye guard."

When Americans took up the Caucasian yoke in the Philippines and for the first time began nation-building in foreign lands, the U.S. experience turned out in large part as Kipling had predicted. Washington appropriated Madrid's imperial cloak and cast it around America's shoulders, to refashion the Republic as an empire. But Americans soon found the cloth to be ill fitting as they grew weary of the intervention in the Philippines.

A Porcupine Wrong-End-To

In 1899, fighting broke out between the United States and a Filipino nationalist army led by Emilio Aguinaldo. When conventional military tactics proved disastrous for the Filipinos, Aguinaldo shifted to a drawn-out guerrilla campaign. This was the first time the U.S. military had ever fought a large-scale conflict outside North America. And it was quite a place to start: an average of only 24,000 U.S. troops faced 80,000 to 100,000 rebels in disease-ridden jungle terrain, spread over hundreds of inhabited islands seven thousand miles away.[55]

According to Max Boot, it was "one of the most successful counterinsurgencies waged by a Western army in modern times."[56]

The rebels were defeated partly because of Aguinaldo's limitations as a guerrilla leader. He was no Ho Chi Minh or General Giap. Instead, Aguinaldo represented the interests of the elite, failed to offer a compelling nationalist vision, and received "lukewarm support from the Filipino masses."[57]

The United States also pursued an effective strategy to win the hearts and minds of the Filipinos through public works. William Howard Taft was involved for thirteen years in this project as governor of the Philippines, secretary of war, and president. A jovial, ambitious, and hot-tempered man, Taft was, at 325 pounds, almost three times heavier than the slender Aguinaldo. Scornful about the fitness of the Filipinos to govern their own affairs, Taft nevertheless sought to uplift "our little brown brother" by overseeing the creation of a police force, introducing health initiatives, and building roads and schools.[58]

In 1901, U.S. brigadier general Frederick Funston, a native of Ohio and a slight man himself at 120 pounds, captured Aguinaldo in an episode straight out of a children's comic book. Funston located Aguinaldo's camp and discovered that the guerrilla leader had requested reinforcements. He then set out with a band of loyalist Filipinos posing as rebel forces arriving with "captured" American prisoners.

Funston gained entry to Aguinaldo's base, and when the head of the insurgency came out to offer his congratulations, Funston's men took Aguinaldo prisoner and whisked him away. Following his detention, Aguinaldo issued a proclamation accepting U.S. sovereignty and calling on the rebels to disarm. The Philippine insurgency weakened after 1902, although resistance continued, notably by Muslims on the southern island of Mindanao.

But it was a dark victory, which cost the lives of 4,200 Americans, 20,000 rebels, and an estimated 200,000 Filipino civilians, mostly from disease and famine related to the war.[59] U.S. troops

Emilio Aguinaldo boarding the USS Vicksburg, *shortly after his capture in 1901*

grew frustrated with the Filipinos' guerrilla tactics, including ambushes, torture, and mutilation. As one American officer noted, "If these people will only organize their forces into an army and get together in some number, and generally speaking, use modern, civilized methods of warfare, our task would be a simple one and comparatively easy"—which is presumably why they didn't.[60]

The United States responded with its own brutal tactics, which eerily resembled those employed by the Spanish against the Cubans. U.S. troops cut the rebels off from the population by concentrating Filipino civilians in fenced compounds, where disease was rife. Although torture was never official U.S. policy, it was widespread, including the notorious "water cure," which involved forcing liquid down the throats of captives.

In September 1901, on the island of Samar, the Filipinos showed that they could match Funston's deceptive approach. In the town of Balangiga, rebels disguised themselves as women, hiding their knives in the coffins of supposed cholera victims. Suddenly, one of the guerrillas snatched an American sentry's rifle and bludgeoned him with it. To the sound of conch shells and church bells, the rebels launched a furious assault on the garrison of seventy-four Americans, many of whom were still eating breakfast.

The U.S. company commander jumped from a second-story window in his pajamas, only to be hacked to death. The American cook resisted by hurling canned goods and wielding a meat cleaver. A group of survivors armed with rifles rallied and formed an infantry square, beating off the insurgents and retreating to the water. But even the boats did not bring safety, as the survivors faced an odyssey of escape, tracked by insurgents on the shore and equally hostile sharks in the water. In all, the rebels killed forty-eight Americans and injured most of the others.

The U.S. response was swift and terrible. The task of pacifying the island was given to Jacob "Hell Roaring Jake" Smith, a career army officer who'd earned the sobriquet because of his booming voice. Smith carried with him a souvenir from the Civil War: a minié ball in his hip. After 1865, shady financial deals, insubordination, and the illegal sale of alcohol almost got Smith thrown out of the military. But he had connections and survived to reach the rank of brigadier general. Smith ordered his men to kill any enemies they found over the age of ten and to turn the interior of Samar into a "howling wilderness."[61]

In reality, the campaign was not quite that severe. Nevertheless, U.S. troops swept destructively across the island, their progress marked by the glow of blazing villages. Thousands of homes were destroyed, along with tons of food and hundreds of carabao (water buffalo). The island was blockaded and the population herded into camps. The insurgency on Samar was crushed, but at a terrible price. Several thousand civilians died as a direct or indirect result of the pacification campaign.[62]

The behavior of U.S. soldiers on Samar was not typical, and most of the 126,000 Americans who served in the war didn't live up to the image of cold-blooded killers. But abuses were still very common. Reports suggested that for every wounded Filipino rebel, fifteen were killed—a telling statistic about the fate of captives.

Divisions in the United States over the annexation of the Philippines broadened and deepened in the face of the Filipino rebellion. Many Americans defended the nation-building mission and favored a long-term occupation of the islands. President McKinley argued that the country should not be swayed from its righteous path by a raggedy band of insurgents. Following McKinley's assassination, new president Theodore Roosevelt described the Philippine War in 1902 as the most glorious in the nation's history. These expansionists could count on support from a majority of the Republican Party; most Presbyterians, Congregationalists, Baptists, and Methodists; a number of famous publishers and university presidents; and many students.[63]

Arrayed against them was a diverse group of critics: the Anti-Imperialist League; much of the Democratic Party, including its nominee for president in 1900, William Jennings Bryan; German Americans fearful that the quest for colonies would bring the United States into conflict with Berlin; a minority of Republicans, such as Carl Schurz; Unitarians, Universalists, and Quakers; most labor leaders; and the majority of professors, writers, and intellectuals. Industrialist Andrew Carnegie bankrolled the Anti-Imperialist League and once offered to purchase the independence of the Philippines by writing a personal check for $20 million.[64]

Opponents of nation-building in the Philippines had often cheered the crusade against Spain but now saw the United States bogged down in an interminable struggle. Mark Twain railed against the brutality and hypocrisy of the Philippine War, describing the intervention as "a quagmire from which each fresh step renders the difficulty of extrication immensely greater."[65] Ernest Crosby parodied "The White Man's Burden" with dripping sarcasm:

> Take up the White Man's burden;
> Send forth your sturdy sons,
> And load them down with whisky
> And Testaments and guns.
> Throw in a few diseases
> To spread in tropic climes
> For there the healthy niggers
> Are quite behind the times.[66]

The anti-imperialist movement struggled, however, to spark a nationwide mass opposition to the Philippine War. McKinley won a clear victory over Bryan in the 1900 presidential election, although this was mainly because of the booming economy. The polyglot anti-imperialist coalition of conservatives and progressives, businessmen and labor union bosses, was fatally divided. Republican Carl Schurz loathed the populist Bryan, whom he called "the evil genius of the anti-imperialistic cause."[67] Carnegie backed McKinley in 1900 because imperialism worried him less than the Democratic Party's economic plans.[68]

The anti-imperialists also faced challenges that would bedevil other antiwar figures in American history. Just like Senators Hillary Clinton and John Kerry in regard to Iraq, critics of the Philippine War were endlessly reminded that they had originally supported the campaign against Spain: they were for the war before they were against it. In an era of extreme patriotism, Republican Party appeals for Americans to do their duty struck a powerful note. The anti-imperialists were castigated as traitors, the toast of the *insurrectos*.

Although the anti-imperialists were unable to end the war, most Americans grew profoundly disenchanted with the thankless task of nation-building in the Philippines. The pro-imperialist *New York Times* admitted in 1901, "The American people are plainly tired of the Philippine War."[69] Theodore Roosevelt concluded that "in the excitement of the Spanish War people wanted to take the islands. They had an idea they would be a valuable possession. Now they think they are of no value."[70]

As the fighting dragged on, McKinley privately remarked that he wished the United States had never occupied the territory.[71] In 1901, Roosevelt commented, "Sometimes I feel it is an intensely disagreeable and unfortunate task which we cannot in honor shirk."[72] As president, he concluded that the islands were a "white elephant" and "our heel of Achilles" in the Pacific: a strategic liability that should be made independent at an early date.[73]

America's appetite for imperialism was sated at the first bite. The Philippines would prove to be the country's first and last great colonial adventure. Roosevelt could have annexed the Dominican Republic—apparently with local consent—but his desire for this endeavor was the same as "a gorged boa-constrictor might have to swallow a porcupine wrong-end-to."[74] The Anti-Imperialist League had lost the battle but won the war.

After 1902, even as the counterinsurgency campaign wound down, the U.S. nation-building mission in the Philippines continued to exhibit serious flaws. It was, for example, often suffocatingly paternalistic, if not outright racist, in tone. Furthermore, the Filipino economy remained dependent on a handful of exports. Massive economic inequalities in Filipino society went uncorrected, and the United States ended up perpetuating the system of rule by oligarchies.

However, if the United States had never intervened in the Philippines, these inequalities would likely not have been resolved. And in other respects, the U.S. occupation ultimately achieved significant gains. Indeed, compared to the heart of darkness that beat oppressively in many of the European colonies, the American regime in the Philippines was "a model of enlightenment."[75] The Philippines had the freest press in Asia and attained the first representative assembly in an Asian colony (established in 1907, with a franchise broadened to literate adult males in 1916). The territory's population doubled from 1900 to 1920, and its standard of living in 1943 was three times higher than that of neighboring countries.[76]

The centerpiece of the U.S. development mission was education, and the Filipino literacy rate rose from 20 percent in 1901 to over 50 percent in 1941 — the highest in Southeast Asia.[77] Thousands of elementary schools were built, and hundreds of Americans traveled to work on the archipelago as educators, in a precursor of the Peace Corps. Not all of them were idealists. Blaine Moore described his pupils as "170 wriggling, squirming, talking barbarians" and focused his energy on mining ventures, rather than imparting the blessings of liberty.[78] Most educators were genuinely committed to teaching English, however, as well as to spreading the gospel of baseball, as a way of luring Filipinos away from the rival pursuit of cockfighting.

U.S. policies of liberalization, modernization, and mass education often dovetailed with Filipino goals, and Washington managed to co-opt large elements of society. Many Filipinos who had fought against the Americans assumed high office in the colonial regime. In public, the Filipino elite exhorted the cause of independence, but in private they were far more ambivalent, fearing the strategic and economic consequences if they broke ties with the United States.[79] Filipino president Manuel Quezon recognized the difficulty in cultivating mass resistance to the U.S. regime: "Damn the Americans! Why don't they tyrannize us more?"[80]

Despite a degree of success, there was waning American enthusiasm for a permanent commitment. One survey of members of Congress in 1907 found that only 20 percent favored keeping the islands.[81] According to the Democratic Party platform in 1912, the occupation had been "an inexcusable blunder which has involved us in enormous expense, brought us weakness instead of strength, and laid our nation open to the charge of abandonment of the fundamental doctrine of self-government."[82] It could have been written by later Democrats in reference to Vietnam or Iraq.

Americans increasingly saw the Philippines as strategically vulnerable and an economic competitor, and many sought to declare U.S. independence from this colonial albatross. The Jones Act of 1916 solidified Washington's commitment to Philippine independence once a "stable government" was formed in the islands. President Franklin Roosevelt remarked in 1934, "Let's get rid of the Philippines—that's the most important thing. Let's be frank about it."[83] Signing into law an act that paved the way for Philippine independence—which ultimately came in 1946, after World War II—Roosevelt renounced the war once championed by his distant cousin: "Our nation covets no territory, nor sovereignty over a people gained through war against their will."[84]

By the 1920s, most historians depicted the acquisition of the Philippines as a disastrous error.[85] Later historians, writing in the wake of Vietnam, were even more adamant that the nation-building mission in the Philippines was fundamentally immoral. The war in Indochina cast its shadow back over history, making earlier U.S. counterinsurgency operations seem like proto–My Lais.[86] Scholars of the U.S. military were the exception to the rule. These embedded historians followed the American troops in the Philippines so closely that they tended to sympathize more with their efforts.[87]

Let Men Die to Make Us Rich

Disillusionment with nation-building in the Philippines was partly just a reflection of the real costs in blood and treasure. But as with southern Reconstruction, declining feelings of vengeance and American idealism also encouraged a skeptical view of the mission and a desire to leave.

The U.S. troops on the front lines in the Philippine War were often motivated by revenge. As one military commentator put it in 1899, "Upon the part of the rank and file of the Americans," there emerged a "feeling of intense personal hatred of their tormentors, and an earnest desire to be turned loose upon them and kill them."[88] But back on the home front, the struggle against the Filipino rebels lacked the good-versus-evil clarity of the Spanish-American War. In 1901, a strongly pro-imperialist editor declared that "the situation is a depressing one from every point of view. Good men are perplexed. Questions of right and wrong, of consistency with American ideals and principles, of stifling the 'passion for independence,' of national responsibility, of prudence—all are hard to decide."[89] As the moral lines blurred, so the desire for retribution against the adversary and the public's commitment to the campaign began to fade.

Apologists for the brutal tactics employed by U.S. troops in Samar and elsewhere often pointed out that Union and Confederate soldiers had carried out similar acts in the Civil War.[90] They were right. Indeed, harsh measures in the Philippines were explicitly justified by Abraham Lincoln's 1863 General Orders No. 100, which authorized the summary shooting of enemies taken without a uniform.

But American brutality looks very different in the context of an interstate crusade compared to a nation-building quagmire. During the Civil War, when the North drank deeply from the crusading elixir, the Union armies that laid waste to the South were seen as avenging angels. But the exacters of punitive justice in the Philippines were viewed as far less righteous. Rather than applaud the callous tactics of U.S. troops, the Senate investigated military abuses in 1902, prompting a revival of domestic anti-imperialism. Jake Smith was court-martialed and forced into retirement. The Philippine campaign was the "first war in which American officers and troops were officially charged with what we would now call war crimes."[91]

The same national idealism that drove the United States to crusade against Spain also ensured that the fruits of the campaign in the Philippines seemed to rot and decay. Partly it was a matter of unrealistic expectations. Addled by war fever in 1898 and almost completely ignorant about Filipino society, Americans thought they would be greeted as liberators and could quickly remake the archipelago in the image of the United States. Suddenly, however, they were confronted by the reality of a tropical climate, disease, insurgency, and death. With illusions going in, the inevitable result was disillusionment and a rising sense of nation-building fatigue.[92]

U.S. officials made the usual error of promising immediate success, thereby planting the seeds of later perceptions of failure. In April 1900, Theodore Roosevelt declared that "the insurrection in the Philippine Islands has been overcome."[93] The following month, General Elwell Otis, commander of U.S. forces in the Philippines, claimed in *Leslie's Weekly,* "The war in the Philippines is already over.... There will be no more real fighting."[94] Contrary to these promises of mission accomplished, months and years of tough warfare lay ahead, engendering profound frustration.[95]

Idealism also encouraged Americans to set a high bar for success in nation-building. During the 1920s, for example, U.S. experts concluded that educational policies were failing in the Philippines because Filipino students were not the equals of their American counterparts. As Stanley Karnow put it, the verdict was "harsh and probably unjust, since it assessed the Filipinos by American standards. But the Americans had no other yardstick than their own."[96]

The Philippine intervention represented a flagrant breach of one particular U.S. ideal: anti-imperialism. For a brief while, it looked as if America's traditional aversion to colonialism would be replaced by a newfound love of empire. The late-nineteenth-century wave of imperialism, which saw the European empires carve up much of the world, also washed U.S. shores. Prominent Americans admired the British Empire, talked of a common Anglo-Saxon mission, and wanted the United States to join the club of colonial great powers — with the occupation of the Philippines seen as the price of admission.

But America's flirtation with imperialism was shallow and insincere. The anti-imperial ideal soon reasserted itself and encouraged a gloomy view of the mission in the Philippines. The Founding Fathers would never have imagined that future Americans, in the words of one senator, "might strut about in the cast-off clothing of pinchbeck emperors and pewter kings."[97] The Democratic Party platform of 1900 declared, with a nod to Lincoln, "No nation can long endure half republic and half empire."[98]

For the first time, critics denounced a nation-building mission as a form of economic imperialism. Foreshadowing the left-wing view of the Vietnam War as a conflict engineered by shadowy corporate interests, William Jennings Bryan argued that the campaign in the Philippines served the interests of the wealthy classes.[99] Mark Twain also saw the mission as a pillaging expedition led by Christian butchers, suggesting new lyrics for "The Battle Hymn of the Republic": "As Christ died to make men holy, let men die to make us rich."[100]

Attacks on American imperialism touched a raw nerve in the national psyche and put supporters of the war on the defensive. The administration refused to call the Philippines a colony and avoided using the term *imperialism* in favor of *expansion*—a word suggesting continuity with the western frontier. When proponents of nation-building described the United States as an empire, it was an empire of liberty, an empire of peace, an empire of the intellect—anything but a typical European empire.

Critics had a perfect analogy to demonstrate the futility of the Philippine mission and its betrayal of American ideals: southern Reconstruction. Minister Thomas Wentworth Higginson argued that the United States should steer clear of the Philippines or face a depressing repeat of its experience of nation-building in the South.[101] Edwin Godkin, founder and first editor of the *Nation,* learned a similar lesson from southern Reconstruction: the United States couldn't rule other peoples. Never again should we send "large bands of characterless adventurers called 'carpetbaggers' to humiliate the vanquished and plunder them."[102]

Senator Benjamin "Pitchfork Ben" Tillman, a murderous white supremacist, saw the nation-building missions in the South and in the Philippines as similarly despotic. Without any apparent irony, Tillman argued that the "shrouds of murdered Filipinos, done to death because they were fighting for liberty," had a silver lining, because Republicans would no longer dare to "preach a crusade against the South's treatment of the negro."[103]

The Cradle of Liberty

Just as the glorious Civil War provided a sharp contrast to the interminable era of southern Reconstruction, so the magnificent crusade of 1898 was a strikingly different experience than the quagmire in the Philippines. Zeal changed to weariness, unity became division, and a noble cause turned into a sordid fight. Whereas the war against Spain conjured up champions like Dewey, Roosevelt, and the Rough Riders, heroes from the Philippines were few and far between. Funston was briefly celebrated after capturing Aguinaldo.

His name emblazons a street, school, fort, and park in San Francisco, and he is buried in the Presidio. But today virtually no one knows who he is. The most famous soldier from the Philippine War may be—revealingly—Jake Smith.

Of course, the Philippine War was much longer and bloodier than the campaign against Spain. But declining feelings of wrath, together with the nation's idealism, meant that Americans were fated to become disillusioned by their experience in the Philippines, even if fewer U.S. troops had died, less money had been expended, and abuses had been largely avoided. The Asian intervention was forgotten with incredible speed and left unmarked by memorials.

The truth is that in 1898, there were no easy options for the United States in regard to the Philippines. An independent archipelago would probably have been short-lived, with the imperial great powers hovering like vultures. There might easily have been a major international war over control of the islands.[104]

Nevertheless, the bloody fight of 1899–1902 could have been averted. The Filipino elite admired the United States, and Aguinaldo initially told his troops that "the great North American nation, the cradle of liberty," was "the friend to our people."[105] One option was self-government under U.S. sovereignty, with a clear promise of future independence. Another possibility was an American protectorate similar to Cuba. In both cases, the United States could have provided significant nation-building assistance in establishing a new state and stabilizing the territory, while aiming to avoid either a civil war or a great power struggle. But guided by a profound sense of crusading idealism, Americans discarded compromise solutions and limited authority, in favor of the absolutist position that the United States should have full control in order to begin its sacred mission.

In 1901, the year that Aguinaldo was captured, a baby boy was born eight thousand miles away in Bethany, Missouri. More than a century later, he would come to enjoy a singular distinction.

CHAPTER 6

To End All War

The baby boy was Frank Buckles. In 1917, at sixteen years of age but claiming he was twenty-one, Buckles enlisted in the U.S. Army during World War I. He was sent to France on the *Carpathia,* the same ship that rescued the survivors of the *Titanic* in 1912. Buckles became an ambulance driver and guarded German prisoners after the armistice—all while he was still just a boy. This is a common enough story perhaps, but with one important difference: of the two million Americans sent to Europe in 1917– 1918, Frank Buckles was the only one still alive in 2010. The physical bond linking us to World War I was down to a single fragile strand.

Despite the tens of thousands of American dead and the conflict's profound global impact, World War I is largely forgotten in the United States. "For a long time," remarked Buckles in 2007, "I've felt that there should be more recognition of the surviving veterans."[1] But in 1917–1918, the campaign generated incredible zeal and passion, as Americans took up the crusader's sword to mold a plastic world and punish the devilish Hun.

The Spirit of '17

When World War I began in 1914, the United States remained on the sidelines, watching in horror as Europe consumed itself. It was called the Great War because no conflict had ever been as terrible. Germany, Austria-Hungary, and the Ottoman Empire were aligned against Britain, France, Russia, and Italy. On the eastern front, the fighting was quite fluid, but in the West, static trench warfare emerged, as men lived and ended their lives burrowed in the earth.

For three years, Americans sought to keep the United States free from contamination by this European horror. Popular songs included "Don't Take My Darling Boy Away" and "I Didn't Raise My Boy to Be a Soldier." President Woodrow Wilson urged neutrality in thought and deed and won reelection in 1916 on the slogan "He kept us out of war." In early 1917, Wilson was still racked with doubt about joining the fray, reflecting a nation that was uncertain and divided.

In April 1917, the United States finally entered the war on the side of Britain and its allies. Wilson believed that Germany had forced the United States toward the precipice with unrestricted submarine warfare against U.S. shipping and the infamous Zimmermann telegram, in which Berlin incited Mexico to attack the United States and reclaim its lost territories in the American Southwest. In addition, only participation in the war could give Wilson a decisive voice at the subsequent peace conference table.

On April 2, Wilson delivered a war message to Congress, his grim demeanor matching the clouds and rain outside. Four days later, on Good Friday, the House of Representatives voted for war by a margin of 373 to 50. Germany's minister of marine said that the U.S. threat was "zero, a complete and absolute nothing, a less than nothing," but American participation proved critical as the Great War approached its endgame.[2]

In 1917, there was no excuse for illusions. For close to a thousand days, Americans had heard horrific accounts of the Somme and Verdun, the systematic industrial destruction, the millions of dead, the soldiers living like rats in a subterranean world, and the European governments rocked to their foundations.

But what were such worries in the face of a sentiment "mightier than logic, wide as light, strong as gravity"? With the outbreak of war, an unmistakable wave of enthusiasm spread throughout all social classes. Congress met Wilson's request for war by exploding into cheers. When the audience at the Metropolitan Opera in New York City heard the news of war, they had the same fevered reaction. Congressional mail overwhelmingly favored fighting. The registration of ten million Americans for the draft went surprisingly smoothly. Women built nationwide organizations to support the war effort, often campaigning for the dual goals of victory and suffrage. The *Nation* noted a "rebirth of American patriotism," with flags flying up and down America's streets.[3]

Secretary of the Treasury William McAdoo claimed that the campaign "is a kind of crusade; and like all crusades, it sweeps along on a powerful stream of romanticism."[4] In 1917, Theodore Roosevelt was almost sixty years old, blind in one eye, and nursing a sore hip from an expedition to the Amazon. But TR rolled back the years, telling the Harvard Club, "If ever there is a holy war, it is this war," and asking President Wilson if he could raise a division and lead it into battle in France.[5] Roosevelt didn't get his wish, but four of his sons joined the fight — the youngest of whom, Quentin, died in the war.

The Destruction of Every Arbitrary Power

Just as in 1861 and 1898, the crusade tradition came to the fore as Americans backed the use of all necessary force to remake the world. Before the United States entered the Great War, Wilson called for "peace without victory," which would leave no side humiliated.[6] In early 1917, Americans even considered fighting a limited war to protect U.S. neutral rights. The United States would compel Germany to end unrestricted submarine warfare, then pull back. But once the trumpet sounded, the idea of engaging in a restricted operation vanished from discussion.

The campaign evolved into a democratic crusade against autocracy and a quest to end all war. In his war message of April 1917, Wilson mixed somberness with grandiosity. The struggle was a choice unsought, a "solemn and even tragical" decision, which had "been thrust upon" the United States. The objective was to "bring the Government of the German Empire to terms and end the war." And as a wider aim, "the world must be made safe for democracy."[7]

In the coming months, Wilson steadily escalated U.S. war aims until the nation was fighting for an extraordinary transformational vision. On June 14, 1917, Wilson called for "a People's War, a war for freedom and justice and self-government amongst all the nations of the world."[8] As one critic noted, the address "implies that America is ready to pour out endless blood and treasure, not to the end of a negotiated peace, but to the utter crushing of the Central Powers."[9]

In January 1918, Wilson outlined his Fourteen Points program, promising to sweep away the old politics of diplomacy and war and rebuild the structure of international relations on the surer foundations of self-determination, disarmament, and a new collective security organization—the League of Nations. The revolutionary agenda was bursting at the seams; in the coming months, the president tacked on an additional thirteen points.[10]

Wilson's expansive objectives drew praise from both political parties and most of the press. A broad consensus emerged in favor of joining the League, although few gave any thought to the details. The *New York Times* called the Fourteen Points speech "the President's triumph," adding later that "when Woodrow Wilson speaks to the American people he speaks for them; their wish, their purpose, their innermost thoughts are expressed in his words, for he has an instinctive understanding of their will."[11]

Parsing public opinion a little, we find the skeptics and the true believers. Dissenters, who rejected a crusading war, included Irish Americans with little love for Britain, German Americans with ties to their homeland, Quakers, feminists, and socialists (who opposed a campaign to enrich the ruling class). Robert La Follette was one of half a dozen senators to vote against the war, prophesying that America's poor were about to rot in the trenches.[12]

It is a brave thing to stand against the crusading tide and shout "No!" La Follette's image was hanged in effigy. A fellow senator suggested that he take up a new position in the Reichstag. When La Follette boarded Washington trolley cars, the other riders sometimes got off. As Americans rallied around the flag, the antiwar movement became increasingly marginalized. Many former pacifists were swept up in the idealism and patriotism of the struggle. Who could not support a war to end war? Automotive magnate Henry Ford had campaigned relentlessly for staying out of the fight, but now he enthusiastically switched his industrial empire from plowshares to swords.[13]

The crusading vanguard plunged into the fight with fearsome enthusiasm. Here were the same white Protestants found at the tip of the spear in the Civil War and the Spanish-American War. The true believers also included northeastern industrial workers and the masters of the banking universe on Wall Street, who saw their interests bound up with the war effort; college students who enlisted en masse; and union leaders such as Samuel Gompers, who had opposed the Philippine quagmire but backed the crusade against Germany.[14]

The two million American troops who arrived in Europe had plenty to occupy their thoughts without worrying about crusading war aims. The slaughter came late for the Americans, but even they confronted the question posed by British war poet Wilfred Owen: "What passing-bells for these who die as cattle?"[15]

The German offensive of 1918 surged, slowed, and finally ground to a halt in the face of Allied resistance and the influx of forces from the New World.[16] As the tide turned in the summer and fall of 1918, American soldiers attacked some of the strongest German defenses on the western front. Edward Rickenbacker, America's World War I "Ace of Aces" with twenty-six kills, swept across the sky in late September 1918 and saw below him the opening salvos of the massive U.S. offensive in the Meuse-Argonne region, northwest of Verdun. From his aerial vantage point, Rickenbacker viewed through the mist what seemed like ants swarming over molehills. Another witness thought the U.S. Army was like "a blanket of destruction ten miles deep, thirty miles long, gliding by inches, skulking by inches—hundreds of thousands of my fellow beings are dragging and tugging this vast carpet of destruction toward the enemy; thrusting its sharp and explosive edge into the enemy."[17]

On the front lines, the war looked very different. The initial success of the U.S. assault soon faltered in the face of furious German opposition. Enemy troops had spent the past four years carefully constructing a killing field, with trench works named after Wagnerian witches: Giselher, Kriemhilde, and Freya. The doughboys advanced through a scarred and apocalyptic landscape into dense woods and shell craters, with visibility limited by thick white fog. German fire cut the young Americans down like so much corn. U.S. troops incurred 120,000 deaths and injuries in just a few weeks.

On October 2, the 305th Infantry attacked what was known as "dead man's hill" in the Bois de la Naza, part of the Argonne Forest. As one soldier recalled, "The only order that could be heard was 'Forward' and Company F was game. It was awful. The poor boys were getting slaughtered as fast as sheep could go up a plank.

No one could ever describe the horror of it. The screams of the wounded were terrible but we stuck to it."[18]

Brigadier General Edmund Wittenmyer, known as "Old Witt," who reputedly feared nothing under the sun, came to the front lines to personally lead the assault. The next morning, Wittenmyer returned to headquarters, sat down, wiped his brow, and said, "Well, anyone who says he likes war is either a damn fool or a damn liar."[19] "Enlightened by the volleyed glare," Private Walter Bromwich wrote to his pastor questioning the very notion of a benevolent God: "How can there be fairness in one man being maimed for life, suffering agonies, another killed instantaneously, while I get out of it safe?"[20]

Despite all of this, the American soldiers on the western front often spoke in their private letters of valor and glory, the cause, and the crusade. They adopted the romantic language of Sir Walter Scott, as if, like the Connecticut Yankee, they had been transported across time to King Arthur's court.[21] Winston Churchill recalled the first American arrivals in France: "Crammed in their lorries they clattered along the roads singing the songs of a new world at the top of their voices, burning to reach the bloody field."[22] Historian William Langer traveled to France as a young man and recalled the eagerness of the troops to get to the front, driven by enthusiasm for adventure and heroism.[23] Wilson described the American soldiers as "disinterested champions of right," who "were recognized as crusaders, and as their thousands swelled to millions, their strength was seen to mean salvation."[24] One cynical aviator thought that the American people had "been fed on bunk until they'd never believe anything that didn't sound like a monk's story of the Crusades."[25]

During the final months of the Great War, Wilson's tone became even more strident. On July 4, 1918, he claimed that there would be "no half-way decision" and "no compromise." The United States was fighting for the "destruction of every arbitrary power anywhere...that can disturb the peace of the world."[26] Reeling under the Allied hammer blows, Germany sued for peace in October 1918. Wilson gave Berlin the stark choice of regime change or "surrender."[27] The president insisted that the Allies would have "the unrestricted power to safeguard and enforce the details of the peace."[28] In the end, the kaiser abdicated, Germany's military was forced to evacuate captured territory and disarm, and Allied troops occupied the Rhineland. Berlin lay incapacitated.

But some American crusaders were still not satisfied. Whereas Wilson saw a democratic Germany quickly joining a new world order built around the League of Nations, Republicans like Theodore Roosevelt and Senator Henry Cabot Lodge wanted Berlin's defeat to be indisputable and demanded unconditional surrender. Here the division was not over a transformational war versus a limited war; it was over the direction in which America's crusading fervor should be channeled.

"Let us dictate peace by the hammering guns," thundered Roosevelt.[29] Lodge argued that the siren song of the Fourteen Points must not entice America onto the rocks of a negotiated settlement: "No peace that satisfies Germany in any degree can ever satisfy us."[30] The head of the American Expeditionary Force in France, General John "Black Jack" Pershing, argued that U.S. troops should continue the struggle and bring Germany "to her knees."[31]

Hardened by the spilling of blood, the American public backed the objective of unconditional surrender. "As the war progressed and the issues grew clearer," remarked journalist Ray Stannard Baker, "I became more and more sincerely convinced of the necessity...that the Germans and all they stood for be defeated."[32] The *New Republic* had originally hoped for a negotiated end to the war, but by October 1918, its editors wanted Berlin to be left "beaten and prostrate."[33]

The Senate, along with most of the press, rejected the German offer to negotiate an armistice, calling instead for Berlin's absolute surrender. Edward "Colonel" House, a close adviser to Wilson, thought that the president was unaware of "the nearly unanimous sentiment in this country against anything but unconditional surrender. He did not seem to realize how war-mad our people had become."[34]

The Horrors of War

A central exhibit in the case for war against Berlin was the barbaric campaign of German submarine attacks that had indiscriminately killed noncombatants, including 128 Americans who died in 1915 when the *Lusitania* was torpedoed. As Wilson declared in his war message of April 2, 1917, "I am not now thinking of the loss of property involved, immense and serious as that is, but only of the wanton and wholesale destruction of the lives of noncombatants, men, women, and children, engaged in pursuits which have always, even in the darkest periods of modern history, been deemed innocent and legitimate."[35]

To destroy this menace, however, Americans were themselves willing to fight a hard war and deliberately target civilians. Back in the Civil War, the method was the destruction of the crops, barns, and mills needed by southerners to live. Here the U.S. fleet greatly strengthened the Allied naval blockade, which caused almost one million deaths in Germany and Austria-Hungary through malnutrition and disease.[36]

The *New York Times* noted that "it is not a pleasant or inspiring task to force the women and children of an entire nation nearer and nearer the point of starvation," yet it remained America's duty "to bring Germany to its complete defeat by the stern enforcement of this method."[37] In January 1918, Colonel House happily told Wilson that in Germany, "it looks as if things are beginning to crack."[38]

Just before the armistice, Helen Bailie, a forty-four-year-old mother, put her two children to bed in Natick, Massachusetts, and wrote in her diary, "I cannot feel compassion for the German people. Tho victims in a way, they...shd themselves have tasted more of the horrors of war."[39]

"I Fear Lest This War Be Over Too Soon"

Why did a campaign that began as an effort to protect U.S. neutral rights unfold into a hard war to achieve goals of almost infinite magnitude? Strategic considerations were an important factor in the U.S. decision to enter World War I and pursue a transformational agenda. U.S. loans to Britain and France from 1914 to 1917 gave influential business and financial constituencies an interest in an Allied victory so that they could recoup their money. Wilson's tougher language in 1918 was partly a response to the harsh peace treaty imposed by Germany on Russia, which signaled Berlin's intention to dominate Europe. The naval blockade also had a clear strategic logic: to coerce Germany. After all, Britain had been blockading Berlin since 1914.

In the fall of 1918, Lothar Persius, a retired German naval captain, offered a different perspective in the newspaper *Berliner Tageblatt*. As he saw it, the United States had intervened not for economic reasons, but because of "the high idealism which on the whole prevails" in the United States. Americans maintained a "spirit of deep religious and moral culture" and rejected war unless it was "a struggle against despotism and slavery."[40]

Many Americans were profoundly uncomfortable with a war fought for narrow strategic purposes or to restore the European balance of power. Secretary of State Robert Lansing said in 1917, "To go to war solely because American ships had been sunk and Americans killed would cause debate.... The sounder basis was the duty of this and every other democratic nation to suppress an auto-cratic government like the German."[41] In 1921, the U.S. ambassa-dor to Britain suggested that the United States had entered the war only to protect American interests. He was subjected to a torrent of vilification at home, and Secretary of State Charles Evans Hughes was forced to clarify that the intervention had been thoroughly idealistic.[42]

Liberal and religious principles cultivated a profound sense of mission in the Great War, propelling Americans toward magnifi-cent war aims. Woodrow Wilson was the standard-bearer of the crusade. Born in Virginia in 1856, Wilson arrived in the White House via the law and the academy. He was an American president who favored British-style parliamentary government; a friend of organized labor and of white supremacists; a master of words who was probably dyslexic; a man of great energy and ill health; a pro-fessor who stepped into the hurly-burly world of politics; a figure with roots in the North, who was the first southerner elected presi-dent since the Civil War; an antimilitarist who reportedly never engaged in a fistfight in his life, yet guided the United States into the greatest war the world had ever known.

Wilson certainly had a practical side and understood the dynam-ics of power politics. But in 1917–1918, he believed that America was engaged in the most righteous war in history. Just a few weeks before the U.S. declaration of war, the decision whether to fight felt like a terrible dilemma to him. Once the Rubicon was crossed, every-thing suddenly became clear. There had only ever been one choice: to pursue a quest for justice that would propagate America's liberal ideals of democracy, economic freedom, and self-determination.

In Wilson's mind, representative governments were inherently more peaceful than autocracies because the public could veto aggressive wars. Whereas half a century before, slavery had posed a fatal threat to American liberty, now a world divided into democ-racy and militaristic tyranny could not stand. The danger for "peace and freedom lies in the existence of autocratic governments backed by organized force which is controlled wholly by their will, not by the will of their people."[43]

Wilson also aimed to spark a global diplomatic revolution. The Great War showed that the security of all states was interdependent: even distant America had been drawn into the maelstrom. The League of Nations would be the keystone of a nobler world civilization, ending the old-style power politics that provoked conflict and bloodshed.

A phoenix would rise from the ashes of Europe, as victory over Germany, regime change in Berlin, and the creation of the League inaugurated a new age of peace and freedom. "I cannot be deprived of the hope that we are chosen, and prominently chosen," Wilson commented, "to show the way to the nations of the world how they shall walk in the paths of liberty."[44] As America's honored dead rose in number, Wilson brought increased devotion to the cause, broadening the scale of the mission and arguing for a "peace worth the infinite sacrifices of these years of tragical suffering."[45]

Many Europeans were skeptical about Wilson's idealism. According to the *Times* of London, the president seemed to believe that the kingdom of justice was close at hand.[46] How could Wilson, in the midst of a cataclysmic war, assume that all the major powers would commit to peace? Wilson's principled vision of the conflict also begged another question: if the moral battle lines were so starkly drawn and Germany was such a mortal threat to American values, why had Wilson waited so long to enter the war? But, then, Americans think very differently about such issues once they seize the crusader's sword.

Wilson's depiction of World War I as a struggle to protect and extend liberal ideals was superbly attuned to the American mind. Following in the devilish footsteps of Spain, Germany became widely seen as the antithesis of America: militaristic, barbaric, autocratic, feudal, and corrupt. War was a redemptive act—for the

United States, for Europe, and for the world. "Never was there such a spectacle in all history," wrote a correspondent for the *New York Times,* "as that of the fresh millions of free Americans flocking to the rescue of beleaguered and exhausted Europe."[47] A cartoon in the *New York World* featured Uncle Sam beating a drum, calling forth Americans from all corners of the land to fight in this new dawn.[48] Twenty-six-year-old Lester Hensler wrote to his parents before heading to France, "I am thankful that I can take a place among men who will bring freedom to the world."[49] U.S. diplomat James W. Gerard wrote to Wilson, "There is a lofty idealism about it which puts this war on the plane of a crusade."[50]

Republicans like Theodore Roosevelt talked more openly of power politics, but the contest between Wilson and Roosevelt was not about idealism versus realpolitik. It was about different conceptions of the American mission. Roosevelt's belief system was founded on idealism: "To my fellow Americans I preach the sword of the Lord and of Gideon."[51]

There were some holdouts. The American writer E. E. Cummings drove an ambulance in France and could make it through only one paragraph of Wilson's idealistic rhetoric before "being taken with a dangerous fit of laughter."[52] Opponents of the war countered Wilson with their own arguments based on liberal principles. La Follette wondered, If this was a war for democracy, would the British Empire be the next target? Antiwar activists also talked in religious terms: the conflict was antithetical to Christ's message of peace and defiled mankind.[53]

But as with earlier crusades, religion inspired Americans to pursue the fight with missionary zeal. The son, grandson, and nephew of Presbyterian ministers, Wilson was a highly religious man who saw America as an apostle with a unique calling to shepherd the less enlightened nations. This sense of a divinely inspired quest helped draw a president who was profoundly opposed to armaments and killing into the hellish struggle. Wilson ended his war message in April 1917 by stating that America had to live by its ideals: "God helping her, she can do no other." It was a reference to Martin Luther's famous statement to the Diet of Worms: "God helping me, I can do no other."[54] French prime minister Georges Clemenceau remarked cuttingly of the president's righteous tone, "God gave us the Ten Commandments, and we broke them. Wilson gives us the Fourteen Points. We shall see."[55]

The Protestant clergy embraced a holy war for a democratic peace. Few missed the symbolism of the United States declaring war on Good Friday, the day of sacrifice. Christ gave his life for mankind. Now the United States would forfeit its blood and treasure to save Europe. Reverend Randolph McKim preached, "It is God who has summoned us to this war. It is his war we are fighting.... This conflict is indeed a crusade. The greatest in history— the holiest."[56]

The U.S. government used an extensive propaganda machine to cultivate these missionary themes and sell the war to the American people. George Creel headed the Committee on Public Information and based his messages not on strategic self-interest, but on morality and idealism—a sure sign of which buttons were seen as most sensitive in the American psyche.[57]

Creel called the war "a Crusade not merely to re-win the tomb of Christ, but to bring back to earth the rule of right, the peace, goodwill to men and gentleness he taught."[58] The 1918 government film *Pershing's Crusaders* opened with scenes of a medieval crusader accompanied by American soldiers, with the subtitle, "The young men of America are going out to rescue Civilization. They are going to fight for one definite thing, to save Democracy from death."[59]

This framing of the conflict as Christ and liberty versus the devil and slavery drew Americans toward a vision of war that

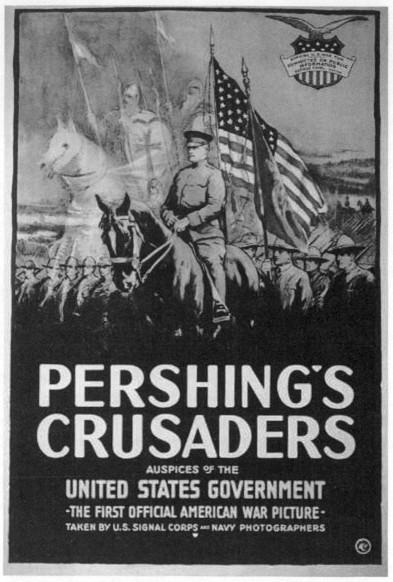

Pershing's Crusaders *(1918)*

rejected limited aims and tolerated the deaths of thousands of
enemy civilians. American Progressives, for example, were opposed
to the very idea of war and could be rallied to fight only by the
highest of ideals. But the same strident idealism made it more dif-

ficult to compromise and end the fighting. Progressive clergyman William Faunce admitted that Christians should oppose war, yet nevertheless America had to "resist the devil and all his works, and that resistance may demand the total personality, soul and body, of a man or a nation."[60] Ray Stannard Baker remarked, "I *hate* war, I love peace and yet at moments I fear lest this war be over too soon—before people are scourged into an awakening."[61]

The American Civil War provided a template for a crusading struggle in 1917. "As our fathers fought with slavery and crushed it, in order that it not seize and crush them," Theodore Roosevelt said, "so we are called on to fight new forces."[62] Wilson told Confederate veterans in June 1917 that God had restored the Union so that the United States could serve the cause of liberty. A former president of Dartmouth College, William Tucker, noted a growing interest in the life of Abraham Lincoln because of "the similarity between the fundamental issues at stake in the present war, and those of the Civil War."[63]

During World War I, the crusading canticle "The Battle Hymn of the Republic" reemerged with incredible resonance. Theologian Lyman Abbott suggested that the song was an international battle hymn for all republics. Just as in 1898, new lyrics were fashioned for this adaptable anthem: "We have heard the cry of anguish, / From the victims of the Hun."[64]

Memories of the Civil War encouraged Americans to strive for the boldest of goals. Roosevelt compared people who talked of a negotiated peace with those who opposed Lincoln in 1864. Lodge argued that the struggle "must end substantially as our civil war ended"—with a clear victory for the forces of right.[65] According to William Widenor, Lodge failed to recognize that "he too was a captive of the American historical experience, especially of the Civil War paradigm. He never once considered the possibility of a war of limited objectives."[66]

The People's Wrath

In his war message, Wilson announced, "Our motive will not be revenge."[67] Indeed, Americans were probably less vengeful during World War I than their French and British allies, who, after all, had a three-year head start in moral indignation. Nevertheless, there was still a powerful streak of wrath in the United States, which grew stronger as the fighting progressed in 1917–1918 and justified both grand objectives and a hard war against enemy civilians.

Germans became widely seen as bloodthirsty and barbaric Huns, the perpetrators of horrendous atrocities in Belgium and elsewhere, and the purveyors of brutal unrestricted submarine warfare. Newell Hillis, pastor of Plymouth Church of the Pilgrims in Brooklyn, New York, claimed that Germany was a "mad dog" that had "reduced savagery to a science."[68] By 1918, there was a definite thirst for German blood. Democratic senator Henry Ashurst warned Wilson that unless the policy was unconditional surrender, the president would be swept away by "the cyclone of the people's wrath."[69] The secretary of labor noted that the press sought "all kinds of punishment for the Germans, including the hanging of the Kaiser."[70] Wilson feared that "intolerant hatred of Germans" would create "American Prussianism."[71]

Moralistic retribution was often directed inward against individuals and groups displaying less than "100 percent Americanism." Sometimes the results were playful—or childish, depending on one's perspective—as hamburgers were rechristened "liberty steaks" and frankfurters became "liberty dogs," in a culinary forerunner of the "freedom fries" phenomenon after 9/11 (when the French refused to support the U.S. invasion of Iraq). Oddly enough, association with the Hun contaminated even disease: German measles became "liberty measles."

There was also a much darker side to the popular mood. "Once lead this people into war," Wilson had predicted, "and they'll forget there ever was such a thing as tolerance. To fight you must be brutal and ruthless, and the spirit of ruthless brutality will enter into the very fibre of our national life, infecting Congress, the courts, the policeman on the beat, the man in the street."[72]

Bach and Beethoven were no longer acceptable. In Lewistown, Montana, a committee organized the burning of German books. In Iowa, the governor banned the speaking of German in public. Robert Prager, a German American, was lynched in Illinois by a mob of several hundred people. Before being killed, he was allowed to write a short letter to his parents: "I must this day, the 5th of April, 1918, die." The ringleaders were found not guilty after their lawyers called the attack "patriotic murder."[73]

Germany's sudden collapse in October and November 1918 was an enormous relief, but it also robbed many Americans of the sense that due vengeance had been meted out. Journalist David Lawrence told Wilson that the "man in the street" did not believe that Germany had "been licked enough."[74] It was a little like Saddam Hussein remaining in power after the Gulf War. Here the kaiser escaped the noose by fleeing to a comfortable exile in Holland.

In January 1919, a group of enterprising doughboys from the 114th Field Artillery Regiment decided to exact their own retribution by traveling to Holland to kidnap him. Aided by U.S. officials who provided the necessary travel documents, the soldiers managed to gain entrance to the kaiser's home. There the kaiser's son served them cigars and water (in the belief that all Americans were teetotalers) and kept the men occupied until Dutch soldiers arrived, when the Americans were forced to leave empty-handed. General Pershing later said that he would have given a year's pay to be on the expedition.[75]

A Pit of Our Own Digging

On November 11, 1918, with the guns suddenly silenced, Captain Rickenbacker flew over the trenches. One group of men dressed in khaki arose from the holes in the ground. Another group of gray-clad figures surfaced on the other side. The two lines slowly moved toward each other until they merged.[76]

Once hostilities ceased, the wave of crusading sentiment abruptly crashed. For several years, Americans wanted to think about anything but the war. Support for transforming international politics seeped away, and Wilson's plans for U.S. entry into the League of Nations were defeated in Congress. In the 1920 presidential election, Republican Warren Harding promised a return to "normalcy" and won 61 percent of the vote—the worst defeat for a Democrat since the Civil War.

During the 1920s, there was a profound backlash against U.S. involvement in the Great War, with the emergence of a strident antiwar literature. Polls taken in the late 1930s found that more than 70 percent of Americans saw entry into World War I as a mistake.[77] The price of the struggle was severe: 50,000 doughboys were killed in the last two hundred days of the war, along with another 62,000 who died of disease (many in training camps in the United States). The crusade cost around $33 billion.

American disillusionment was caused not so much by the blood and treasure expended as by a sense of what this sacrifice had meant. Before 1917, the Great War was widely seen as a nationalistic European struggle. Wilson had temporarily covered this sullied conflict with the cloth of American idealism. Now the cloth was suddenly removed, the original interpretation reemerged, and many felt tricked by a moralistic sleight of hand. In May 1919, the *Nation* wrote of Wilson, "The one-time idol of democracy stands today discredited and condemned." His hypnotic rhetoric was no longer effective; the president was merely a "compromising politician."[78]

Expectations went unmet. The Great War did not end all war. Imperialism continued as the British and French empires absorbed the German colonies. The world was not transformed—or at least not in the intended manner. George Creel wrote in 1920 that when the fighting ended, America "stood on the hilltops of glory," but "today we writhe in a pit of our own digging, despising ourselves and despised by the betrayed peoples of earth."[79]

The campaign of 1917–1918 didn't fit easily into America's crusading pantheon, and over time World War I became a largely forgotten struggle. Despite the fact that the Great War resulted in more American deaths than the wars in Korea and Vietnam combined, there is no national memorial to World War I on the Mall. There is only a tribute to those who served from the District of Columbia, which now sits in disrepair and is often overlooked.[80]

Banana Wars

On July 28, 1915, Vilbrun Guillaume Sam, the president of Haiti, was cowering in the bathroom at the French legation in Port-au-Prince when the mob arrived. Led by men dressed in black funeral frocks, who had just buried their children, murdered by the regime, the screaming crowd hauled Sam from the bathroom. Then they dragged him through the streets and cut him to pieces with machetes, removing his hands, feet, and head and sticking various appendages on an iron fence. The grisly spectacle was the finale to seven years of near anarchy in Haiti and prompted the United States to intervene and stabilize the country.

The grand crusade of World War I was not the only military campaign during this era. Disillusionment with the mission in the

Philippines had closed the book on American imperialism. But the United States didn't abandon nation-building entirely. From 1898 to 1934, it undertook more than twenty-five interventions in the Caribbean, which came to be known as the "banana wars." Although the United States did not seek permanent control, several of the occupations were ambitious in scope and duration, most notably those in Cuba (1899–1902, 1906–1909, and 1917–1922), Haiti (1915–1934), the Dominican Republic (1916–1924), and Nicaragua (1912–1933).

Nation-building followed a similar pattern. Fraudulent elections, chaos, and the threat of civil war prompted the United States to send in the Marines. As Washington saw it, a stable, secure, democratic region would enhance the prosperity of Americans and Latin Americans alike, protect the crescent of territories that shielded the Panama Canal, and expunge foreign—especially European—influence.

Guided by the quest for order, President Theodore Roosevelt in 1904 declared that the United States would exercise "an international police power" against "chronic wrongdoing" in the Western Hemisphere, or as Woodrow Wilson later put it, "teach the South American Republics to elect good men."[81] Poet Wallace Irwin offered a different spin on things: "I can't talk your heathen lingo, / But I'll do my best—by jingo, / Stop that fightin', San Domingo!"[82]

Pirates of the Caribbean

Like southern Reconstruction and the intervention in the Philippines, nation-building in the Caribbean became widely seen as a futile quagmire. Labor leaders, Progressives, intellectuals, and publications like the *Nation* were especially critical, but by the end of the 1920s, hardly anyone was willing to defend the results. These several dozen operations produced not one enduring popular hero and no national memorials. Most of the banana wars were quickly forgotten.

To a large degree, the perception of failure matched the reality. The United States repeatedly failed to align the aims of the mission with the hopes of the local people—something Washington had shown some capacity to do in the Philippines. Instead, U.S. actions sparked considerable anti-Americanism. The Haitians, for instance, had little love for their American occupiers. One soldier recalled arriving in Port-au-Prince: "We marched over the cobblestoned streets of the waterfront through walls of human silence and dead-eyed stares."[83]

The tone of the U.S. operations was often arrogant, chauvinistic, paternalistic, ethnocentric, insensitive, presumptuous, and demeaning. Latin American views were treated with superior disdain. Cartoons depicted Uncle Sam as a kindly parent overseeing his idle children. The *New York Times* claimed that intervention was necessary to keep the Latin Americans "harmless against the ultimate consequences of their own misbehavior."[84]

Washington sometimes behaved in an explicitly undemocratic manner. In Haiti, the United States ran an authoritarian government that suppressed the opposition and starkly limited the freedom of the press. The United States also employed the old Haitian practice of forced labor for road-building, provoking resistance. Racism was endemic, undermining efforts to win over Haitian elites or the mass of blacks. Even the Haitian president was not allowed entry to the segregated American Club in Port-au-Prince.

The U.S. press backed the interventions in Haiti and the Dominican Republic at first but became fiercely critical by 1920, as muckraking journalists exposed abuses by American forces. In the 1920 presidential campaign, Republican Warren Harding criticized the "rape" of Haiti and the Dominican Republic and promised that as president, he would not "cover with a veil of secrecy repeated acts of unwarranted interference in domestic affairs of the little republics of the Western Hemisphere."[85] Charles Evans Hughes, secretary of state from 1921 to 1925, concluded that U.S. interests in Latin America "do not lie in controlling peoples."[86]

The intervention in Nicaragua proved to be an especially frustrating experience. After the Marines pulled out of Nicaragua in 1925, the country descended once more into civil war, and American forces soon returned. One Nicaraguan general, Augusto Sandino, rejected the U.S. presence and started a guerrilla war. The charismatic Sandino became a hero to anti-Americans and the international left, and a symbol of resistance to Yankee domination. Sandino lacked popular support, however, among the mass of Nicaraguans. As he told his men, "Most of the people of Nicaragua don't like us."[87] Still, Sandino had significant backing in the north of the country, and U.S. efforts to democratize Nicaraguan society pushed the nation's conservative elites to make common cause with Sandino against the foreign occupier.

The United States lost 136 Marines in a futile bid to stamp out Sandino's movement. The rebel general attacked mines owned by U.S. investors, in one case leaving the following note: "Dear Sir: I have the honor to inform you that on this date your mine has been reduced to ashes."[88] Sandino ambushed isolated U.S. and Nicaraguan government forces. His men looted widely and killed civilians suspected of collaboration. Nicaraguan and American troops responded in kind, yet the elusive Sandino kept slipping away. When Marines reached one of Sandino's mountain headquarters, they found it guarded by straw dummies.

In the United States, the Nicaraguan intervention provoked demonstrations and picketing of the White House. If the Marines were fighting Nicaraguan "bandits," noted Senator Burton Wheeler, perhaps they could be better employed in Chicago.[89] America's experience in Nicaragua and elsewhere led formerly ardent interventionists to throw up their hands. As assistant secretary of the navy from 1913 to 1920, Franklin Roosevelt had been a militant supporter of the banana wars. But Roosevelt changed his mind in the 1920s, concluding that the operations failed to help the local people and simply sparked hatred for the United States. Capturing the emerging national mood, FDR declared in 1928, "Never before in our history have we had fewer friends in the Western Hemisphere."[90]

After Roosevelt won election as president in 1932, he announced that the United States would act as a "good neighbor" by bringing the curtain down on these missions: "The definite policy of the United States from now on is one opposed to armed intervention."[91] If the Latin Americans wanted to elect good men, it was up to them. The *Denver News* described the reaction to the exit of U.S. forces from Port-au-Prince: "Neither the Haitians, the American public, nor the marines themselves will feel very badly about it if they never go back."[92]

Since the 1930s, most historians have been scathing in their criticism of the banana wars, with Wilson and the other interventionist presidents seen as either naive or rapacious. Would the Caribbean societies have been better off if the Marines had stayed at home? One historian has argued that the answer is a definitive yes: "For eight years [the Dominicans] lost the opportunity to guide their own destiny and to work toward creating a more democratic, just, and stable society."[93]

Good Neighbors

There are, however, some important qualifiers of this gloomy picture of nation-building failure that are often ignored by critics. Of course, the ideal solution was not U.S. occupation, but indigenous progress toward democracy and prosperity. It's dubious, however, whether the Dominican Republic—or, for that matter, Haiti,

Nicaragua, or Cuba—had any reasonable chance of following this path in the early twentieth century. In the absence of U.S. intervention, the most likely scenario was civil war or dictatorship. For all the sins of the American regimes, it's not self-evident that the interests of the Latin American people were better served by home-grown insurgency or autocracy.

Furthermore, any judgment of U.S. nation-building should recognize the incredible difficulty involved in stabilizing Caribbean societies. Washington intervened in the most chaos-ridden and impoverished countries in the region, which would now be called "failed states." Since independence from France in 1804, for instance, Haiti had steadily disintegrated, as its infrastructure and plantations crumbled and large-scale agriculture was replaced by subsistence farming. There were only three automobiles in Haiti when U.S. forces landed in 1915, compared to 2.5 million in the United States. Haiti had never been democratic. Instead, the custom was for disaffected elites to hire *cacos,* or peasant warriors, and overthrow the regime in a coup d'état before taking their own brief turn in the sun. Of the twenty-two rulers of Haiti from 1843 to 1915, only one served out his term of office.

In this tough environment, the U.S. occupations enjoyed a degree of success: "Yankee enterprise and money poured into the region.... Local economic activity boomed and export levels soared.... Washington's efforts *did* reduce the Caribbean's level of political violence and international tension. Germany never got a foothold there, and neither it nor any other power challenged the North American claim to Caribbean supremacy."[94]

The U.S. regime in Haiti built one thousand miles of roads, along with hospitals, rural clinics, lighthouses, courthouses, the first radio station in the country, and the first automatic telephone exchange in Latin America. The number of automobiles increased a thousandfold (from three to three thousand). When Haitian *cacos* resisted the United States, the Marines led a destructive counterinsurgency operation that killed three thousand rebels, while also producing a degree of stability in rural areas that had been unknown for generations.[95]

Meanwhile, from 1916 to 1924, U.S. troops in the Dominican Republic pacified the country, reorganized the tax system, revived economic growth (although the wealthy benefited most), constructed several hundred miles of new roads, improved ports and railroads, established a sanitation system, built seven hundred schools, and oversaw the freest elections in the history of the country.

If American nation-building was a principal cause of the problems in the Caribbean, then presumably when Washington ceased intervening, the result would be an uptick in prosperity and freedom. Franklin Roosevelt's good neighbor policy provides a test of this claim. Believing that harmonious relations would bear fruit for U.S. interests, FDR renounced intervention and adopted an attitude of neutrality toward the internal affairs of the Latin American states. As a result, the United States improved its image in the region, and Latin America generally lined up in the anti-Nazi alliance in World War II.

But the good neighbor policy was no boon for development or democracy. With the threat of U.S. intervention lifted, the region's motley collection of strongmen loudly applauded and then promptly solidified their rule. The public works programs fell into disuse, the roads crumbled, and the telephone systems collapsed. In Nicaragua, the withdrawal of the Marines facilitated Anastasio Somoza's bid for power, and he dominated the country for twenty years. FDR reportedly said that Somoza was "a sonofabitch but he's our sonofabitch," and he welcomed the dictator to stay overnight in the White House.[96] In 1940, Roosevelt entertained Dominican Republic autocrat Rafael Trujillo, even though this self-styled "Genius of Peace," "Protector of Fine Arts and Letters," and "First and Greatest of Dominican Chiefs of State" was responsible for the deaths of thousands of Haitian civilians in border incidents.[97]

A newspaper in Mexico City described the good neighbor policy as "a league of 'mestizo' dictators, with the United States destined to guarantee the slavery of Latin American peoples."[98] One Cuban wondered why Roosevelt had become "the Good Neighbor of tyrants."[99]

The correlation of U.S. *non*intervention with the rise of dictatorship provides a conundrum for the critics of American nation-building. One common retort is that reforms during U.S. interventions produced more effective national police forces, which paved the way for Somoza and his ilk to take power. Thus Washington can be blamed both for intervening and for the autocracy that arose when it didn't intervene.

There is some truth to this charge. Washington did not recognize the consequences of turning a police force into the strongest institution in the country. But dictatorship had existed in Caribbean societies before the Marines arrived, and even if certain domestic reforms ultimately aided the rule of strongmen, these policies didn't diminish the chances of democracy so much as the odds of civil war. Authoritarian rule was not the U.S. objective in Latin America. Rather, disillusionment with seemingly endless quagmires led Washington to accept dictatorship as the least bad outcome.

"Not as Easy as It Had Seemed"

The U.S. nation-building missions in the Caribbean should not be lauded as successes. The avoidable mistakes, abuses of freedom, and arrogant and racist style meant that far less was achieved than was possible. In some respects, the interventions are a model for how *not* to conduct a nation-building operation. Partly, therefore, American perceptions of a quagmire in Latin America simply reflected the situation on the ground.

But as with southern Reconstruction and the intervention in the Philippines, skepticism was reinforced by a combination of declining wrath and national idealism. During World War I, when the desire for vengeance was whipped up by German outrages and domestic propaganda, few Americans criticized the starvation blockade that killed thousands of civilians. But attacks by Caribbean insurgents failed to provoke the same cyclone of wrath. The Latin American missions seemed far removed from a battle between good and evil, sapping the retributive impulse and, as a result, the will to continue. Abuses by U.S. troops were widely criticized rather than celebrated, and they led to congressional hearings in the 1920s. One senator railed against the use of aircraft in Nicaragua "to bomb innocent women and children from the air."[100]

An American idealist was never going to be satisfied by the outcomes in Haiti, Nicaragua, and elsewhere. First of all, the United States' sacred principles encouraged unrealistic expectations. Most Americans had little if any understanding of the complexities of local culture and politics in the Caribbean and the difficulties involved in transplanting U.S. institutions. People often assumed that American troops would be welcomed with smiles, if not with flowers. The Caribbean, rich in natural resources, just needed a little Yankee know-how and a sprinkling of elections to spark an economic takeoff and a virtuous cycle of wealth creation and democratic freedom.[101] The U.S. minister to Nicaragua claimed that the country would "rapidly advance in wealth and population were there security of life and property."[102] As one historian noted, U.S. officials believed that American ingenuity could transform Haiti "if only Haitians would follow the formula of the American success story."[103]

Smedley Darlington Butler, called "the Fighting Quaker," was involved in many of the banana wars and became, at the time of his death in 1940, the most decorated Marine in American history. According to one legend, Butler was tasked with getting the Haitian president to sign a treaty. Butler arrived with the treaty, but the president, who was reluctant to sign, hid in the bathroom. After waiting for an hour, Butler located a ladder, climbed through the bathroom window, and found the president sitting on the commode, fully dressed and smoking a cigar. Faced by Butler, the treaty, and a fountain pen, the president promptly signed.[104]

Butler also spent time running the police and fire departments of Philadelphia, which, with its rampant municipal corruption and dens of vice, was not dissimilar to some of the failed states he visited. Raiding the speakeasies of Philadelphia's social elite, including the Ritz-Carlton and the Union League, won Butler few friends among the cocktail set, and the Marine later noted that cleaning up the city "was worse than any battle I was ever in."[105]

At first, Butler shared the confidence of many of his countrymen about the potential of U.S. intervention in Haiti, believing that the United States would create "a first-class black man's country...[of] clean little towns, with tidy thatched-roof dwellings."[106] Indeed, when U.S. forces approached Port-au-Prince by sea, it looked beautiful from a distance. But up close it was completely filthy—a metaphor for the combination of American idealism, ignorance, and unwarranted expectations. As historian Alan McPherson noted, "The high hopes raised by the initial intervention in Haiti only compounded the disillusionment that soon followed."[107] U.S. anticipation of a rapid transition to democracy and stability was almost impossible to realize. Elections, after all, had a very different function in the Caribbean compared to the United States. Traditionally, they didn't determine who would hold office, but instead ratified, through corrupt practices, a seizure of power that had already happened.[108]

U.S. leaders encouraged these overly optimistic expectations with promises of imminent triumph. For instance, in the campaign against the insurgents in Nicaragua, officials kept claiming that Sandino had been killed or defeated, or had fled into exile. But reports of Sandino's death were greatly exaggerated and contributed to a growing credibility gap on the part of the government.[109]

The Caribbean missions failed to produce the hoped-for change. President Calvin Coolidge concluded that "policing Central America was not as easy as it had seemed."[110] Secretary of State Frank Kellogg noted, "There is a great deal of criticism in this country about the way in which these operations are being dragged out with constant sacrifice of American lives and without any concrete results....People cannot understand why the job cannot be done, and frankly I do not understand myself."[111] The official commission of inquiry into the Haitian mission found that despite some gains, "the high hopes of our good works in this land have not been realized."[112] A disillusioned Smedley Darlington Butler spent his final years warning against the perils of nation-building. "I helped in the rape of half a dozen Central American republics," he said.[113]

In World War I, the battle for America's sacred principles justified almost any sacrifice. Most people supported the *negative* mission to destroy Prussian militarism and the barriers to freedom. But in Latin America, Washington was engaged in a *positive* mission to export its principles by building hospitals, overseeing elections, and tackling corruption. Rather than fight for its ideals, Washington had to live up to them, and it usually fell far short.

Americans were often struck by the chasm that existed between U.S. values and the situation in the target country. One administrator called the forced-labor system in Haiti "un-American."[114] Progressive journalist William Allen White was a member of the commission of inquiry into the intervention in Haiti and concluded that the whole endeavor was futile: "We are in the 20th century looking toward the 21st. They are in the 18th century with the ideals of the Grand Louis always behind them as models."[115] An American officer supervising the 1930 elections in Nicaragua commented that "poverty and ignorance have reduced [the local people] to such a primitive state that abstractions such as democratic government, the free ballot, etc., have no meaning for them."[116]

To critics on the left, the Caribbean interventions were a form of economic imperialism, which breached America's core principles. The *Nation* saw capitalistic exploitation as the primary motivation: "This is imperialism of the rankest kind."[117] It's not difficult to see why people reached this conclusion. The overbearing style of the United States was reminiscent of the Roman legions being sent to quell squabbling tribes. Washington was obviously concerned about its broader economic relations with Latin America, seeking to protect U.S. investments, cultivate markets, guarantee control over petroleum reserves, and replace European with U.S. financial influence.

But the Caribbean missions don't easily fit the label of imperialism. The United States never intended to rule permanently. Indeed, Washington was often reluctant to intervene and acted at the behest of one or more factions in a civil war. Furthermore, interventionists like Woodrow Wilson had little time for big business and made unlikely stooges for corporate plutocrats. Perhaps most damning of all for the economic imperialism argument is that U.S. investments in several of the target states were minimal—for instance, amounting to just a few million dollars in Haiti. Protecting trade and investment was not the primary driving force behind the missions. They were mainly about politics and American security—more diplomacy than dollars.

Broader dynamics reinforced a despondent view of the Caribbean operations. Just as the economic downturn of 1873 eroded support for southern Reconstruction, so the Great Depression made Americans more skeptical about the value of intervening abroad. The banana wars were a distraction from critical challenges at home. The economic crisis also undermined American confidence in the nation's historic mission to spread U.S. ideals. Perhaps the United States was not the last best hope for liberty after all. Here the Depression intensified a retreat from nation-building that was already well under way before the Wall Street crash of 1929.

Skepticism was further stoked by the rising tide of isolationism in the United States. At a time when Americans across the political spectrum, from socialists to conservatives, regretted U.S. entry into World War I as a disastrous folly and looked to avoid foreign entanglements, it became harder to justify the endless stabilization missions in the Caribbean.

Perceptions of failure produced a powerful backlash against American nation-building. The use of force to coerce Latin American countries into electing good men went the same way as efforts to protect civil rights in the South and build an American empire. By the early 1930s, the United States was not concerned with an orderly transfer of power to the new Caribbean regimes. Neither did it focus on protecting the fragile gains made during the operations. Americans just wanted to leave as quickly as possible.

Difficult Steering

World War I and the banana wars were like yin and yang. At least while it lasted, the Great War was a glorious experience, akin to the Civil War and the Spanish-American War. By contrast, the interventions in the Caribbean were a grim trial, similar to southern Reconstruction and the mission in the Philippines.

The Caribbean operations caused few American deaths, and there was little need to raise taxes. But like death and taxes, U.S. regret about the interventions was a certainty. These operations revealed the sins of commission. For all its success in constructing public works and establishing law and order, the United States was rarely able to win local hearts and minds. But the era also revealed the sins of omission. If the tale of the banana wars is at best a mixed picture, the story of the good neighbor policy is similarly ambiguous, as dictatorship became strongly entrenched in the region.

How could Americans use force without getting drawn into interminable local squabbles? Could Washington shape politics in other societies and not make a mockery of its ideals of anti-imperialism and self-determination? Could the United States successfully align its objectives with the aspirations of the target population? These dilemmas and more went unresolved as the United States stumbled toward an effective nation-building formula. As Theodore Roosevelt put it, "We have passed the time when a nation with even an imperfectly developed conscience is content simply to exploit for its own benefit a country that it has conquered; and the effort to govern such a country in its own interest without falling into mawkish sentimentality implies some mighty difficult steering."[118]

In the late 1930s and early 1940s, Franklin Roosevelt's vision shifted away from Latin America and toward Europe and the Far East, where fascist aggression provoked America's greatest crusade — one that recruited the most unlikely of warriors.

CHAPTER 7

When the Saints Go Marching In

For a budding American crusader, Patrick Hitler had an unfortunate last name. Born in Britain, he was Adolf Hitler's nephew. After a sojourn in the Third Reich during the 1930s, Patrick ended up in the United States, where he lectured on the topic "Why I Hate My Uncle." Following Pearl Harbor, Patrick tried to enlist in the U.S. military, but his application was denied because his family background raised eyebrows.

Rather than take no for an answer, Patrick appealed directly to President Franklin Roosevelt: "I am the nephew and only descendant of the ill-famed Chancellor and Leader of Germany who today so despotically seeks to enslave the free and Christian peoples of the globe.... More than anything else I would like to see active combat as soon as possible and thereby be accepted by my friends and comrades as one of them in this great struggle for liberty."[1]

Following the president's intervention, Patrick was allowed to serve. He joined the U.S. Navy in 1944 and survived the war. Patrick then changed his last name and moved to Long Island, where he had four children. The offspring reportedly made a pact not to marry or have any children of their own, so that the Hitler bloodline would finally end.[2]

Can anyone doubt the purity of America's fourth crusade when Hitler's own nephew signed up to rescue the world from enslavement? In our minds, World War II was the good war, the golden age, and the greatest generation. The home front was united as one, and the soldiers were driven by a compelling cause.

And in many respects it was a model crusade. Despite hundreds of thousands of American deaths and injuries, public support for the war effort barely wavered. Large majorities backed the use of all necessary force to compel unconditional surrender, democratize Germany and Japan, and create a new international organization, the United Nations. Indeed, the desire for vengeance may have been more powerful in the Pacific campaign than in any other interstate war in U.S. history. But compared to earlier crusades, the sense of idealistic mission was less ardent in World War II, and many U.S. troops fought with a cool and even cynical perspective.

Not for One Dragon's End

American society in the 1930s appears an unfertile soil from which a great crusade would spring forth. In 1936, 95 percent of the public opposed getting involved in a future European war for any reason whatsoever. Even by 1941, after two years of fighting in Europe, Germany's conquest of France, and its invasion of the Soviet Union, less than a third of Americans wanted to declare war on Berlin.[3]

On Sunday, December 7, 1941, as the early-morning sun shone down on the U.S. naval base of Pearl Harbor in Hawaii, 353 Japanese aircraft launched a surprise attack that damaged or destroyed 21 U.S. ships and nearly 350 aircraft and killed more than 2,400 Americans, including 1,177 men who died when the *Arizona* exploded.[4]

The antiwar sentiment of the 1930s was suddenly cast aside, as Americans wrote a new verse of the crusader's epic song, embracing a global campaign on a scale even grander than the Civil War and the Great War. In the wake of the Japanese assault and Germany's declaration of war against the United States, the public mood was angry, determined, and patriotic. One congressional representative delivered a poem on the radio, replete with familiar imagery.

> *The High Crusade whereon we have embarked calls forth the free.*
> *In hosts, with spears and flaunting flags arrayed;*
> *Not for one dragon's end, one victory.*
> *One last great war, but to unending war*
> *Without, within, till God's white torch supreme*
> *Melts the last chain: and the last dungeon door*
> *Swings slowly wide to the triumphant dream.*[5]

Public support for expansive war aims swelled up and continued to rise during the war. The United States was less threatened by German and Japanese militarism than its allies, Britain and the Soviet Union, but if anything, Americans were even more determined to struggle for a transformational victory. As historian Paul Schroeder put it, "No great power fought the war for more grandiose...aims and ideals for the postwar world."[6]

In World War I, Woodrow Wilson and Theodore Roosevelt had dueled over whether to crusade for a new international organization or the unconditional surrender of Germany. After 1941, there was broad consensus that the United States should pursue both objectives.

A policy of unconditional surrender was potentially dangerous because it might embolden the enemy and lengthen the war. But only one day after Pearl Harbor, when tapping sounds could still be heard from U.S. sailors trapped in sunken ships, FDR promised Congress that Americans would fight "in their righteous might" for "absolute victory."[7] The strategy was formalized a year later, in January 1943, at the Allied conference at Casablanca, when Roosevelt called for "the unconditional surrender by Germany, Italy, and Japan."[8] In private, the British government feared that the policy would redouble German and Japanese resistance. But the objective of unconditional surrender won the backing of around three-quarters of the American public.[9]

During the 1930s, Americans opposed entry into the League of Nations, but once the Japanese bombers struck, beliefs changed almost overnight. For Democratic senator Joseph Ball, the creation of a new international organization was "the greatest crusade since Jesus sent his twelve disciples out to preach the brotherhood of man."[10] There was a steady rise in support for U.S. membership in a reformed League, from around 55 to 60 percent in 1942, to 60 to 70 percent in 1943, to 80 to 90 percent in 1945.[11]

In striking contrast to Wilson's tortuous efforts to join the League of Nations, U.S. membership in the United Nations sailed through the Senate in the summer of 1945 by a vote of 89 to 2. It illustrates the advantages of locking down congressional commitments while an interstate war is ongoing—before the crusader wave has crashed.

The vanguard led the fight for unconditional surrender and the United Nations. True believers like Vice President Henry Wallace and Republican presidential candidate Wendell Willkie were part of a broad internationalist movement, which included the United Nations Association, the American Legion, labor unions, and many religious leaders, as well as wealthier and better-educated Americans. As information about the Holocaust emerged, American Jews also knew what they were fighting for.[12]

But these committed crusaders don't represent the whole picture. Today everyone understands the stakes of World War II: stopping fascism and ending the Holocaust. After 1941, however, only about 60 to 70 percent of the public had "a clear idea what the war is about," while a substantial minority was unsure. Women were less certain than men about the wisdom of joining the United Nations and more willing to contemplate a negotiated peace with the enemy. Americans with at least one parent born in an Axis country also were warier about unconditional surrender. Meanwhile, a rump of surviving isolationists, mostly midwestern Republicans, saw membership in the United Nations as a dangerous step toward a global superstate.[13]

Burning the Cities We Learned About in School

While the nation was at peace, Americans repeatedly condemned the bombing of civilians as fundamentally immoral. But after Pearl Harbor, ethical inhibitions were largely discarded. This was no time for what Lincoln called "elder-stalk squirts charged with rose water." Instead, as poet Randall Jarrell wrote, "In bombers named for girls, we burned / The cities we had learned about in school."[14]

In March 1945, hundreds of American B-29 bombers set off

The killing of civilians looks very different when framed by an interstate crusade rather than a nation-building quagmire. Here, the airmen that bombed Germany in World War II are celebrated in a 1994 stamp.

from the Mariana Islands and flew toward Tokyo, where they ignited a deadly firestorm that engulfed the city and killed 80,000 people. The bodies floating in the rivers and canals of Tokyo were indistinguishable from burnt wood. The stench of smoldering flesh was so overwhelming that U.S. aircrews wore oxygen masks to avoid vomiting.[15]

Bombing raids in the summer of 1945 deliberately spared Hiroshima, so that the Japanese could bear witness to the power of a single atomic bomb. The Americans had to save the city in order to destroy it. Photographer Yoshito Matsushige was in Hiroshima on the day of days. People jumped into a swimming pool when the explosion happened, he reported, but the heat evaporated the water, leaving their bodies at the bottom of the pool, "like boiled fish."[16] America had become death, the destroyer of worlds. To Japanese civilians, the U.S. military must have seemed like the Martians in H. G. Wells's 1898 story *The War of the Worlds:* an alien adversary whose machines killed with cool, depersonalized zeal.

But if anything, the American public believed that the military was too timid in targeting civilians. The occasional critic who questioned the carnage was widely derided as a naïf or fool. Most U.S. servicemen praised the dropping of the atomic bomb for ending the war and possibly saving their lives. The *Christian Century* argued that no line could be drawn between discriminate and indiscriminate bombing: "If we fight at all, we fight all out."[17]

Crusade for a New World Order

In the time-honored fashion, during World War II liberal and religious ideals propelled many Americans toward maximum war aims and all necessary force. At heart, Roosevelt was a Wilsonian and a liberal internationalist. In 1920, as the Democratic vice presidential candidate, he campaigned for U.S. membership in the League of

Nations, before being swept away by the crash and dissipation of the Great War's crusader wave. FDR presented World War II as a moral cause, telling Congress in January 1942, "There never has been—there never can be—successful compromise between good and evil. Only total victory can reward the champions of tolerance, and decency, and faith."[18] Roosevelt's public prayer on D-Day held that with "faith in our united crusade," Americans must endeavor toward "a peace that will let all of men live in freedom."[19]

The Nazis and the Japanese were exemplary foils for the U.S. crusader: seemingly perfect antitheses of America's sacred principles. In 1942, 63 percent of the public thought that the United States was fighting for "an ideal," while only 21 percent believed that its main motivation was "self-defense."[20] FDR claimed that the struggle was for the "Four Freedoms": the freedom of speech and worship, and the freedom from want and fear. According to the Office of Facts and Figures, these objectives "have a powerful and genuine appeal to seven persons in ten."[21]

Norman Rockwell celebrated the quadruple goals in a series of paintings that appeared in the *Saturday Evening Post* in 1943. The artist's favorite was *Freedom of Speech,* where a working-class man rises to speak, while his white-collar neighbors listen respectfully. Rockwell received sixty thousand letters about the paintings, most of them very positive. Some people claimed they now understood the meaning of the war.[22]

Dwight Fee, a veteran of World War I, wrote to his enlisted son, "You are serving in a great cause. Because of you and those like you millions of fathers and mothers and children again will be able to think and speak freely without fear; to live their lives without oppression."[23] When the first American casualty of the war was buried in London, his fellow volunteers sang the crusader's anthem, "The Battle Hymn of the Republic."[24]

Religious leaders often depicted World War II as a struggle between democracy and totalitarianism, in which the fate of

Christianity was at stake. The Lutheran Church called on its supporters "to dedicate themselves wholly, with every resource of heart and mind and conscience, to the defeat and destruction of this evil."[25] The Methodist Church had been a founding member of the crusading vanguard since the attack on Fort Sumter in 1861. Now it pressed Washington to create a new international organization to end war and protect individual freedom. The campaign, called "Crusade for a New World Order," helped to rally American Protestants behind membership in the United Nations.[26]

Memories of past crusades legitimized grandiose objectives and the use of all necessary force. Just as Abraham Lincoln reemerged in popular consciousness during the Great War, so in World War II there was a revival of interest in the life and ideals of Woodrow Wilson. Having concluded in the 1930s that entry into World War I had been a disastrous blunder, Americans changed their minds after 1941 and decided that Wilson had been right all along. Now the United States had a second chance to pursue the internationalist dream. Following World War I, as FDR put it, "we gave up the hope of achieving a better peace because we had not the courage to fulfill our responsibilities in an admittedly imperfect world. We must not let that happen again, or we shall follow the same tragic road again—the road to a third world war."[27]

Darryl Zanuck produced the 1944 movie *Wilson* with a $3 million budget, making it the second-most-expensive film up to that time, surpassed only by *Gone with the Wind*. Here Wilson was reborn as a highly charismatic hero, betrayed by the villainous Henry Cabot Lodge. The movie was critically acclaimed and won a number of Oscars.[28]

Blood upon the Risers

But *Wilson* was a flop at the box office, and this commercial failure symbolized the tempering of the missionary impulse in World War II. Compared to earlier crusades, Americans were cooler and more cynical, and less given to wild-eyed idealism.

FDR was far more pragmatic than Wilson, seeing his predecessor's Fourteen Points as a standard of perfection like the Ten Commandments: something to be striven for but never completely attained. Underpinning grand U.S. war aims in World War II was a clear recognition of power politics. The strategy of unconditional surrender was designed in part to maintain the alliance between the Anglo-Americans and the Soviets by avoiding bitter disputes over the process of negotiating peace. FDR always planned for the great powers to run the show at the United Nations. Targeting civilians also had an obvious strategic logic: to undermine the Axis war effort. If anything, the British had even less hesitation in carpet bombing Hitler's Germany.

Among U.S. troops, it was hard to find the strident idealism, and the romantic and chivalric tenor, of earlier crusades. The army's Information and Education Division interviewed thousands of soldiers during the war and found little understanding of the conflict in terms of abstract principles. In one survey, only 13 percent of the soldiers could name more than two of the Four Freedoms.[29] Novelist James Jones was not consoled by the thought of dying for the cause: "After you are dead there is no such thing as Liberty, or Democracy or Freedom." Instead, men fought because "there is nothing else for you to do."[30] Meanwhile, the editor of the *Christian Herald* toured the theaters of war and found "overwhelming indifference to organized religion" among the men.[31]

As always, prosaic concerns featured heavily in a soldier's mind. One man received a long letter from his fiancée, which ended casually with the statement, "I was married last week." To ease the pain, the letter went on: "My husband won't mind you writing to me occasionally. He's a sailor and very broadminded."[32]

The troops weren't singing "The Battle Hymn of the Republic" as they marched into combat. Paratroopers were more likely to be belting out "Blood upon the Risers," written to the tune of "Battle Hymn" and describing a soldier whose parachute fails: "Gory, gory, what a hell of a way to die." The most popular song of World War II was the highly sentimental "White Christmas"—a stark contrast to the upbeat "Over There" from World War I.[33]

There were musical exceptions. John Steinbeck was on a troopship heading across the Atlantic to Britain in 1943. A United Service Organizations (USO) unit entertained the white troops below, while Steinbeck sat with the segregated black soldiers on deck. Suddenly, one of the black men began to sing "When the Saints Go Marching In." A cry went out: "Sing it brother." The men, lying on their backs on the deck, all joined in. Steinbeck wrote, "The song becomes huge with authority. This is a war song. This could be *the* war song."[34]

For some Americans, memories of World War I and its aftermath tempered their idealistic zeal. People recalled the rhetorical excesses, the propaganda, and, most of all, the incredible disillusionment with the last crusade, as dreams ended up being trampled underfoot. Words like *sacred* and *cause* rang a little hollow. Religious leaders believed they had succumbed to nationalistic drumbeating during the Great War. Chastened, they turned against war itself in the 1920s and 1930s and supported World War II with a resolute but calmer tone.[35]

America's citizen-soldiers fought for their buddies. They fought to get back to their lives at home. And they fought because there was a job to be done. But the sense of idealism had not disappeared. Faith in America's liberal and religious principles was latent, helping to explain why the GIs accepted conscription and military authority and saw the war as fundamentally justified. Lieutenant Robert Shannon wrote from Iwo Jima, saying there was patriotism among the men, but not "the kind that is amassed in the throats of people when our national ensign is unfurled, or like as many sheep, cheer at a passing parade—but rather the kind which lies deep and still in the hearts of our defenders."[36]

"We are told that the American soldier does not know what he is fighting for," noted General Dwight Eisenhower after the German concentration camps were liberated in 1945. "Now, at least, he will know what he is fighting *against*."[37] Having seen the piles of dead bodies, an American sergeant said that he had never been so sure "of exactly what I was fighting for."[38]

From a range of motives, America's soldiers battled with astounding bravery. The men who stormed ashore on D-Day sometimes landed miles from the target site, driving themselves forward against machine gun fire and mortars. Their compatriots flung themselves from aircraft, burdened by up to one hundred pounds of weaponry and supplies. Parachutists had to win a murderous lottery just to land safely, before they faced lethal resistance on fields lit by the natural light of the moon and the artificial glow of tracers and flamethrowers.

Like Autumn Leaves

Although the sense of idealistic mission was restrained for many soldiers, vengeance was anything but muted, especially in regard to the Japanese. Before 1941, Americans actually viewed the Japanese more favorably than the Germans, Italians, and Jews.[39] But the assault on Pearl Harbor provoked widespread fury. President Roosevelt described it as "a date which will live in infamy" and an "unprovoked and dastardly attack."[40] Rage intensified in the face of grotesque Japanese atrocities against soldiers and civilians and the fanatical style of Japanese warfare. Only 4 percent of the British and American soldiers captured by the Germans died in captivity, versus 27 percent who were unfortunate enough to fall into Japanese hands.[41]

In the days after Pearl Harbor, a survey by *Time, Life,* and *Fortune* described an America that was "deeply resentful of the treachery. Vengeance-bent, confident of victory, dazzled by cataclysm."[42] In 1942, 28 percent of Americans said they hated the Japanese. The Office of War Information helpfully provided the press with appropriate words to describe the Asian adversary ("brutal,"

Government war poster

"fanatical," and "cruel"), along with words to avoid ("monkey-man," "slant-eyes," and "Jap-rat").[43]

As one of the characters in Gilbert and Sullivan's musical *Mikado* sings, "My object all sublime . . . / To let the punishment fit the crime." There was an unmistakable sense of payback as American bombers struck Japanese cities. Red Foley's hit song "Smoke on the Water" promised that the United States would "make a graveyard of Japan." *Time* magazine called the firebombing of Tokyo "a dream come true," because "properly kindled, Japanese cities will burn like autumn leaves."[44] President Harry Truman described the delivery of the atomic bomb in August 1945: "We have used it against those who attacked us without warning at Pearl Harbor, against those who have starved and beaten and executed American prisoners of war, against those who have abandoned all pretense of obeying international laws of warfare."[45]

Of course, most of those reduced to shadows in Hiroshima had committed none of these crimes. But by this stage, the line between combatant and noncombatant was completely blurred. When the war was over, 23 percent of Americans said they regretted that more atomic bombs had not been "quickly" dropped on Japan before they "had a chance to surrender."[46]

The desire for retribution developed a genocidal edge. In 1945, a quarter of American soldiers said that their main objective was not to force the enemy's defeat, but simply to kill as many Japanese as possible.[47] Around 10 to 15 percent of the American public openly told pollsters that all Japanese men, women, and children should die.[48] In April 1945, the head of the War Manpower Commission, Paul McNutt, favored "the extermination of the Japanese *in toto*," clarifying that he meant the Japanese *people*, not just the military.[49]

During the postwar occupation of Japan, one American dentist engineered his own private revenge. He was asked to make a set of dentures for Hideki Tojo, the Japanese wartime leader, who was now in U.S. custody. The dentist engraved the phrase "Remember

Pearl Harbor" in Morse code on the dentures because "not many people had a chance to get those words into his mouth."[50]

In World War II, a combination of strategic interests, missionary sentiment, and vengeance produced broad support for maximum objectives and all necessary force. A war of limited goals or restrained tactics was inconceivable. As Vice President Henry Wallace declared in 1942, "No compromise with Satan is possible."[51] Even after the horrific fighting at Iwo Jima in 1945, Americans geared up for an invasion of Japan. Secretary of State James Byrnes told Truman that the president would be "crucified" domestically if the United States abandoned the policy of unconditional surrender and began negotiating with Tokyo.[52]

The Good War

Following victory against Japan, the crusader wave crashed, and the desire to transform the world drained away. Americans wanted normalcy and clamored for rapid demobilization. Within a month, only 7 percent of the public thought that the most important issue facing the country was foreign policy. "The tide of public opinion was impossible to stem," remarked Truman. "Every momma and poppa in the country had to have her boy home right immediately."[53]

Studs Terkel called his oral history of World War II *"The Good War."* The quotation marks were designed to reinforce the irony that despite our recollections, war is never good. But World War II did pass into our collective memory as the good war and the nation's perfect crusade. Americans still recall a campaign of moral clarity and total commitment, where a flag-waving nation at arms battled for democracy.[54]

For the United States, it *was* a good war, at least relative to the other combatants. The 400,000 American dead represent one fatality for every fifteen Germans and every fifty Russians who were killed. In critical arenas, such as the war at sea, the war in the air, and the campaign against Japan, the U.S. contribution to victory was truly decisive. Washington ended the conflict with unparalleled power.

But just as memories of the Civil War faded into a hazy image of gray and blue, so recollections of World War II began to blur. Lost in the celebratory song were several discordant notes. It was the Soviet Union, not the United States, which was primarily responsible for the defeat of Nazi Germany. Russian troops killed four out of every five German soldiers who died in the war. The fighting in Europe revolved around two brutal totalitarian states trying to batter each other into submission. The ultimate outcome was, quite predictably, not freedom in eastern Europe, but the domination of whichever tyrannical regime was left standing.[55]

This was not the greatest generation for civil rights. African Americans were segregated in the U.S. military and largely kept in supporting roles. When blacks gave blood, the Red Cross separated it from whites' blood to avoid disturbing racists. One restaurant in Kansas refused to serve black U.S. troops but happily served German POWs who were detained nearby.[56]

And then there was the sheer horror of the good war. After witnessing a battlefield in France, General Eisenhower observed that someone could walk for hundreds of yards while stepping only on decaying flesh.[57]

World War II was a profoundly necessary war. Wrestling with the ambiguities doesn't diminish the heroism of the fight against fascism—it just makes it more real. But like Americans in the 1890s, living under the shadow of the Civil War, the post-1945 generation looked back on World War II as a model for combat—with significant consequences when the crusader's standard was unfurled once again only five years later.

Attacking in Another Direction

The 1950–1953 Korean War illustrates what happens when an interstate war deviates from the crusader script. In June 1950, Communist North Korea crossed the 38th parallel and invaded non-Communist South Korea. For U.S. president Harry Truman, it was a rerun of Nazi aggression in the 1930s, and this time there would be no appeasement.

It started out as a classic crusade. American World War II hero Douglas MacArthur headed a UN army, including troops from the United States, Britain, Australia, Canada, and a dozen other countries. The U.S.-led force liberated South Korea and then pushed across the 38th parallel to overthrow the Communist regime in North Korea. U.S. ambassador to the United Nations Warren Austin said that "the United Nations must see that the people of Korea attain complete individual and political freedom."[58] More than three-quarters of Americans approved of the intervention in Korea, and more than 60 percent supported the goal of regime change.[59] Singer Jimmie Osborne released the celebratory record "Thank God for Victory in Korea."

But Osborne had sung too soon. As the American crusader raced recklessly toward the Yalu River, bordering China, he placed his head in the Chinese noose. Hundreds of thousands of Chinese troops smashed into UN forces in October and November 1950, sending them hurtling back down the peninsula in one of the worst military defeats in American history. U.S. Marines fought desperately against overwhelming odds in northeastern Korea, in temperatures hovering around minus thirty degrees, with fifty-mile-per-hour winds. After withdrawing south, the commander of the First Marine Division sounded an optimistic note: "Gentlemen, we are not retreating. We are merely attacking in another direction."[60]

Based on America's traditional way of war, we might expect Washington to have responded with a massive escalation of both tactics and objectives. And indeed, the United States stepped up its campaign of strategic bombing, which obliterated every major North Korean city and killed hundreds of thousands of civilians.[61] In the euphemism of the day, enemy civilians had been "de-housed."

But fearing the dangers of an expanded war and encouraged by Allied sentiment, Truman slammed the brakes on the crusade. The Korean War would be strictly limited, with the United States seeking a negotiated peace based on a return to the prewar status quo. Strategically, it was the right decision, avoiding an extended commitment in Asia and perhaps averting World War III.

Limited war, however, violated the crusade tradition. For the first time in an interstate war since the 1860s, the United States was *not* employing all necessary force to achieve a transformational outcome. As the campaign descended into an attritional stalemate in the fall of 1950, public support collapsed.[62] It was not just the battlefield losses — after all, the United States had suffered many reversals in the early months of World War II. It was also the manner in which the war was being fought. Why should Americans, as the saying went, "die for a tie"?

Republicans railed against the Democratic president for abandoning the crusade. As one scholar noted, conservatives took "World War II as exemplary, a model to be followed throughout the postwar period."[63] "It is too much to expect that our people will accept a limited war," declared eight Republican senators in 1951. "Our policy must be to win. Our strategy must be devised to bring about decisive victory."[64] Republican senator Robert Taft saw limited war as unnatural and un-American, resembling "a football game in which our team, when it reaches the 50-yard line, is always instructed to kick. Our team can never score."[65]

No one was more opposed to Truman's limited war strategy

than the commander of UN forces, Douglas MacArthur. The general wanted to hit the crusade button by bombing and blockading China and aiding an invasion of the mainland by anti-Communist Chinese based in Taiwan. As MacArthur put it, "Once war is forced upon us, there is no other alternative than to apply every available means to bring it to a swift end. War's very object is victory, not prolonged indecision."[66]

MacArthur touched a sensitive nerve in the American psyche. A majority of people wanted to escalate the war and bomb China. The number favoring the use of atomic weapons in Korea increased from 27 percent in 1950 to 49 percent in 1951.[67] When Truman fired MacArthur for insubordination in 1951, most Americans sympathized with the general, not the president.[68] Twenty-one-year-old sergeant Don Gore wrote to his girlfriend, "General McCarthur [sic] told them that this Korean war was a stupid war and unconstitutional because they wouldn't let us win the war and wouldn't let us lose it. . . . Without General McCarthur to lead us I ain't going."[69] On April 20, 1951, more than half a million people lined the streets of Washington to welcome home MacArthur, the jilted crusader. When the general addressed Congress, one representative gushed, "We heard the voice of God."[70]

By hammering home the point that escalation in Korea risked the outbreak of World War III, Truman ultimately succeeded in dampening the crusading sentiment. During the spring of 1951, congressional hearings over the firing of MacArthur provided the administration with a platform to set out the case for restraint. Support for a truce to end the war, leaving Korea divided at the 38th parallel, rose from 43 to 51 percent. By 1953, in the wake of 37,000 deaths, Americans were sick of the war and backed the armistice signed by new president Dwight Eisenhower.[71] It left the Communist regime in power in North Korea, with its leader, Kim Il Sung, about to be depicted as a living god.

The Korean War never took its place in America's crusading

pantheon. Few popular songs emerged from the campaign. Movies about Korea are usually dark, like *The Steel Helmet* (1951), in which most of the main characters end up dead. Cartoonist Bill Mauldin wrote, "There's no victory in the old-fashioned sense, anyway, because this isn't that kind of war. It's a slow, grinding, lonely, bitched-up war."[72]

Napalm Sticks to Kids

It's just over two inches long by one and a half inches wide and weighs about two ounces. In the Vietnam War, the Zippo lighter was a ubiquitous object. To the GIs, it was a protective amulet that was said to deflect bullets. Its metal case also offered a few square inches where a soldier could express his feelings about the war. The men engraved images and words on their lighters at sidewalk kiosks in South Vietnam or by hand. The inscriptions captured the thoughts of young American males trapped in a confusing war:

"I didn't come to Vietnam to die for my country, I came to make the other S.O.B. die for his."

"If I had been at Kent State, there would have been one hell of a body count."

"If you got this off my dead ass, I hope it brings you the same luck it brought me."

"Napalm sticks to kids."

Today in Vietnam, engraved Zippos are widely sold to American tourists at sidewalk stands. Most of the lighters are fakes, not true relics of the war. Still, the vendors hope that Americans will, as John F. Kennedy once promised, "pay any price."[73]

American visitors perusing the merchandise in Vietnam are the second wave of American travelers to descend on the country. The first group arrived in much greater numbers during the 1960s, and they were armed to the hilt. Vietnam was the largest and most important U.S. nation-building mission of the Cold War era.

Victory in World War II and the emerging global rivalry with the Soviet Union spurred a highly ambitious program of reconstruction and stabilization operations, on a scale that dwarfed earlier nation-building efforts. Beginning with Truman, U.S. presidents saw international communism as a potentially fatal threat to national security and liberal goals of democracy and individual freedom. The fear that Communist revolution would spread like a wildfire transformed developing states of secondary strategic importance into vital firebreaks to halt the inferno.

When the French withdrew from Vietnam in 1954, the country was divided into Communist North Vietnam and non-Communist South Vietnam. Washington provided massive material assistance to South Vietnam from its birth. In the late 1950s, the Communist-led Vietcong began an insurgency in South Vietnam. In response, U.S. involvement steadily escalated until there were more than half a million American ground troops in the country in 1968.

Dueling Traditions

Perceptions of the Vietnam War in the United States were complex and confusing, with many Americans backing an escalation of the war effort, while millions of antiwar activists condemned the immorality of the campaign and marched in favor of withdrawal. But this is no surprise, because, unusually, the conflict invoked *both* traditions.

Vietnam was an interstate war between the United States and North Vietnam, backed by Communist Russia and China. And it was also a nation-building and counterinsurgency mission inside South Vietnam. It was, therefore, seen as a crusade *and* a quagmire, with the two rival traditions competing for dominance in the American mind.

The first interpretation saw Vietnam as an interstate war, similar to the world wars and Korea. Communist North Vietnam, Russia, and China had committed aggression against the freedom-loving South Vietnamese. Secretary of State Dean Rusk claimed that the issue was "a very simple one indeed. Hanoi, with Peiping's support and help," refused "to leave its neighbor alone."[74] As Richard Nixon later put it, "We failed to understand that the war was an invasion from North Vietnam, not an insurgency in South Vietnam. North Vietnam...shrewdly camouflaged its invasion to look like a civil war. But in fact the Vietnam War was the Korean War with jungles."[75]

Framing the conflict as an interstate war invoked the crusade tradition, heightening support for escalation, including more ground troops, more bombing, and even a march on Hanoi. Admiral Thomas H. Moorer believed that, as in the interstate wars of old, Americans should have taken the campaign into "the north, where everyone was the enemy, where you don't have to worry whether or not you were shooting friendly civilians.... The only reason to go to war is to overthrow a government you don't like."[76]

In the early stages of the campaign, most Americans thought of Vietnam as being essentially an interstate war. In February 1965, only 7 percent of Americans believed that attacks on U.S. forces were "mainly part of the civil war in South Vietnam," while 26 percent blamed "the Communist government of North Vietnam," and 53 percent held "the Chinese Communist government" responsible.[77]

Indeed, the origins of U.S. intervention in Vietnam echoed the run-up to previous interstate wars. An alleged attack by North

A pro–Vietnam War rally in Indianapolis in 1966. Photograph by Yoichi R. Okamoto. Courtesy of the Lyndon Baines Johnson Library and Museum.

Vietnam on American naval vessels in the Gulf of Tonkin in 1964 was reminiscent of the destruction of the *Maine* in 1898, the *Lusitania* in 1915, and the *Arizona* in 1941. Following what President Lyndon Johnson described as "hostile actions" by the North Vietnamese in the Gulf of Tonkin, there was overwhelming backing in

Congress for a resolution authorizing the use of force, and the president's approval ratings jumped in a classic rally effect. Consistent with the interstate war interpretation, support for the campaign in Vietnam held up into 1967, with rising sentiment in favor of escalation.[78]

But there was another way to understand the war. The rival perspective saw Vietnam as fundamentally a nation-building mission in the midst of an insurgency. This second view was far more troubling to Americans, prompting fears of a quagmire with no clear progress, in which the United States would only get bogged down.

Folk music overwhelmingly portrayed the Vietnam War as a protracted nation-building mission, with blurred moral lines and no end in sight. Tom Paxton sang in "Lyndon Johnson Told the Nation" about "searching for the Vietcong in vain." Country Joe McDonald's "I-Feel-Like-I'm-Fixing-to-Die Rag" depicted a highly confusing conflict: "And it's one, two, three / what are we fighting for."[79]

Just as we might expect, opinion poll questions that cued people to think of Vietnam as an interstate war produced higher levels of support than questions that framed the conflict as a nation-building mission. In March 1966, 73 percent of Americans thought we should continue to fight "if Red China decides to send a great many troops" to Vietnam, while only 8 percent favored withdrawal. But just two months later, a poll found that 54 percent of the public believed we ought to leave if "the South Vietnamese start fighting on a big scale among themselves," while only 28 percent wanted to "continue to help."[80]

Over time, Americans shifted from viewing the Vietnam War as an interstate crusade to seeing it as a nation-building quagmire. A key event was the 1968 Tet Offensive. The Vietcong insurgents attacked targets across the country, including the U.S. embassy in Saigon. The military outcome was a disaster for the Vietcong, which lost tens of thousands of troops. But the assault sent a powerful message: the struggle was a civil war, the insurgency was extensive, and the South Vietnamese government was illegitimate.

In the wake of Tet, television journalist Walter Cronkite commented, "To say that we are mired in a stalemate seems the only realistic, yet unsatisfactory, conclusion."[81] The U.S. media concluded that efforts to protect the South Vietnamese population from the insurgents were futile. The *Christian Science Monitor* reported on February 13, 1968, that "pacification has been blown sky high."[82] According to Senator Mike Mansfield, it was not America's responsibility "to win a victory for any particular Vietnamese group, or to defeat any particular Vietnamese group."[83]

Consistent with the quagmire interpretation, in 1968 support rose for withdrawal from Vietnam.[84] By this stage, the conflict had sparked a massive antiwar and draft-resistance movement, which included the ideological radicals of the New Left, the pacifist Quakers, and many ordinary Americans who had paid a terrible personal price. An Ohio mother who had lost her son in Vietnam wrote to President Johnson, "Do you know how my days are spent? First I clean my Son's [sic] room then I walk around praying and hoping the phone will ring and I'll know this is a bad dream.... We don't belong over there, so please bring the boys out of there."[85]

For U.S. troops on the ground, Vietnam increasingly resembled a meaningless morass, with no clear mission and no obvious front lines. Stephen Daniel arrived in Vietnam full of confidence, but within a few months he was disillusioned, writing to his parents about the death of a fellow Marine: "He didn't deserve dieing in a damn country not worth fighting for. He didn't deserve diein' for people who won't even fight for themselves."[86]

What passing-bells for those killed in a lost war? The objective of many GIs became survival and escapism. Search-and-destroy missions evolved into search and evade. Drugs offered a psychotro-

An anti–Vietnam War rally in 1967. Photo by Frank Wolfe. Courtesy of the Lyndon Baines Johnson Library and Museum.

pic diversion, with Zippos providing another function—lighting up joints. Perhaps half the enlisted men used marijuana, while thousands became heroin addicts.

Most U.S. soldiers continued to fight bravely, but discipline broke down and the chain of command eroded. Driven by anger at reckless tactics, as well as racial tension and drugs, troops even killed their own officers. It was known as "fragging," after the fragmentation grenades that were often employed for the task. Cases of fragging doubled from 1969 to 1970, to more than two hundred. One infantryman wrote, "Our commanding officer is insane. Gungho lifer looking for nothing but a body count of enemy so he can make a stupid promotion....I know for one fact with the hatred his men have for him, that if we ever got in a fire fight someone will knock him off. It happens quite a bit and I'm for certain It'll [*sic*] happen here. I've never seen such hatred."[87]

Episodes of *Star Trek* captured changing perceptions of the Vietnam War from crusade to quagmire. In "The City on the Edge of Forever" (1967), Doctor McCoy travels back through time to earth in the 1930s, where he saves the life of an idealistic peace activist. The unintended result, however, is that pacifism sweeps American society, the United States never enters World War II, and Nazi Germany emerges victorious. The only way to save the earth is for Captain Kirk and Spock to travel back in time and let the peace activist die, allowing history to return to normal. The lesson is clear: Vietnam is analogous to World War II, and the anti-war movement, however attractive and principled, serves to aid global aggressors.

"The Omega Glory," first screened in 1968, presents a different view of Vietnam. Kirk and his colleagues are drawn into a civil war between two tribes, the Yangs and Kohms, who clearly stand for the Yankees and Communists. Rather than glorify the anti-Communist struggle, the episode presents the Yangs as even more savage than the Kohms. The Yangs fight for a tattered American flag and worship fragments of the Pledge of Allegiance and the Constitution. But these texts mean nothing to them. The interminable war has reduced American ideals to hollow platitudes.[88]

After the fighting in Vietnam ended, the war became widely seen as a disastrous quagmire. By 1982, nearly three-quarters of Americans agreed that "the Vietnam War was more than a mistake, it was fundamentally wrong and immoral."[89] Few heroes emerged from the campaign. A rare exception was the American prisoners of war. The POWs who survived inhumane conditions in Vietnam were widely celebrated and honored. In interstate wars, prisoners share the limelight with daring warriors winning battles on the front lines. But in nation-building missions, they shine brightly as the lone diamonds in the mire.

The claim that Vietnam was essentially an interstate war persisted in influential quarters. In his book *On Strategy: A Critical Analysis of the Vietnam War,* Colonel Harry Summers argued that the primary threat had always been North Vietnam. Washington should have left the insurgency to the South Vietnamese and brought the real enemy to its knees by declaring war on Hanoi, employing massive firepower, and broadening the conflict into Laos. The job of U.S. soldiers was not to engage in nation-building, but "to fight, and win on the battlefield."[90] Summers's view became the conventional wisdom in the military.

Ronald Reagan also favored the interstate crusade interpretation of Vietnam. In a 1980 speech about the war, he made no mention of insurgents or nation-building, civil war or quagmire. Instead, Vietnam was a "noble cause" in which a "small country, newly free from colonial rule, sought our help in establishing self-rule and the means of self-defense against a totalitarian neighbor bent on conquest."[91] U.S. troops "came home without a victory not because they'd been defeated, but because they'd been denied permission to win."[92]

In summary, Americans were motivated to fight in Vietnam—and fight to *win*—against an external state aggressor, but they cared little about the internal politics of the country. The dueling crusade and quagmire interpretations help to explain why supporters and critics of the war often seemed to be talking past each other. They were looking at two different wars, and they were influenced by two different traditions.

Vietnam was just one of the nation-building fronts of the Cold War. Having reduced much of Germany, Japan, and Italy to ruins from 1941 to 1945, Washington set about rebuilding these countries as liberal democratic states. The United States also intervened to buttress pro-Western governments in South Korea, Lebanon, and the Dominican Republic.

How did Americans perceive these broader Cold War interventions? In a very rare exception to the quagmire rule, Americans saw nation-building in West Germany and Japan as a success. In 1946, majorities of the public were satisfied with how the United States was handling the occupation of its former enemies.[93]

By the 1970s, however, in the wake of Vietnam, there was a growing sense that military interventions to fight insurgencies and build democracy in the developing world had failed. Scholars described the emergence of a "Vietnam syndrome," with Americans eager to avoid a repeat of their traumatic experience in Southeast Asia. For example, in 1974 only 10 percent of Americans remembered the 1965 intervention in the Dominican Republic as a "proud moment" in American history.[94]

Adventures in Chaos

In a sense, there's no great mystery in explaining the dominant view of Cold War nation-building as a debacle. Vietnam was truly a spectacular failure. The United States withdrew before a non-Communist South Vietnam had been guaranteed. The war unleashed an astounding amount of death and destruction, killing several million Vietnamese along with more than 58,000 Americans. It entailed the expenditure of $140 billion and created massive social unrest in the United States. Tragically, the settlement terms that Washington received in 1973 were actually worse than the terms North Vietnam offered back in 1965.[95]

Of course, the United States encountered one of the toughest nation-building scenarios imaginable, defending a weak and illegitimate government against an incredibly committed opponent. Even so, Washington made a number of critical mistakes. For instance, the U.S. military fought the campaign, in large part, as a conventional interstate war, employing firepower indiscriminately and neglecting the counterinsurgency arena.[96]

Vietnam has dominated perceptions to such an extent that Americans sometimes dismiss Cold War nation-building as a disaster in toto. But in other cases, Washington achieved considerable success. West Germany, Japan, and Italy were all transformed from authoritarian fascist societies into prosperous, liberal democratic allies of the United States and important markets for U.S. goods. In the wake of Allied occupation, Austria also became a Western-style democracy, although it was neutral in the Cold War. The United States thereby helped to end war in Europe—a triumph for the ages. As James Dobbins and colleagues concluded, "The German and Japanese occupations remain the gold standard for post-war reconstruction."[97]

The United States also played a critical role in South Korea's transition from impoverished despotism to wealthy democracy with a huge nation-building effort, which promoted land redistribution, education reform, and even the introduction of Boy Scout and Girl Scout organizations. Just like the Germans, Japanese, Italians, and Austrians, the Koreans were not passive recipients of America's nation-building largesse. They were active participants, who adapted American ideas to their own traditions. Although it took several decades for democracy to become firmly rooted in South Korea, without U.S. assistance, the country might have shared the twilight fate of North Korea.[98]

Another successful outcome was achieved in a much briefer mission in Lebanon in 1958. U.S. troops were deployed there at the request of the pro-Western Lebanese president and America's allies to avert a civil war and revolution. After U.S. Marines waded ashore on the beaches of Beirut, through throngs of startled sunbathers, Washington engineered a political compromise that was acceptable to all major Lebanese factions, and the country was fairly stable until civil war broke out in 1975. Only one American died from hostile action.[99]

The U.S. intervention in the Dominican Republic in 1965 produced a mixed result. The United States landed twenty thousand troops in the midst of a civil war, aiming to protect Americans caught up in the disturbances and, most important, avoid a Castro-style revolution. Proponents of the Dominican intervention claimed that it averted a bloodbath. Critics countered that the threat of Communist takeover or massacres was exaggerated and the mission caused a negative reaction in Latin America. After 1965, the Dominican Republic was fairly peaceful. Despite the country's many problems, elective government, if not true democracy, has since prevailed.[100]

Quiet Americans

Americans' disillusionment with nation-building in the 1970s was primarily driven by the staggering losses incurred in Vietnam. But a familiar set of cultural factors also reinforced negative beliefs. Compared to interstate wars like World War II and Korea, vengeance faded as a motivating force when the focus shifted to nation-building. After 1945, for example, anger toward the Japanese subsided with incredible speed. When Washington announced in 1946 that Emperor Hirohito would not be tried as a war criminal, the public shrugged its shoulders. As historian John Dower noted, the fascist madman had become the U.S. patient.[101]

Similarly, Americans on the home front were rarely driven to fight in Vietnam by a desire for revenge. The war was too morally complex and confusing to spark a retributive response. The population that Americans were supposedly saving, the South Vietnamese, appeared ungrateful or actively hostile. The adversary could be cast as a nationalist force struggling to free its society from imperialism. Every enemy atrocity was seemingly matched by an American atrocity. Senator Robert Kennedy remarked, "We are not in Vietnam to play the part of an avenging angel, pouring death and destruction on the roads and factories and homes of a guilty land."[102] As historian Michael Sherry put it, "During the Vietnam War, most Americans seemed to hate each other more than the enemy."[103]

Although wrath declined as a factor, idealism was ever present in the minds of Americans and encouraged gloomy evaluations of nation-building. As with southern Reconstruction, the Philippines, and Latin America, idealism raised the bar for success. Americans were enthusiastic nation-builders only if the target country ended up looking like the United States. West Germany and Japan soon achieved this standard, with ordinary Germans and Japanese eating hot dogs and buying motorcars in stable and prosperous democracies. Americans were duly impressed. But these two countries were already modern states before U.S. forces ever arrived. Beneath the ruined cities of the Axis powers lay firm foundations for building rich and free societies—foundations that were notably absent elsewhere.

Political scientist Douglas Macdonald found that Americans often judged the results of Cold War nation-building harshly. Washington typically followed one of two main strategies: it either bolstered friendly governments by providing aid, or it pressured the regime to introduce liberal reforms. The problem was that Americans wanted to see both democracy and stability. The result was a catch-22. Bolstering was viewed as a failure because the target country didn't become democratic. Reform was seen as a mistake because it created short-term problems of stability. With both strategies perceived as ineffective, Washington kept lurching back and forth: bolstering then reforming, bolstering then reforming.[104]

As idealists, Americans sometimes expected too much too soon. In the years after 1945, the United States seemed able to achieve anything. The degree of American confidence and naïveté about nation-building was captured in Graham Greene's 1955 novel, *The Quiet American*. A young American idealist, Alden Pyle, is sent to Vietnam in the early 1950s to build a democratic movement independent of the French colonialists or the Communists. Pyle is convinced that he can help to save the East for democracy, but all his hopes turn to nought, and he ends up dying.[105]

A decade after the novel was published, many Americans continued to hold overconfident assumptions about the nation-building mission in Vietnam. They underestimated the strength of the insurgency and exaggerated the speed and extent of change the United States could bring about. Yes, the French had been defeated in Vietnam, but as one Pentagon official noted, "The French also tried to build the Panama Canal."[106]

When U.S. officials expected too much, they became disillusioned. When politicians promised too much, other Americans became disillusioned. The LBJ administration was repeatedly overly optimistic in its public statements about the progress of the Vietnam War, touting an endless stream of statistics about infiltration rates and body counts to show that victory was just around the corner. William Westmoreland, commander of U.S. forces in Vietnam, claimed in late 1967, "The end begins to come into view."[107] Relative to such declarations, the Tet Offensive looked like a disastrous failure. There was no light at the end of the tunnel after all.

Americans often saw the tactics employed in Vietnam—including saturation bombing, the use of napalm, massacres such as My Lai, and the destruction of villages—as a violation of their core ideals. Vietnam veteran Colin Powell wrote in his autobiography, "We burned down the thatched huts, starting the blaze with Ronson and Zippo cigarette lighters."[108]

But Americans were outraged only because these acts occurred during a nation-building mission. The United States never destroyed the Red River dikes in North Vietnam, for fear of killing thousands of noncombatants. But in the Korean War, North Korean dikes were systematically bombed, causing massive civilian deaths, with little dissent. Indeed, American atrocities were rarely reported at all in Korea, but from an early point in Vietnam, the media highlighted cases of alleged abuses.[109]

Napalm is associated with Vietnam, but it was invented in World War II and was widely used in Europe and the Pacific without any controversy. During the Tet Offensive, when a South Vietnamese general summarily shot a Vietcong officer who had killed several people while wearing civilian clothes, the act symbolized the brutality of the war. But in 1944, when U.S. forces shot Germans captured in American uniforms during the Battle of the Bulge, no one considered it an atrocity.

The phrase "U.S. war crimes" immediately conjures up the 1968 My Lai Massacre in Vietnam. One veteran, Edgar Jones, recalled: "We shot prisoners in cold blood[,]...killed or mistreated enemy civilians, finished off the enemy wounded, tossed the dying into a hole with the dead." But Jones was not writing about My Lai. He was describing the Pacific campaign in World War II, adding that Americans "boiled the flesh off enemy skulls to make table ornaments for sweethearts, or carved their bones into letter openers."[110] We don't associate good wars with atrocities, even if the actual number of misdeeds is much higher.[111]

Critics on the left condemned Cold War nation-building as a flagrant breach of the American ideal of anti-imperialism. The radical interpretation of the Vietnam War held that anticommunism was just a cover for an intervention designed to serve capitalist interests and create imperial ties of dependency and domination. This argument tends to exaggerate the unity of American business, the influence of the business community on policy making, and the consistency of Washington's decision making. If U.S. officials were fighting to preserve an exploitative capitalist order, they forgot to mention the scheme in the documentary record.[112]

Most conservatives supported Cold War interventions to contain communism, but concerns were raised that nation-building violated the American ideal of limited government. Harry Summers described the war effort in Vietnam as "the international version of our domestic Great Society programs where we presumed that we knew what was best for the world in terms of social, political, and economic development and saw it as our duty to force the world into the American mold—to act not so much the World's Policeman as the World's Nanny."[113] This argument echoed criticism of southern Reconstruction as welfarism. Almost a century before, the *New York Evening Post* claimed that the South should "get out of the federal nursery."[114]

Conservatives were especially scathing about the foreign aid component of Cold War nation-building. During the Korean War, Senator Harry F. Byrd argued that South Korea's inability to defend itself after years of foreign aid demonstrated the ineffectiveness of handouts.[115] In 1958, Otto Passman, congressman from Louisiana, told a State Department official, "Son, I don't smoke and I don't drink. My only pleasure in life is kicking the shit out of the foreign aid program of the United States of America."[116] Senator Richard B. Russell of Georgia believed that aid was wasteful and costly and had become a national "disease."[117] In 1963, Russell called foreign aid "that all-time monster of world wide bureaucracy," which made foreign economies "dependent" on U.S. assistance.[118] The critique was strikingly similar to conservative attacks on domestic welfare programs.

The shadow of past quagmires further darkened perceptions. J. William Fulbright's opposition to the war in Vietnam was shaped by his memory of southern Reconstruction. The senator from Arkansas accepted the myth of Reconstruction as a disastrous period of repression and black rule. According to Fulbright, Vietnamese resistance to arrogant U.S. imperialism was analogous to the struggle of southern whites in the post–Civil War period. Washington couldn't remake Vietnam in the U.S. image any more than it could refashion race relations in the South. One member of the White House staff captured Fulbright's thinking about Vietnam: "The American presence is those hated carpetbaggers and damn Yankees."[119]

Minding Its Own Business

Americans spent the bicentennial in 1976 much as they spent the centennial in 1876: retreating from nation-building. Polls showed a sharp uptick among those who wanted the United States to "mind its own business" internationally.[120] By now, Zippos were increasingly inscribed NEVER AGAIN.

The cliché is that military leaders prepare to fight the last war. But in the 1970s and 1980s, the U.S. military wanted to do anything but fight the last war. The senior army leadership ordered all material on counterinsurgency held at the special warfare school at Fort Bragg, North Carolina, to be destroyed.[121] The cruel mistress of Vietnam reminded Americans of the woman they really loved— World War II. The military planned incessantly for a major campaign against the Soviets in Europe, even though this was the least likely military contingency.

There was time, however, for one more quagmire, when the United States intervened in Lebanon from 1982 to 1984. Following a successful operation by Marines to facilitate the evacuation of Syrian troops and Palestinian Liberation Organization (PLO) fighters from Beirut, the Marine barracks was struck by a massive car bomb in October 1983, killing 241 Americans. The public reaction fit the quagmire mold. After initially rallying around the flag, support for the intervention eroded, and the last Marines withdrew in February 1984.[122]

Secretary of Defense Caspar Weinberger opposed nation-building in Lebanon, and in a November 1984 speech, he gave the quagmire tradition his official blessing. In what became known as the Weinberger-Powell Doctrine, the secretary of defense, together with his then aide and later chairman of the Joint Chiefs of Staff Colin Powell, established a series of ground rules for the use of force. Vital national interests must be involved, clear and achievable objectives ought to exist, popular support had to be guaranteed, and an exit strategy should be established. These tests would filter out almost every nation-building mission.[123]

The United States also engaged in two quick crusades. In 1983, Reagan ordered a Marine assault on Grenada to prevent an armed revolution from turning the Caribbean island into a second Cuba. Despite many errors, including American deaths due to friendly fire, the invasion broadly followed the crusader script, with all necessary force achieving regime change, and public support remained high.[124]

Six years later, in December 1989, President George H. W. Bush began Operation Just Cause to overthrow the government of Manuel Noriega in Panama. Before the invasion, 59 percent of the American public was opposed to intervention in Panama, but once U.S. forces began the attack, 80 percent thought it was justified.[125] As with Grenada, there were many mistakes, but decisive force led to regime change and Noriega's capture, and Bush's popularity rose to 80 percent.[126]

A Black Wall

Just a few hundred yards away from the upbeat World War II Memorial on the Mall, there's a black wall with more than 58,000 names on it. The stark disparity between America's experience of World War II and Vietnam represents the contrast between the ultimate good war and the definitive bad war.

As with earlier interstate campaigns, in World War II Americans favored maximum objectives and tolerated the killing of enemy civilians. As with previous nation-building missions, in Vietnam Americans grew disillusioned, were sensitive to abuses by U.S. troops, and eventually supported withdrawal.

The first issue of the *Captain America* comic book in 1941 showed the hero slugging Hitler with a right hook. "Cap" led the crusade against fascism in Europe and the Pacific, often battling his archenemy, Red Skull. But two decades later, the hero barely made an appearance in Vietnam. Cap concluded that the Vietnam War should be ended not with a crushing victory, but with a peace settlement. As the hero put it in 1970, "I've spent a lifetime defending the flag…and the law! Perhaps I should have battled less…and questioned more!"[127]

World War II was fought with more cynicism and less idealistic fervor than World War I. But in hindsight, World War II came to be seen as the purest of crusades: its dazzling radiance blocking out cautionary memories of the Great War. It reinforced the traditional model of interstate conflict, shaping expectations in Korea and beyond.

Meanwhile, the lesson of Vietnam was, Don't nation-build. But if we look at the broader picture of operations in West Germany, Japan, Italy, Austria, South Korea, Lebanon, and the Dominican Republic, the clearer lesson is, Don't nation-build *in Vietnam*.

In 1991, President George H. W. Bush hoped to bury the Vietnam syndrome forever and create a new world order with a decisive victory over America's latest nemesis, Saddam Hussein. But a new world order would not be the only thing born out of the Gulf War.

CHAPTER 8

Black Gold and Black Hawks

T he USS *Acadia* served in the 1991 Gulf War as a naval support vessel, with a crew of 1,250 personnel, including 360 women. When the ship returned to its home base of San Diego, 36 female sailors—10 percent of the women on board—were missing because they had become pregnant. Much to the navy's irritation, the press labeled the *Acadia* the "Love Boat."

During the five-month buildup of troops in the Gulf in 1990–1991, the number of pregnancies among U.S. female military personnel may have run as high as 1,200. In other words, for every American soldier who died in combat in the Gulf War (148), 8 U.S. personnel were expecting. And nearly a quarter of American deaths were the result of friendly fire (a euphemism that may also apply to those removed from the military theater due to pregnancy). The Gulf War was meant to bury memories of Vietnam forever, but it brought new meaning to the 1960s slogan "Make love, not war."[1]

The disparity between fecundity and fatality tells us less about the role of women in the U.S. military than about the remarkably low number of casualties incurred besting Iraq. How did such a mismatch campaign come to be?

In August 1990, Saddam Hussein invaded and annexed Kuwait. The Iraqi dictator was short of cash after the 1980–1988 Iran-Iraq War and believed that a brazen assault on his oil-rich neighbor would provide a quick fix. If Saddam had attacked Kuwait earlier during the Cold War, he might have manipulated the superpower rivalry to hold on to his prize. But with an impeccable sense of timing, the Iraqi leader invaded just when the Cold War was winding down and Moscow was ready to cooperate with Washington in a major international effort to liberate Kuwait.

Saddam also failed to understand Americans. The dictator believed that the United States would not militarily intervene because it was psychologically crippled by Vietnam. And if Washington did resist, any war with the United States would be a rerun of Lebanon in 1982–1984, when U.S. Marines withdrew after the barracks bombing.[2] But Americans respond to interstate wars very differently than they do to nation-building missions like Lebanon. The public was likely to perceive a conflict with Iraq as a crusade, not a quagmire, and favor the use of all necessary force to achieve grand objectives, including regime change in Baghdad. In his song "Don't Give Us a Reason," Hank Williams Jr. offered Saddam some advice: "You can take that poison gas, and stick it in your sassafras."[3]

After the invasion of Kuwait, U.S. president George H. W. Bush turned to the United Nations, which passed comprehensive economic sanctions against Baghdad and authorized the use of force to liberate Kuwait if Saddam did not withdraw. With British prime minister Margaret Thatcher's advice ringing in his ears — "Remember, George, this is no time to go wobbly" — Bush spent months carefully building a large coalition force in the Gulf for a counteroffensive.[4]

God Bless the USA

Before the trumpet sounded, Americans were far from a nation of eager crusaders. Many experts predicted that a war against Iraq could turn into a long and bloody struggle, with thousands of U.S. casualties. In the fall of 1990, public opinion was evenly split on whether to fight or give sanctions more time. In January 1991, the Senate authorized the use of force against Iraq by a narrow margin of 52 to 47.[5]

President G. H. W. Bush walking alone in front of the Washington Monument, January 1991. Courtesy of the George Bush Presidential Library and Museum.

On January 17, Operation Desert Storm began with a massive air campaign against Iraqi targets. The initiation of hostilities sparked a dramatic shift in American public opinion in favor of an all-out assault on the enemy—echoing what we saw in 1861, 1898, 1917, and 1941. The U.S. media tumbled, danced, jumped, and cheered. Reporters claimed it was "our war," with the home front and the sacred troops united in resisting aggression. One American base commander gave journalists a gift: flags carried by planes bombing Baghdad. "You are warriors, too," he told them.[6] About 95 percent of all television news stories that discussed the U.S. military praised its performance.[7]

Many people felt an intoxicating sense of collective unity as Americans rallied around the flag, the president, and the military. Lee Greenwood's tune "God Bless the USA," originally released in 1984, was dusted off and became the theme song of the war. The yellow ribbon symbolized grassroots participation in the struggle. Stacey Roder, a television producer in Buffalo during Desert Storm, observed, "You couldn't *buy* a yellow ribbon in this town.... This community came together like I've never seen it before.... It's very easy to get caught up in that."[8]

Kent State University in Ohio, where four antiwar protesters were shot dead by National Guardsmen in 1970, is forever associated with the stark divisions of Vietnam. But 60 percent of the students at Kent State backed the Gulf War.[9] There was an almost audible sigh of relief that the United States was out of the nation-building business and battling a tyrant once more.

The public began to see President Bush as a cross between Lincoln and FDR. Bush's approval ratings jumped 18 points, to 82 percent. The number of people who felt that the war was worthwhile increased from 46 percent to 71 percent. Impressively, after taking the nation into war, there was a 27-point surge in Bush's score for "making progress" at "keeping the nation out of war."[10] The rally effect was so powerful that the administration tried to dial down the euphoria, reminding people that there could be sig-nificant casualties.[11]

Americans favored the use of all necessary force to achieve maximum war aims. Before Desert Storm broke, Bush promised, "This will not be another Vietnam. This will not be a protracted, drawn-out war."[12] The head of the U.S. Central Command, H. "Stormin' Norman" Schwarzkopf, told an interviewer in November 1990, "I can assure you that if we have to go to war, I am going to use every single thing that is available to me to bring as much destruction to Iraqi forces as rapidly as I possibly can in the hopes of winning victory as quickly as possible."[13] Schwarzkopf kept a framed copy of William T. Sherman's crusading maxim in his office: "War is the remedy our enemies have chosen. And I say let us give them all they want."[14]

In a highly symbolic move, the bombing campaign was called Instant Thunder, to distinguish it from the prolonged air operations in Vietnam, called Rolling Thunder. A CNN team was in Baghdad and relayed vivid images of the first attacks. The sky was lit up with antiaircraft fire, but the Iraqi military was shooting almost blindly into the night. Its air defense centers had already been knocked out, and U.S. stealth bombers were virtually undetectable.[15]

As in previous interstate wars, Americans were unfazed by enemy civilian deaths, which amounted to around 2,200. When U.S. planes bombed the Al-Firdos bunker in Baghdad on February 13, killing two hundred to three hundred Iraqi civilians, more than 80 percent of the American public thought that the bunker was a legitimate military target. If Iraqi resistance had proved stubborn, there is little doubt that Americans would have tolerated far higher civilian casualties. People were even willing to contemplate the use of extreme measures. Opinion was evenly split on whether the United States should employ "tactical nuclear weapons against Iraq if it might save the lives of United States troops": 45 percent said yes, 45 percent said no.[16]

On February 24, coalition forces began the ground campaign phase. Shocked and awed by air strikes and a lightning armored assault, Saddam's troops fled out of Kuwait in disarray. Some Iraqis were so eager to give up, they surrendered to U.S. reconnaissance drones. With Kuwait quickly liberated, this seemed like a model crusade in America's pantheon of triumphs. But although the victory was impressive, it was not complete. Bush called a halt to the fighting after freeing Kuwait, leaving Saddam Hussein in power.

It was the right decision. First, U.S. allies opposed an expansion of the war. To march on Baghdad would have destroyed the coalition the president had so painstakingly put together. Second, the United Nations mandate covered only the liberation of Kuwait, not regime change in Iraq, so a war ostensibly fought to defend international law would have ended up as an illegal campaign. Third, escalation would have risked a broadened conflict with

President G. H. W. Bush speaking to the British prime minister by phone during a February 1991 meeting in the Oval Office, White House. Courtesy of the George Bush Presidential Library and Museum.

unpredictable consequences. Saddam might have used chemical weapons in a last-ditch defense. Fourth, victory would have left the United States in charge of creating a new government in postwar Iraq—a task for which it was not in the least prepared. As Secretary of Defense Dick Cheney put it, "How many forces are you going to have to leave there to keep it propped up, how many casualties are you going to take through the course of this operation?"[17]

Despite the strategic logic of restricting the war, Americans were uncomfortable with a limited campaign that left the tyrant in power. As the fighting progressed, crusading sentiment swelled up, and the number favoring a march on Baghdad rose to well over 70 percent.[18] Even when pollsters explicitly reminded people that the United Nations had authorized only a war to free Kuwait, a majority of the public still wanted to fight for regime change. And of this majority of hawks, most were willing to sacrifice thousands of U.S. lives to remove Saddam from power.[19] By comparison, in Britain, among the United States' strongest allies in the Gulf War, only 27 percent of the public wanted to escalate the campaign and overthrow the Iraqi dictator.[20]

Americans were not, however, eager to roll up their sleeves and start nation-building in Iraq: overseeing elections, resolving ethnic conflicts, and all the rest of it. Instead, they spent barely a moment thinking about what would happen after Saddam fell. They wanted regime change, not nation-building.

In April 1991, shortly after the cease-fire, two very revealing polling questions were put to the same group of Americans. The first asked respondents if they wanted to restart the war with Iraq and force Saddam from power; 54 percent said yes. The second inquired whether the United States should aid Kurdish and Shiite rebels in Iraq who had risen up to overthrow Saddam. Logically, one might expect support for this strategy to be even higher because it implied there was popular backing in Iraq for regime change, as well as allies on the ground to share the burden of fighting. But only 32 percent of Americans wanted to aid the Iraqi rebels, while 53 percent were opposed.[21] Why the disparity?

Asking whether U.S. forces should march on Baghdad invoked the crusade tradition and the preference for maximum objectives. The mention of rebels triggered the quagmire tradition, fears of intervening in another country's civil war, and memories of Vietnam. The lesson for other countries seemed to be, If you want the United States to overthrow your regime, don't start a rebellion.

Surface-to-Air Prayer

American thinking about the invasion of Kuwait was not based primarily on strategic logic. At first, Bush tried to defend the intervention using arguments about national interests, including protecting the Middle East balance of power and global energy supplies. But polls and focus groups showed that this approach gained little traction with the public.

The president was pushing the wrong buttons in the American psyche. Bush shifted gears and began highlighting Iraqi aggression and the malevolent nature of Saddam Hussein, describing the conflict as "good versus evil, right versus wrong, human dignity and freedom versus tyranny and oppression."[22] As the *New York Times* put it, "The pragmatic President who plied Realpolitik for the first two years of his Administration is suddenly on a moral crusade."[23] The new missionary tone hit home. In December 1990, Americans thought that the United States was motivated more by a desire to protect oil supplies than by principle. But during the war, people changed their minds and overwhelmingly thought that the United States was guided by ideals.[24]

But which ideals were Americans fighting for? A war to save the world for Kuwaiti-style feudal monarchy didn't have the right ring to it. Fortunately, barely a quarter of Americans knew that

Kuwait was a monarchy.[25] The administration instead highlighted the rule of law in international politics and the protection of small countries from invasion. After all, this was the first time in the history of the United Nations that one member state had annexed another. A U.S. serviceman wrote from Saudi Arabia, "We came here to protect the freedom of the people of Kuwait and Saudi Arabia. Freedom is for everyone around the world, not just Americans."[26]

Missionary sentiment was reinforced by the belief that, as Bush put it, the United States and its allies were "on the side of God."[27] During the war, reporters often wrote about Americans turning to religion and, in one case, employing "surface-to-air prayer." Nearly 5 percent of the war coverage on one Buffalo television station involved images of people praying.[28]

Marching on Baghdad would not only protect and extend our ideals; it would also smite Saddam with the terrible swift sword of vengeance. The Iraqi dictator was a picture-perfect villain, who invaded a weaker neighbor, treated Kuwaitis with brutality, took Americans hostage, fired Scud missiles at Israel and Saudi Arabia, and burned oil fields. Bush used metaphors such as rape to describe Saddam's crimes and stir the emotional desire for revenge. In American eyes, Saddam was a demonic force. When people were asked to give the dictator a favorability score from 0 to 100, the median rating was usually 0.[29] In a January 1991 poll of West Virginians, Adolf Hitler only narrowly defeated Saddam Hussein for the title of most evil leader of the twentieth century (43 percent to 36 percent).[30]

"People in Nebraska want this guy dead," reported Senator Bob Kerrey about opinion in his home state.[31] Revealingly, Americans who strongly supported the death penalty, and were therefore unusually retributive, were also the leading champions of regime change in Baghdad and of bombing near civilian areas when necessary. The death penalty and the overthrow of Saddam were both means of punishing evildoers, and collateral damage was an acceptable price for justice.[32]

When Americans looked at Saddam, they saw the shadow of Hitler and concluded that the two tyrants should share the same fate. President Bush repeatedly compared the Iraqi dictator to the German dictator, the occupation of Kuwait to the activities of the German SS, and a policy of drawn-out sanctions to appeasement.[33] Meanwhile, the *New York Times* and the *Washington Post* printed more than two hundred stories on the analogy between Saddam and Hitler.[34] It didn't help Saddam's case that he had read and admired *Mein Kampf*. Before the war, between 63 and 72 percent of Americans believed that the comparison to Hitler was "a good way" to look at the situation. By February 1991, this figure rose to 81 percent, and about the same number thought that World War II was a closer analogy to the Gulf War than was Vietnam.[35]

Missionary idealism, vengeance, and parallels with World War II encouraged Americans to seek the total defeat of the adversary. To advance American values, the tyrant must be deposed. Any lesser outcome would be unjust, given Saddam's crimes. Would our forefathers who stormed ashore on D-Day have left the great dictator in power? After the Gulf War ended with a limited victory, Bush wrote in his diary, "It hasn't been a clean end—there is no battleship *Missouri* surrender. This is what's missing to make this akin to WWII, to separate Kuwait from Korea and Vietnam."[36]

Not all Americans supported escalation. Bush genuinely saw the conflict in moral terms, but what mattered most to him were strategic interests, and these favored restraint. In a survey after the war ended, American elites were asked whether they backed the decision to leave Saddam in power. Interestingly, those elites with specific expertise in foreign policy were more likely to favor the decision, recognizing the importance of restricting the Gulf War. But for most Americans, this outcome clashed with the moral narrative of the campaign.[37]

Going to Bed with Rita Hayworth

The disintegration of the Iraqi army and the rapid end of hostilities on February 27, 1991, may have been the best thing that ever happened to the Iraqi dictator. The war was so short and U.S. casualties were so low that the fighting was over before American opinion, especially at the elite level, could harden in favor of regime change. Saddam stayed in power only because he lost so badly.

Americans were left with mixed feelings after the Gulf War. In many respects, the campaign was the anti-Vietnam: a cathartic experience that closely followed the crusader template. U.S. troops returned home to a hero's welcome. On March 31, Whitney Houston dedicated her first televised concert as a solo artist to the soldiers and their families. Among the songs was that old crusading classic, "The Battle Hymn of the Republic."

In hindsight, people strongly supported the decision to fight in the Gulf—so much so, that it affected their memories. Before the war began, the country was split evenly between hawks favoring the use of force and doves wanting to continue with sanctions. But after the cease-fire, people recalled by a margin of four to one that they had *always been hawks*.[38]

The facts that Bush had applied the brakes and that Saddam had survived helped to make the victory feel hollow. Like cheap sparkling wine, the euphoria soon fizzled out. Samuel Kaplan, a professor at Swarthmore College, described the national mood: "[It] reminds me of what Rita Hayworth once said about herself: 'Men go to bed with Rita Hayworth and wake up and find it's only me.' America went to bed with a great victory and woke up with a victory that no longer seems so great and a world filled with problems that we basically aren't able to do anything about."[39]

Americans ultimately concluded that Bush was wrong to stay the crusader's sword. Just after the fighting ended in February 1991, 46 percent of Americans believed that the United States should have toppled Saddam. By April, the figure was 56 percent. By July, it was 76 percent.[40] In 1992, 69 percent of Americans thought that the Gulf War wasn't even a victory, because Saddam remained in power.[41] Dan Welch, a tank commander with the First Infantry, wrote home after the cease-fire, "I think we've made a mistake and not finished this the way it should have been ended.... He's still alive, and unless somehow the rebels finish what we've started, we may be back."[42]

A crusader scorned is an unforgiving voter. The major reason Bush lost to Bill Clinton in 1992 was the economy. But ironically, the failure to topple Saddam may have helped bring regime change to the United States. Bush grumbled that he was "sick and tired" of not getting more credit for the Gulf War, but the public didn't listen.[43] Saddam taunted his nemesis throughout the presidential campaign and greeted Bush's defeat with huge celebrations in Baghdad.

Desert Storm seemed to show that the U.S. military could stick to what it does best—crusading. In 1992, chairman of the Joint Chiefs of Staff, Colin Powell, published a National Military Strategy titled "Decisive Force." Powell concluded that the United States should overwhelm its opponents through the rapid application of massive firepower.[44] Officials toasted America's envelopment maneuvers in Kuwait as a rerun of Hannibal's destruction of the Romans at Cannae. But the global environment was changing in ways that made both Cannae and the Gulf War anachronisms. The new security challenges arose not from interstate wars, but from failed states, insurgents, and terrorists. The future of military campaigning lay in combating the AK-47, the rocket-propelled grenade, and the improvised explosive device.

New World Order

On December 9, 1992, U.S. naval commandos slipped ashore as an advance guard for the humanitarian intervention in Somalia. But a small army was waiting for them on the beach, employing bright lights that blinded the commandos. Fortunately, it was an army of journalists and cameramen. In a bid to win the public relations battle in Somalia, officials had tipped off the press. The result was a cross between Omaha Beach and Oscar night.

The end of the Cold War and international cooperation in the Gulf led President Bush to promise a "new world order, a world where the rule of law, not the law of the jungle, governs the conduct of nations."[45] Having often criticized Cold War interventions, American liberals suddenly became enamored with using force for the global good. The United States launched its fifth wave of nation-building operations in Somalia (1992), Haiti (1994), Bosnia (1995), and Kosovo (1999).

Given America's experience in nation-building from southern Reconstruction through Lebanon, the public's response to the "new interventionism" was predictable. After one year of the mission in Haiti, just 41 percent of Americans thought the intervention was a success—and this figure was even lower for Somalia, Bosnia, and Kosovo.[46] These operations sparked bruising political battles between President Bill Clinton and the Republican Congress. The U.S. military establishment also was deeply suspicious about the turn toward nation-building. Americans searched for the right word to describe these missions and soon found it. "We are in a quagmire," commented Congressman Romano Mazzoli about the U.S. intervention in Somalia, "and we will not get out of that quagmire by getting further and deeper into it."[47]

The Greatest Joy in My Life

It's tough to square these widespread perceptions of failure with the reality of what happened on the ground in Somalia, Haiti, Bosnia, and Kosovo. These nation-building missions achieved many of their goals and produced substantial beneficial effects at modest costs.

Let's start with the East African state of Somalia, which came to symbolize America's supposedly disastrous experience in nation-building. After the end of the Cold War, Somalia disintegrated into clan-based warfare, with widespread famine. In response, President Bush announced that the United States would intervene to secure the delivery of humanitarian relief, and U.S. forces played an active role in Somalia from December 1992 to October 1993.

The result was, on balance, a partial success. By helping to end the famine, U.S. forces saved around 100,000 lives. (Some estimates put the figure in the low tens of thousands, others at more than a million.) Americans built or repaired Somali infrastructure, including roads and schools, and trained 3,500 police officers. The number of refugees was halved. "Never before, perhaps," wrote political scientist John Mueller, "has so much been done for so many at such little cost."[48]

When President Bush visited Somalia in December 1992, he was greeted by adoring crowds. One journalist noted the declining specter of famine: "As Mr. Bush drives from the airstrip to an orphanage, there will be no bodies ready for the daily pickup of the dead, swathed in dirty rags and tied like parcels with string at each end, lying on the narrow dusty strips of road."[49] By contrast, when UN Secretary-General Boutros Boutros-Ghali arrived a few days later, his motorcade was pelted with stones and fruit—a sign of Somali frustration with earlier UN efforts.[50]

In 1993, as the mission in Somalia expanded into more

ambitious nation-building terrain, the new administration of Bill Clinton failed to clarify a long-term strategy.[51] It's important to note, however, that Somalia is probably the most difficult environment in the world to attempt nation-building. The territory is completely impoverished, lacking in the most basic infrastructure and variously described as a "failed state" and a "geographical expression." Many of the policy failures in Somalia in 1993 were not the fault of the United States, which scaled back its military presence from 30,000 to 4,000 troops and handed over responsibility for the operation to other coalition states.

In the end, forty-three Americans died in Somalia, including eighteen in the "Black Hawk Down" incident, or battle of Mogadishu, in October 1993. Even this infamous military action accomplished its main objective by capturing several Somalis linked to earlier attacks on UN forces. But the cost in American lives was far higher than expected, as U.S. troops engaged in a complex firefight in Mogadishu. Overall, however, as American diplomat Chester Crocker wrote, the intervention in Somalia "knocked a hideously costly, stalemated clan war off dead center and opened the field for local initiatives."[52]

Back at home, the Somalia mission was not perceived as a partial success — one that saved the lives of thousands of Somalis for every American who died. Instead, it was widely viewed as one of the greatest military disasters since Vietnam. Even before the battle of Mogadishu, Americans supported a withdrawal from Somalia by a margin of almost two to one.[53] Opposition surged further with news of the eighteen dead soldiers. Images of the captured U.S. pilot, Michael Durant, and American bodies being dragged through the streets were the lead story on all the major networks. Congressmen referred to the pictures as they angrily called for withdrawal from Somalia.[54]

Rick Coe, a park ranger in Houston, felt that the intervention had turned into "a nightmare, a quagmire, a death trap."[55] Only 25 percent of Americans thought that the operation to "provide humanitarian relief" in Somalia was successful, while 66 percent considered it a failure.[56]

A year after the battle of Mogadishu, in 1994, President Clinton ordered U.S. forces into Haiti. The objective was to restore the democratically elected government of Jean-Bertrand Aristide, who had been overthrown by a coup, and to end the flight of Haitian refugees to the United States. The U.S. nation-building mission in Haiti, which lasted from 1994 to 1996, produced mixed results. Aristide's government was reinstalled without substantial bloodshed, humanitarian suffering was mitigated, the exodus of refugees was halted, elections were held, and efforts were made to rebuild the health and sanitation infrastructure and to train a new police force — all at a cost of only four American lives. Political killings fell dramatically in Haiti, from one thousand per year to just one per year.

The American intervention achieved its restricted goals, which were admittedly palliative rather than curative. As in Somalia, because most of the U.S. forces pulled out in 1996, the long-term gains of the intervention were limited. It's notable that within just a few weeks of U.S. troops *arriving* in Haiti, a plurality of Americans thought that the operation was a failure.[57]

Even while U.S. forces were entering Haiti, attention was already shifting to the bloody civil war in the former Yugoslavia. The epicenter of the conflict was Bosnia and Herzegovina, where Serbs, Croats, and Bosnian Muslims had engaged in savage fighting since 1992. For years, the international community vacillated between delivering humanitarian assistance while staying above the fray, and confronting the Serbs, who were blamed for aggression and human rights abuses. Finally, in 1995, NATO bombing and a Croat offensive forced Serbia to the negotiating table, and in the most unlikely of places—Dayton, Ohio—a deal was reached that ended the war. To uphold the agreement, the United States contributed forces to a multilateral peacekeeping operation in Bosnia, known as IFOR (Implementation Force).

This was another tough mission. Bosnia had endured years of ethnic cleansing, systematic rape, and the massacre of civilians. Yet by 1998, the country was basically stable, gross domestic product (GDP) had doubled, unemployment was falling, a free media had been established, and public elections had been held. In 2005, the European Union started negotiations for Bosnia's eventual entry into the EU. U.S. fatalities were precisely zero.[58]

Ordinary life returned to Bosnian villages devastated by years of war. Meho Sinanovic came home after four years of hiding in the woods. "What had changed?" Meho was asked. "IFOR is here," he replied. Meho's wife described his return as "the greatest joy in my life."[59] Major Tom O'Sullivan served in Bosnia. He sent a letter and a U.S. flag to his son for the boy's seventh birthday. O'Sullivan wrote, "This flag represents America and makes me proud each time I see it.... Some Americans don't know much about the sacrifices it represents or the peace it has brought to places like Bosnia."[60]

Despite the success story in Bosnia, Americans were skeptical. In one 1998 survey, 63 percent of the public believed that U.S. troops had been killed in Bosnia, with an average estimate of 172 deaths. Meanwhile, only 42 percent of the public knew that the civil war in Bosnia had ended. No wonder 69 percent were dissatisfied with how the mission was going.[61]

Although the virus of ethnic conflict was in remission in Bosnia, it spread to the Serbian province of Kosovo. Many Serbs consider the territory to be part of their sacred homeland, but most of the population is Albanian Muslims. By 1997, a low-level civil conflict had broken out between the Serbian government and the

Kosovo Liberation Army. Serb leader Slobodan Milošević told Wesley Clark, NATO's Supreme Allied Commander Europe, "We know how to handle these Albanians, these murderers, these rapists, these killers-of-their-own-kind. We have taken care of them before.... In Drenica, in 1946, we killed them. We killed them all.... Oh, it took several years, but we eventually killed them all."[62]

In 1999, in response to Serbian human rights abuses, NATO launched a major air campaign against Serbia. After three months, Milošević announced the withdrawal of Serb forces from Kosovo. The United States contributed troops to an international peace-keeping operation in the province, similar to the one in Bosnia.

Once again, by any reasonable standards, the operation was a success. The conflict in Kosovo was largely contained, and most of the Kosovo Albanian refugees returned home. The economy stabilized, and thousands of police were trained.[63] U.S. fatalities were again zero. But as with Somalia, Haiti, and Bosnia, the American public was unconvinced. Scholar Robert Entman noted that "the administration received remarkably little praise for its victory."[64] In 2000, only 37 percent of Americans agreed that the United States and its allies had made "progress in achieving the goals they started out with" in Kosovo.[65]

Consider for a moment what would have happened without these American interventions. Many thousands of Somalis would not be alive today. Haiti would not at least have tasted democracy. Bosnia and Kosovo could easily have returned to violence. Meho Sinanovic may once again have had to flee for his life. Despite the great complexity of these four missions, a total of only forty-seven Americans died. During this period, more Red Cross workers than U.S. soldiers were killed while nation-building.[66]

Sorrows of Empire

All of this begs a question: if we are willing to tolerate an average of forty U.S. service members dying in accidents and suicides every two weeks with barely a murmur, why were the deaths of forty-three Americans in Somalia, in a mission that saved 100,000 lives, seen as a catastrophe?[67] Alternatively, if we would have celebrated the overthrow of Saddam, even if thousands of Americans had been killed, why didn't we rejoice when intervention in the Balkans stabilized an entire region of Europe with no American deaths?

The answer lies in understanding how the nation-building operations looked from the vantage point of the United States. Wrath and idealism played a very different role in Somalia, Haiti, Bosnia, and Kosovo than they did in the Gulf War. U.S. troops in the Gulf seemed like avenging angels delivering righteous punishment to Saddam, but retribution was not a powerful motivator in the nation-building missions because the good guys and the bad guys were hard to identify. After the battle of Mogadishu, for example, polls showed some desire to punish the Somalis responsible, but this sentiment evaporated if retribution would slow the withdrawal of U.S. forces.[68] As Osama bin Laden observed in 1996, "Clinton appeared in front of the whole world threatening and promising revenge, but these threats were merely a preparation for withdrawal."[69]

American idealism virtually doomed the nation-building operations to be seen as a failure. For a start, expectations were often completely unrealistic. Sarah Sewall, deputy assistant secretary for peacekeeping and humanitarian assistance from 1993 to 1996, noted that "Washington fundamentally underestimated the difficulty of the new 'peace enforcement' operations." She added, "I say this as a former Clinton Administration official who initially argued that the UN should be able to assume a peace enforcement role."[70]

Forgetting the decades it took for the wounds of the Civil War to heal, Americans sometimes expected adversaries in foreign ethnic conflicts to lay down their weapons and embrace peace and reconciliation once international forces arrived. "In a more religious time it was only God whom we asked to deliver us from evil," noted journalist William Shawcross. "Now we call upon our own man-made institutions for such deliverance. That is sometimes to ask for miracles."[71] The anticipation of marvels and wonders meant that people were unmoved by the more down-to-earth but still valuable gains that were made.

People often set a high bar for success based on idealistic standards. One critic, for example, issued a damning verdict: "After eight years of experimentation it is time to conclude that an ambitious nation-building program is not a sufficient condition to transform a country into a self-sustaining, democratic member of the family of nations."[72] To achieve such an extraordinary result in a country like Somalia, however, would require divine intervention.

Another critic judged the missions in Somalia and Haiti as a "failure." What was the metric? "To call a nation building effort a success... we need to see that the military occupation of the target country was followed by the establishment of an enduring democracy."[73] But how likely was "an enduring democracy" in Somalia, a country that has never known democracy and was so devastated that some people have called it a mere "geographical expression"? It's like judging a volunteer's work in a homeless shelter as a failure because the recipients of assistance didn't get admitted to Harvard.[74]

One might think that U.S. leaders would try to reduce public expectations and implore people to lower the bar for success. But instead, they often make the situation worse with extravagant promises and grandiose rhetoric. In 1993, U.S. ambassador to the United Nations Madeleine Albright suggested that the mission in Somalia was "an unprecedented enterprise aimed at nothing less than the restoration of an entire country as a proud, functioning and viable member of the community of nations."[75] President Clinton claimed that the operation in Kosovo was designed to "save the people of Kosovo, to defeat ethnic cleansing, to start the new millennium in the right way, as a time of human rights and human dignity and allied confidence that together we can build a future worthy of our dreams for our children."[76] Well, good luck with that.

Americans on both the left and the right berated these nation-building missions as deviations from the country's core ideals. From the left, critics like Noam Chomsky assailed U.S. "humanitarian imperialism."[77] However, although the United States may have attained *primacy* after the Cold War, this is quite different from *empire*. Nation-building in the 1990s deviated in striking ways from traditional imperialism—for instance, U.S. cooperation with allies and institutions like the UN, the significant role played by human-itarianism, and Washington's desire to leave all four target countries as quickly as possible.

Left-wing critics of American imperialism often assume that when we intervene in a country, the local people will invariably turn against us. But this wasn't true in Kosovo, where the ethnic Albanian majority is immensely grateful for the U.S. nation-building mission. The Kosovo Albanians could be the most pro-American people anywhere outside the United States. U.S. flags fly everywhere. You can drive down Bill Clinton Boulevard, visit the eleven-foot-high statue of Clinton in Priština, and stay at the Hotel Victory, which has a replica of the Statue of Liberty on its roof.[78]

The anti-imperialists, quite reasonably, wanted the Somalis, Haitians, Bosnians, and Kosovars to decide their own fate, free of Yankee colonial control. But self-determination is not meaningful where there is mass famine, repressive dictatorship, or sustained eth-nic conflict. In extreme circumstances, foreign intervention may be necessary to empower local people.

Meanwhile, voices on the American right often criticized U.S. nation-building operations for violating the ideal of limited government. During the 1990s, there was bipartisan consensus in favor of domestic welfare reform. As Clinton declared in his 1996 State of the Union address, "The era of big government is over."[79] It was, therefore, an unfortunate time for the United States to ask its warriors to give handouts to foreigners.

According to the *Los Angeles Times,* "By the mid-1990s, many Republicans...saw Bill Clinton's humanitarian interventions as the equivalent of welfare programs—as attempts by big government to carry out social engineering."[80] Scholar Michael Mandelbaum decried the interventions in Somalia and elsewhere as "international social work"—appropriate for Mother Teresa but not the United States.[81] The U.S. should focus on crusading, not wasting time and energy, in Condoleezza Rice's derisive phrase, "escorting kids to kindergarten."[82]

But why shouldn't the U.S. military become skilled at social work in order to prevent civil war from erupting? Would a withdrawal of international forces from the Balkans free the people from oppressive big government or create profound insecurity and risk a resumption of fighting? Ronald Reagan once joked, "The nine most terrifying words in the English language are: 'I'm from the government and I'm here to help.'" But for Kosovo Albanians, who faced ethnic cleansing at the hands of Belgrade, among the more comforting words in the English language are, "I'm from the U.S. government and I'm here to help." Neither is there anything inherently wrong with troops watching over children at school. After all, in 1957 soldiers from the 101st Airborne Division escorted black kids to school in Little Rock, Arkansas, and protected them from racist mobs.

In the Gulf War, memories of World War II inspired Americans to march on Baghdad. But during the interventions in the 1990s, the shadow of historical nation-building failures—and imagined failures—darkened perceptions. Senator Lauch Faircloth of North Carolina argued that there was little point in occupying Haiti, with its "history of being ruled by voodoo priests, witch-doctors, and blood-thirsty dictators." The United States had tried this strategy in 1915–1934, but Haiti remained "a squalid, wretched place." Representative Thomas Petri of Wisconsin even quoted the findings of the U.S. commission that investigated the Haitian occupation in 1930: "In part, the high hopes of our good works in this land have not been realized."[83]

And, of course, there was Vietnam. In theory at least, memories of the debacle in Vietnam could have made missions in the 1990s look like successes by reducing our expectations and setting a low bar for a positive outcome. But rather than viewing *success relative to Vietnam,* Americans saw *failure analogous to Vietnam.*

For one thing, the U.S. media frequently evoked memories of the fighting in Indochina. During the first year of the nation-building mission in Somalia, the *New York Times* published 102 stories that mentioned Somalia and Vietnam (the relevant figure for Haiti was 39, for Bosnia 104, and for Kosovo 77). By contrast, the *Times* of London ran stories about these operations that also mentioned Vietnam less than half the time—for example, on 34 occasions for Kosovo.[84]

The public was also willing to accept that the current operation was similar to the quagmire in Indochina. The situation in Somalia three weeks after the October 1993 battle of Mogadishu was as different from Vietnam as one could imagine. U.S. casualties in Somalia were more than a thousand times lower than in Vietnam. The Somali militias were a far cry from the superbly committed and organized Vietcong. Clinton had even announced that the United States was ending the mission in Somalia and pulling out. Nevertheless, 62 percent of the public believed that the intervention in Somalia "could turn into another Vietnam."[85]

It wasn't just Somalia. President George H. W. Bush opposed

intervention in Bosnia because "I do not want to see the United States bogged down in any way into some guerrilla warfare. We lived through that once."[86] Fully 49 percent of Americans considered it very or somewhat likely "that Kosovo will turn into another Vietnam."[87]

Though not easy to prove, it's likely that memories of Vietnam encouraged more skeptical judgments of later nation-building efforts. For instance, polling questions that subtly evoke Vietnam by asking if America is getting "bogged down" tend to produce more critical responses than other questions that do not employ this loaded language.[88]

The experience in Somalia provided further ammunition to denounce subsequent operations in Haiti, Bosnia, and Kosovo. After one American soldier was wounded in Haiti, Republican senator Kay Bailey Hutchison claimed, "This is a very similar pattern, Mr. President, to what took place in Somalia. At first, the Somalis welcomed us. Then they took up arms against us, with disastrous results." Senator Robert Dole similarly criticized the intervention in Haiti: "Like Somalia, our objectives are vague. Our mission is constantly changing...and we are relying on the United Nations to call the shots down the road. It is hard to avoid the observation that 'Haiti is Creole for Somalia.'"[89] Ambassador Richard Holbrooke talked of a "Vietmalia syndrome," combining cautionary memories of both debacles.[90]

"We've Got to Get You Out of Here"

Like earlier verses in America's epic military song, the post–Cold War phase began with a crusade and ended with a quagmire — or in this case, four quagmires. The interstate war against Iraq roused Americans to reach for the crusading sword. Doubts about the wisdom of fighting evaporated as the public rallied behind the cause.

Not only did Americans support a campaign to liberate Kuwait, but they wanted to go even further and overthrow Saddam.

President Bush was damned if he did march on Baghdad and damned if he didn't. When the president called off the dogs of war, the victory seemed hollow. But if he had overthrown Saddam, Bush would have landed the United States in an unpopular nation-building mission in Iraq. Just ask his son.

There was no crusading zeal when the United States began nation-building in Somalia, Haiti, Bosnia, and Kosovo. There was no sustained rallying around the flag. There was no desire to strive toward a majestic result, using all necessary force. Instead, there was a growing sense of disillusionment and failure, and a fear that America had become bogged down once again.

In Somalia and Haiti, the quagmire tradition proved to be a kind of self-fulfilling prophecy, where American skepticism encouraged withdrawal, undermining the actual success of the mission. One can reasonably debate the optimum strategy for the United States to achieve its objectives in Somalia. Washington could have attempted a policy of concerted nation-building, using decisive force to disarm the local factions. Or it might have shifted to a more conciliatory approach, accompanied by a long-term commitment of time and resources. Either way, a rapid U.S. pullout in 1993 was *not* the most effective way forward.

America's enemies drew their own lessons from the exit. In his 1996 fatwa against the United States, Osama bin Laden described the withdrawal from Somalia as evidence of American "impotence and weaknesses." After a few minor battles, he said, "you left the area carrying disappointment, humiliation, defeat and your dead with you."[91] Meanwhile, the retreat from Somalia encouraged Saddam Hussein to believe that the United States would never successfully invade Iraq. In the run-up to the 2003 Iraq War, Saddam handed out copies of the movie *Black Hawk Down* to his generals to show that the regime was safe.[92]

The quagmire tradition also twisted how Americans learned from history. The perception of failure in Somalia, Haiti, Bosnia, and Kosovo provoked a backlash against further nation-building. Some 59 percent of the public found the following argument convincing: "Our experience in Somalia shows that UN peacekeeping operations do not work very well and that American soldiers may be killed and humiliated. We should not take the risk that we will have a repeat of the same mess we got ourselves into in Somalia."[93]

Officials were reluctant to replicate the supposed mistake. A week after the battle of Mogadishu in October 1993, the USS *Harlan County* arrived in Haiti with two hundred U.S. and Canadian troops to facilitate a planned transition to democratic rule. When a gang of armed thugs turned up at the docks of Port-au-Prince claiming that Haiti would become "another Somalia," Washington got nervous and promptly retreated.

Tragically, memories of failure in Somalia deterred the United States from intervening to stop the 1994 genocide in Rwanda. If people had more accurately seen the Somalia operation as a partial success, they might have contemplated effective action. Canadian general Roméo Dallaire, who commanded a small UN force in Rwanda during the genocide, claimed that with just five thousand well-equipped troops, he could have ended the slaughter and saved hundreds of thousands of lives.[94]

In influential quarters, the backlash against nation-building gathered force. The Clinton administration issued Presidential Decision Directive 25 in 1994, stating that it was not U.S. policy to expand its involvement in "peace operations."[95] Among conservatives, nation-building became reviled as a kind of international welfare program. For example, in 2000 presidential candidate George W. Bush said, "I don't think our troops ought to be used for what's called nation-building."[96] The military was designed to fight and win wars, Bush thought, and when it tried stabilizing foreign countries, morale suffered. In July 2001, Bush, now president, told the U.S. commander in Kosovo, "We've got to get you out of here."[97]

Soon, however, Bush would don a hero's costume in a new crusade against global evil—one that landed the president in his very own quagmire.

CHAPTER 9

The Bush Warriors

O n February 18, 2002, with the Taliban regime vanquished in Afghanistan, the German newsmagazine *Der Spiegel* ran a cover titled "The Bush Warriors: America's Crusade Against Evil," picturing U.S. administration officials as popular heroes. President George W. Bush was center stage as Rambo, with an enormous machine gun. Secretary of Defense Donald Rumsfeld was Conan the Barbarian, wearing a necklace made from the teeth of his enemies and carrying a sword dripping with blood. Hovering at the back, National Security Advisor Condoleezza Rice was Xena (Warrior Princess), and Secretary of State Colin Powell was Batman. Rounding out the group was Vice President Dick Cheney as the Terminator—an unlikely comparison, because the Terminator's advanced targeting system allowed it to distinguish between man and quail.

The U.S. ambassador to Germany, Daniel Coats, visited the offices of *Der Spiegel.* He wasn't there to complain about the satirical cover or the article criticizing American unilateralism. Instead, the ambassador announced that the administration was thrilled by its depiction as superhero crusaders and that "the President was flattered to be pictured with such a body." Coats promptly ordered thirty-three large posters

Der Spiegel, *February 18 (#8), 2002. Used with permission.*

of the image to be sent back to Washington, at the reported request of Rumsfeld, Powell, Cheney, and Rice.[1]

Bush's coalition of the thrilling was pitted against Islamic terrorists and state sponsors of terrorism. During the 1990s, Osama bin Laden and the Al Qaeda group set up base in Afghanistan, with the blessing of the Taliban regime. Al Qaeda organized a series of terrorist attacks that culminated in 9/11. In novelist Martin Amis's words, the defining moment came with "the advent of the second plane, sharking in low over the Statue of Liberty." In that moment, an aviation disaster transmuted into a new era defined by terror: "Its glint was the worldflash of a coming future."[2] Navy petty officer Gregory Cleghorne recalled, "Now, up there on floors so high no hook and ladder could ever reach, a man in a tattered and burned white business shirt stands in a broken window with flames licking at him and smoke billowing around him. I see someone let go, briefly flying."[3] Dates began to live in infamy: 9/11 in the United States, 3/11 in Spain, and 7/7 in Britain.[4]

The Bush administration responded with a global campaign against terrorism, punctuated by two major conflicts, the first in Afghanistan beginning in 2001 and the second in Iraq beginning in 2003. Just as in earlier eras, Americans experienced the interstate war and the nation-building phases of these missions in polar-opposite ways. Public support was high when the United States overthrew the Taliban in Afghanistan and raced to Baghdad. Prewar doubts swiftly vanished, as idealism and vengeance inspired the use of all necessary force in a quest for regime change. But when the conflicts transitioned to nation-building, the mood grew profoundly gloomy, as wrath faded and the operations failed to live up to America's sacred values.

It wasn't just the public that saw these wars in the time-honored manner. The Bush administration was a pure exponent of the crusade and quagmire traditions. Officials were determined to overthrow tyrants, defeat evil, and transform the world. But the administration was also allergic to the idea of nation-building. This was a very American combination of beliefs—and one that had disastrous consequences.

From the Fields of Gettysburg to the Mountains of Afghanistan

On September 10, 2001, the idea of invading Afghanistan was as fantastic as the notion on December 6, 1941, of making a graveyard of Japan. But within a few weeks of 9/11, Americans picked up the crusading sword to smite the Taliban regime in Kabul. On the left and the right, people kept time with the new antiterrorist music. Huge majorities of Americans backed a long-term global campaign against terrorism, even if there were thousands of U.S. casualties.[5] Every member of Congress—with one exception, Democrat Barbara Lee—authorized the president to use military force against terrorists. It was a neat parallel with the start of an earlier crusade, in 1941, when only one member of Congress, Jeannette Rankin, voted against war with Japan.

CBS anchor Dan Rather was often castigated by conservatives as a totem of the "liberal media," but Rather announced, "George Bush is the president.... [Wherever] he wants me to line up, just tell me where."[6] Powerfully affected by 9/11, Pat Tillman turned down a lucrative football contract to enlist in the U.S. Army as a Ranger. A true patriot, Tillman had run around the battlefield of Gettysburg as a child. Now he would take the fight to the terrorists.[7] At the memorial service for 9/11 at the National Cathedral in Washington, the choir struck up a tune that has seen the nation through many great trials: "The Battle Hymn of the Republic."

The interstate war against the Taliban regime in Afghanistan, which began on October 7, 2001, broadly followed the crusader template. The United States fought for maximum war aims: to overthrow the adversary and establish a new representative government. Small numbers of U.S. troops, in cooperation with the rebel Afghan Northern Alliance and backed by massive airpower, captured Kabul in mid-November. By December 7, Kandahar had fallen, and the Taliban retreated to the mountains of southern Afghanistan.

The United States stood like a colossus, seemingly omnipotent. Here in Afghanistan, the graveyard of empires, American firepower turned Taliban redoubts into blistered necropolises, while the United States suffered only a handful of casualties. Michael

O'Hanlon of the Brookings Institution called it "a masterpiece of military creativity and finesse."[8] During the interstate war phase, more than 80 percent of Americans approved of the mission.[9]

The Road That Runs Through Baghdad

Barely had Kabul fallen than the Bush administration began preparing for a second crusade: against Saddam Hussein's regime in Iraq. In 2002, the United States labeled Iraq part of the "axis of evil," along with Iran and North Korea, and accused Saddam of pursuing weapons of mass destruction.[10] Weapons inspectors had withdrawn from Iraq in 1998, but they returned in 2002 following a new UN Security Council resolution. Washington was unwilling, however, to endure a prolonged inspections process and shifted irrevocably to a war footing. After failing to gain a second UN resolution authorizing an invasion of Iraq, Bush pressed ahead in concert with an ad hoc coalition of states.

Befitting a crusader, the Bush administration was interested only in magnificent objectives in Iraq. The toppling of Saddam's government would trigger a domino effect of freedom in the Middle East. Neoconservatives both inside and outside the administration had long been pushing a transformational agenda. "The road that leads to real security and peace," wrote Robert Kagan and William Kristol in 2002, "[is] the road that runs through Baghdad."[11]

When Americans later grew disillusioned with the Iraq War, they sometimes looked back on the invasion as an extremist policy dreamed up by a neoconservative cabal. But Americans were Bush's willing crusaders. Long before Bush was elected, and long before 9/11, Americans saw Saddam as a major threat and his removal as the solution to that threat. In the twelve years between the 1991 Gulf War and the 2003 Iraq War, there were more than one hundred polls asking whether the United States should reintroduce ground troops to overthrow Saddam Hussein. Incredibly, in every single case, a majority of Americans said yes.[12]

In 1998, Bush was still governor of Texas when President Clinton signed the Iraq Liberation Act, which called for regime change in Iraq and provided funding to opposition groups. Debating Bush in the 2000 presidential election, Al Gore declared, "Now I want to go further. I want to give robust support to the groups that are trying to overthrow Saddam Hussein."[13] In October 2002, Congress authorized war with lopsided votes in the Senate (77 to 23) and the House (296 to 133). Democratic hawks included Bill and Hillary Clinton, Madeleine Albright, and *New York Times* columnist Thomas Friedman.

For some Americans, Iraq had initiated hostilities years before. Saddam had tried to annex Kuwait and assassinate George H. W. Bush; he had violated UN resolutions; and he had helped to orchestrate 9/11 — or so many believed. In 2001, close to 80 percent of Americans thought that it was "very likely" or "somewhat likely" that Saddam was personally involved in 9/11, and these figures remained high through 2003.[14] In 1991, Bush senior had prematurely brought the crusade to a halt. Now it was time to conclude the second act and bring down the curtain.

But other Americans were not so sure. Beneath the strain of public bellicosity, there was considerable ambivalence about the use of force in Iraq. Americans were wary about an invasion without allied backing, and close to half of the public supported efforts to achieve U.S. goals without war.[15]

"I hate the idea of war," wrote U.S. Army sergeant Denis Prior, "and I can't wait for it to begin."[16] When the first shot was fired in Iraq on March 20, 2003, doubts about a unilateral military campaign faded, and Americans rallied around the war effort. As in Afghanistan, the campaign followed the crusading model. There was no question of a limited war or a compromise peace deal with Saddam. Victory would be complete. Iraqi forces crumbled, and the coalition reached Baghdad by April 9. Max Boot extolled the overthrow of Saddam in a campaign of speed and maneuver that made the great German World War II general Erwin Rommel "seem positively incompetent by comparison."[17] The commander in chief of the U.S. Central Command, Tommy Franks, described Operation Iraqi Freedom as "unequalled in its excellence by anything in the annals of war."[18]

As the Abrams tanks began rumbling across the desert, about seven in ten Americans backed the invasion. Public support peaked at 74 percent after Bush announced an end to major combat operations on May 1.[19] Not every American was on board. Democrats, nonreligious people, women, and blacks were significantly more cautious about the war. At the other end of the scale was the committed crusading vanguard, which included the usual suspects: Republicans, evangelicals, men, and whites.[20]

Before the invasion of Iraq, the majority of Americans opposed war if thousands of Iraqi civilians would die.[21] But concerns about protecting the innocent from the horrors of battle began to evaporate once hostilities actually began. Some 2,000 to 7,000 Iraqi non-combatants were killed in the interstate war phase, yet 82 percent of the American public thought that the U.S. military was successful at minimizing civilian casualties, and a clear majority believed that the United States had achieved a victory.[22] As in the 1991 Gulf War, there was no need to test the boundaries of America's willingness to kill noncombatants because the ailing Iraqi war machine disintegrated with such haste.

The Light Shines in the Darkness

Why did Americans see the wars against the Taliban and Saddam Hussein as crusades for regime change? Strategic interests were clearly important. After all, the invasion of Afghanistan was fundamentally a response to 9/11. Similarly, the Bush administration was motivated to occupy Iraq by a perceived security threat emanating from Saddam's rogue government, weapons of mass destruction, and international terrorism.

But as with earlier interstate wars, strategic logic only provides part of the answer. First, consider the attitude of foreign policy "realists." These scholars and policy makers believe that national interests usually determine the behavior of countries. But in 2003, many prominent realists *rejected* the Iraq War because it *undermined* U.S. interests—suggesting that some other force was propelling America toward regime change.[23]

Second, before the invasion of Iraq, most Americans thought that the campaign was unlikely to decrease the risk of terrorist attacks against the United States. And they believed that military action could easily provoke Saddam to hand weapons of mass destruction to terrorists. Yet the public still supported the war.[24]

Third, many Americans were not responding to objective reality, because they saw the world inaccurately. Common misperceptions included the idea that Saddam was implicated in 9/11 and had strong ties to Al Qaeda.[25]

America's sense of idealistic mission powerfully shaped perceptions of the interstate wars in Afghanistan and Iraq. The *threat* to our ideals was immense. They attacked us because we love freedom. Al Qaeda, the Taliban, and Saddam Hussein were evil and despotic—the very antithesis of Americanism. And the *opportunity* to extend our ideals was similarly compelling. By slaying tyrants and exporting liberal principles of representative government, American military power could cut the Gordian knot of autocracy and extremism in the Middle East.[26]

Bush was a man on a mission. Although perceived strategic threats were the core reason for invading Afghanistan and Iraq, idealistic factors powerfully influenced the president's broader understanding of these wars. "I believe the United States is *the* beacon for freedom in the world," he said. "And I believe we have a responsibility to promote freedom that is as solemn as the responsibility is to protecting the American people, because the two go hand-in-hand."[27] As Bush saw it, "A free, democratic, peaceful Iraq will not threaten America or our friends with illegal weapons[;] ... will not be a training ground for terrorists, or a funnel of money to terrorists, or provide weapons to terrorists[;] ... will not destabilize the Middle East[;] ... [and] can set a hopeful example to the entire region and lead other nations to choose freedom."[28]

The neoconservative conviction that the United States is an agent of liberal evangelism is broadly consistent with our traditional sense of mission. Indeed, the neoconservative vision of the Iraq War contained elements that appealed even to many on the left. Just as Woodrow Wilson's war to make the world safe for democracy rallied the Progressive movement during World War I, so a conflict to free the Iraqi people co-opted a substantial number of liberals in 2003.

Only about one in ten Americans claimed that religious beliefs were the most important influence on their thinking about the Iraq War. And, in fact, doves were just as likely as hawks to cite religion as a reason for their position. When Catholics and black Protestants heard from their clergy on the issue of Iraq, they tended to hear *anti*war messages.[29] The horrors of combat also tested many people's religious beliefs. "My faith doesn't equal that of Job's," wrote one woman who lost her son in Iraq. "I question. Why has God cut the fruit from my vine? Taken the only child that remained?"[30]

For white evangelicals, however, religious faith strengthened the sense of crusading mission. Pro-war messages issued forth from the evangelical pulpit, establishing a narrative of the Iraq campaign as a righteous struggle. Evangelicals strongly supported the overthrow of Saddam Hussein and tended to worry less about inflicting Iraqi civilian casualties.[31]

The religious missionary spirit extended to one influential

evangelical: George W. Bush. The president stressed that the war on terror was not a religious war. He praised Islam repeatedly. But Bush also explicitly cast the campaign in providential terms, as the chosen people's quest for redemption. Few can doubt the intensity of Bush's personal faith or the role of religion in solidifying his desire for a transformational struggle. Back in the Civil War, abolitionists believed that the Union army was a divine tool. Now Bush saw the United States as a vessel propelled forward on the rough seas by the breath of God.

On September 20, 2001, he claimed, "Freedom and fear, justice and cruelty, have always been at war, and we know that God is not neutral between them."[32] A year later, the president adopted language from the Gospel of John: "And the light shines in the darkness. And the darkness will not overcome it."[33] And in 2003, he suggested that U.S. troops "carry a message of hope, a message that is ancient and ever new. In the words of the prophet Isaiah, 'To the captives, come out, and to those in darkness, be free.' "[34] The president reportedly informed the Palestinian prime minister, "God told me to strike at Al Qaeda and I struck them, and then he instructed me to strike at Saddam, which I did."[35]

Regime change in Afghanistan and Iraq would be the latest chapter in America's great story of emancipation. As Bush put it, "Our commitment to liberty is America's tradition, declared at our founding, affirmed in Franklin Roosevelt's Four Freedoms, asserted in the Truman Doctrine and in Ronald Reagan's challenge to an evil empire."[36] He took a page out of his father's playbook by cultivating the analogy to World War II: September 11 was the new Pearl Harbor; the enemy was "Islamo-fascism" and the "axis of evil"; critics of war were appeasers.[37]

It's tempting to dismiss this missionary talk as mere rhetoric. But Bush was, by most accounts, a true believer, telling journalist Bob Woodward that freedom "is not America's gift to the world. Freedom is God's gift to everybody in the world. I believe that."

Bush went on to explain: "As a matter of fact, I was the person that wrote that line, or said it. I didn't write it, I just said it in a speech. And it became part of the jargon. And I believe that. And I believe we have a duty to free people. I would hope we wouldn't have to do it militarily, but we have a duty."[38]

Looking for a Fight

There was a second powerful incentive to remove the Taliban and Saddam Hussein from power: a desire to gain revenge for 9/11. It would be hard to imagine a crime more likely to spark a retributive impulse than a sudden and deliberate surprise attack that slaughtered thousands of innocent civilians in the homeland of the United States, destroying one national symbol, the World Trade Center, and damaging another, the Pentagon. If this were not unmitigated evil, what was?

Bush's rhetoric was imbued with the language of the righteous avenger. He spoke about evil in 30 percent of his speeches from September 11, 2001, to June 16, 2003.[39] "Justice demands that those who helped or harbored the terrorists be punished—and punished severely," declared the president two days after the terrorist attacks. "The enormity of their evil demands it. We will use all the resources of the United States and our cooperating friends and allies to pursue those responsible for this evil, until justice is done."[40]

Americans were looking for payback for 9/11. Studies revealed that anger, not fear, was the dominant reaction to the terrorist attacks.[41] Country music offers an insight into the minds of the 45 million Americans who listen to country music radio stations every week. In "Courtesy of the Red, White, and Blue," Toby Keith sang, "We'll put a boot in your ass / It's the American way." Darryl Worley's "Have You Forgotten?" included these lines: "Some say this country's just out looking for a fight / After 9/11, man, I'd have to say that's right."[42]

The military response to 9/11 was initially called Operation Infinite Justice, until someone wisely pointed out that only God could provide infinite justice. The name was changed to Operation Enduring Freedom. The two titles nicely capture the retributive and idealistic sides of the crusading coin.

American wrath was not sated by the fall of the Taliban. There was plenty of moralistic retribution left to combat the next evil-doer, Saddam Hussein. One disk jockey, who played "Have You Forgotten?" every hour, was asked about the lack of direct evidence connecting Saddam to Al Qaeda. He replied, "The audience is so wrapped up in the emotion of what it's about, I don't think they're nitpicking at this point.... Everybody's viewing all the bad guys in a big bucket."[43]

Tellingly, Americans who strongly backed the death penalty, and were therefore especially retributive, also tended to support regime change in Baghdad. Capital punishment and the overthrow of Saddam Hussein would both serve the cause of infinite justice. Meanwhile, the greater antiwar sentiment among women resulted to a large extent from diminished feelings of vengeance.[44]

These idealistic and retributive beliefs meant that limited war against the Taliban and Saddam Hussein—with an objective short of regime change—wasn't even an option. Washington cannot compromise with pure evil or a dictator who is the reincarnation of Hitler. The United States must unleash the fateful lightning and crush the serpent with its heel.

Bush claimed that America's "enemies will not be stopped by negotiation, or concessions, or appeals to reason. In this war, there is only one option—and that is victory."[45] Vice President Cheney echoed these sentiments: "The war against terror will not end in a treaty. There will be no summit meeting, no negotiations with terrorists. This conflict can only end in their complete and utter destruction."[46]

End of the Show

In October 2008, *Der Spiegel* ran a follow-up story on America's crusading superheroes. But the cover image, titled "The Bush Warriors—End of the Show," told a very different tale from the one in 2002. The president appeared as a haggard-looking Rambo, leaning on his machine gun and using his ammunition strap as a sling. Cheney, the Terminator, was weary, with a cracked lens in his glasses. Condi was a battered and bruised Xena, carrying a broken sword. Colin Powell was nowhere to be seen, his Batman suit hanging empty at the back. Rumsfeld was a limping Conan the Barbarian, already half offstage. *Der Spiegel* described a newly pessimistic mood among Americans in the face of wearying foreign conflicts. No one in the Bush administration ordered a full-size version of this image.[47]

The two *Der Spiegel* covers symbolize the transition in the American experience of the wars in Afghanistan and Iraq. As the campaigns evolved from interstate crusades to nation-building quagmires, public opinion followed a familiar arc of hope and disappointment.

The War That Never Ends

Once the Taliban retreated south in 2001 and the mission in Afghanistan shifted toward nation-building and counterinsurgency, Americans were, at first, fairly optimistic. In October 2002, 70 percent of the public thought the operation was "successful."[48] There was some significant progress during this period, with fairly

Der Spiegel, *October 27 (#44), 2008. Used with permission.*

democratic elections in 2004–2005, at least by Afghan standards, and tentative signs of economic development. Three million Afghan refugees returned home. The country ceased being a launchpad for international terrorism.[49]

But over time, there was a steady erosion of public confidence and support. By December 2008, most people thought the Afghan campaign was "not successful."[50] The transition from good war to bad war was personified by Pat Tillman. He died in Afghanistan in April 2004, struck down by a devastating enemy assault. Or at least that was the story initially offered by the U.S. military. It soon came to light, however, that Tillman was killed by friendly fire. The army secretary described the official misinformation as "a perfect storm of mistakes, misjudgments and a failure of leadership." The military, as Tillman's father put it, "blew up their poster boy."[51]

To some extent, increasing gloominess mirrored the changing reality on the ground. After 2005, there was a sharp rise in insurgent attacks and a decrease in security in parts of southern Afghanistan. Indeed, 2008 was the deadliest year for U.S. forces since 2001. By December 2009, more than nine hundred Americans had died in Afghanistan. Opium production rose steadily, surpassing 90 percent of the global total.[52] The Afghan elections of 2009 were marred by fraud.

The United States never committed enough forces to Afghanistan. In 2002, there were only 10,000 U.S. soldiers in the country, along with 5,000 international troops. This compared to 60,000 men sent to Bosnia and 50,000 to Kosovo in the 1990s.[53] During a critical period, when the Taliban was regrouping in the south, insufficient forces limited the Afghan government's ability to offer basic services and ensure law and order.

But we should pause before dismissing the intervention in Afghanistan as a failure. First, Afghanistan is one of the most challenging environments for nation-building. The country was reduced to an utterly ruinous state by civil war and Taliban rule. Around 70 percent of the population cannot read or write. The literacy rate was higher in America in 1650.[54] Even with a perfect nation-building campaign, the chances that Afghanistan would soon resemble the United States, or for that matter Russia, India, or China, were zero. A more realistic goal would be that in a decade or two, Afghanistan might draw closer to the level of development in Bangladesh.

Second, there have been some important successes. During the Taliban era, only one million children were in school, including almost no girls. In 2009, the figure was six million, a third of whom were girls. The number of Afghans with access to basic health care increased from 9 percent in 2003 to 80 percent in 2009. Afghanistan is incredibly poor, but its gross domestic product (GDP) has tripled since 2002 and is growing at almost 10 percent a year. Critically, only 6 percent of Afghans support the Taliban. Most Afghans back the international mission and believe that the situation in their country is improving.[55]

Third, the U.S. death toll in Afghanistan has been modest by historical standards. The average of around 100 fatalities a year in Afghanistan is a small fraction of the 1,000 or so U.S. service members who die in accidents and suicides every year, the 7,000 per year killed in Vietnam, or the 100,000 annual fatalities in World War II.

Fourth, we can contrast the current mission in Afghanistan with the previous superpower intervention in the country—by the Soviet Union beginning in 1979. In a bitter counterinsurgency campaign against the Afghan mujahideen, fifteen thousand Soviet troops were killed and one million Afghan civilians died before Moscow withdrew in 1989. One American soldier wrote about the different experiences of Afghan villagers following the Soviet and U.S. interventions. After the Russians invaded, the villagers "took to the surrounding caves, hiding from Soviet aircraft that strafed and bombed most every village they came across, including theirs." By contrast, the local men and women "told us that since America has come to Afghanistan, fighting for *their* freedom and way of life, the village has prospered like it never has before and they are very grateful for our presence."[56]

Americans grew disillusioned with the Iraq War soon after the conflict switched from an interstate war to a nation-building mission in April and May 2003. When the statue of Saddam in Baghdad's Firdos Square fell on April 9, television news anchors frequently alluded to it as a historic event reminiscent of the fall of the Berlin Wall. Brit Hume declared on Fox News, "This transcends anything I've ever seen." Pictures of the toppling of the statue were shown repeatedly all day (once every 4.4 minutes on Fox News from 11 a.m. to 8 p.m.).[57]

But this event also initiated the nation-building phase in Iraq. Just a few weeks later, on July 7, 2003, *Time* ran a story titled "The War That Never Ends." Approval of the war effort declined fairly steadily after 2003, with brief bounces when Saddam Hussein was captured in December 2003 and Iraqi elections were held in January 2005.[58]

Country music songs about Iraq became more downbeat, reflective, and confused, as performers looked to faith as a guide. John Michael Montgomery's "Letters from Home" describes a soldier reading letters from his family: "there ain't nothing funny / When a soldier cries / And I just wipe me eyes." Darryl Worley, who wrote "Have You Forgotten?" later sang "I Just Came Back from a War," which has a very different tone: "I just came back from a place where they hated me / And everything I stand for."[59]

U.S. Army sergeant Brian Turner published a collection of poems about his experiences in Iraq, revealing the psychological strain of counterinsurgency: "Ordinary people seem friendly: 'and any one of them / may dance over your body tomorrow.' "[60]

Perceptions of Iraq as a quagmire weren't conjured up out of thin air; they reflected very real failures on the ground. Of course, stabilizing Iraq was always going to be a tough mission. The country had been devastated by years of oppressive tyranny, war, and sanctions. Bloodshed was bound to follow the end of Saddam's regime, however it came about. And the United States did achieve some positive results in Iraq, such as overseeing reasonably free and fair elections in 2005.

But Washington made a number of serious and avoidable errors that dramatically worsened the prospects for success, including a lack of planning for postwar nation-building and counterinsurgency, and the disbandment of the Iraqi army. Andrew Krepinevich argued that U.S. forces focused too heavily on destroying insurgents, rather than providing security to the Iraqi people— mistakes similar to those made in Vietnam.[61] After 2003, Iraq descended into chaos and civil war. The conflict proved exceptionally costly, with more than four thousand Americans dead, tens of thousands of civilian fatalities, and a price tag approaching $1 trillion.

Casualty statistics can dehumanize individual tragedies. Sergeant John McCary, who served in Al Anbar province in Iraq, grew frustrated at the brutal violence perpetrated by the insurgents. He wrote home in January 2004, "We are dying. Not in some philosophical, chronological, 'the end comes for all of us sooner or later' sense. Just dying."[62]

Aaron Weaver was killed when his Black Hawk helicopter was shot down in Iraq. On Weaver's body was a letter to his fifteen-month-old daughter, saying, "You are the meaning of my life. You make my heart pound with joy and pride. No matter what happens to me or where we go, you will always know that I love you."[63]

When Sam Ross joined the U.S. military after a tough childhood, he finally found a place where he belonged. Ross participated in the invasion of Iraq as part of the Eighty-second Airborne Division. In the heady days of overthrowing Saddam's regime, Ross basked in the appreciation of many Iraqis. But on May 18, 2003, he was blinded and lost a leg when unexploded ordnance suddenly detonated. He returned to a hero's welcome in Dunbar,

Pennsylvania, but his life soon spiraled downward. After a number of suicide attempts, Ross was eventually committed to a psychiatric hospital. UCLA professor Gordon Lee Fain wrote a poem titled "Ballad of Private Ross" that captures the randomness of wartime destruction: "Just a coin toss, / Heads it was someone else, tails it was Ross."[64]

Every soldier's death causes a second loss back in the States. When Marines informed Carlos Arredondo that his son had been killed in Iraq, he was overcome by grief: "I just took off running. I was yelling and screaming." In his rage, he grabbed a hammer from the garage and started to attack the Marine van. He poured gasoline over the vehicle and set it alight. In the process, Carlos himself caught fire, with burns covering a quarter of his body.[65]

Beginning in 2007, there was a significant turnaround in Iraq, and a dramatic reduction in the level of violence. In the "Awakening," Sunni groups allied with U.S. forces against Al Qaeda. The United States' "surge" policy involved an increase in U.S. troop levels and a new strategy focused on providing security to the Iraqi population.[66] If the failures of 2003–2006 reveal the limits of America's expertise at stabilizing foreign societies, the progress from 2007 to 2010 indicates the capacity of the United States to learn and adapt.

Unusually for a nation-building mission, the American public did recognize the success of these efforts, at least in terms of restoring order. In 2007, only 34 percent of people thought that U.S. attempts to stabilize Iraq were going "very well" or "somewhat well." By 2009, this figure had risen to more than 60 percent.[67]

But even when Americans acknowledged a degree of progress in Iraq, there were no celebrations. Church bells didn't ring. Flags didn't adorn homes and storefronts. Instead, people stopped thinking about the Iraq War at all, as the conflict dropped off the media and public radar. And Americans remained very skeptical about the overall value of the mission. Despite a striking fall in violence, in September 2009 just 24 percent of the public thought that the Iraq War was "worth the loss of American life and other costs of attacking Iraq"—the lowest percentage of people ever expressing that sentiment.[68]

Greeted as Liberators

American beliefs about nation-building in Afghanistan and Iraq hewed fairly closely to the changing reality on the battlefield. But this doesn't mean that people were carefully tallying the gains and losses. Like a powerful magnet, declining wrath and national idealism produced a downward pull on perceptions of success, independent of anything that happened on the ground. The two nation-building operations were fated to be viewed as failures, even if key mistakes had been avoided or fewer Americans had died.

Vengeance inspired Americans to overthrow the Taliban and Saddam Hussein, but this vitalizing force dissipated as soon as the dragons were slain and the wars switched to nation-building. Two years after the invasion of Iraq, the most retributive Americans— those who strongly supported the death penalty—tended to believe that the removal of Saddam was the right thing to do. But they were *not* more likely to want to stay and stabilize Iraq.[69]

Once Saddam's statue fell in Firdos Square, the conflict soon lost its moral clarity and sense of righteous justice for the crimes of 9/11. The demonic Saddam Hussein was a far more attractive target of wrath than the faceless rebel factions. Even though the insurgents committed the most heinous atrocities against civilians and U.S. troops, it's striking how little anger ordinary Americans mustered toward the rebels. Just as in Vietnam, pro-war and antiwar Americans seemed to hate each other more than the insurgents.

Antiwar activists, for instance, were rightly horrified by the murder of civilians in Iraq. But protesters displayed little fury toward the Iraqi insurgents who were actually doing most of the killing, instead reserving much of their anger for the United States, which was trying to stop the mayhem.

Of course, a stronger desire for retribution against Iraqi insurgents would probably have been counterproductive, by encouraging punitive policies. But such sentiment might also have bolstered support on the home front.

Meanwhile, American idealism had its usual corrosive effect on perceptions of success, by encouraging illusory expectations about the ease with which Afghanistan and Iraq could be remodeled as stable democracies. Many people were overconfident as the nation-building mission began in Iraq. In March 2003, just 10 percent of the public thought that "military action in Iraq" would take more than a year, and only 9 percent predicted that more than three thousand U.S. troops would die.[70] In other words, around 90 percent of Americans were surprised by the costs of the war.

According to the tenets of liberal idealism, democracy is a universally desired system. Once the impediment of tyranny is removed, therefore, a natural state of liberty can emerge. Many Americans hoped that elections would have a dramatic positive impact, as ordinary Afghans and Iraqis discovered the joys of U.S.-style democracy. Support for the war in Iraq increased at the time of the January 2005 national elections, and 53 percent of Americans thought the vote showed that "Bush's policy in dealing with Iraq is working." But unsurprisingly, the elections weren't a panacea, and the insurgency dragged on. The result was disappointment and a sharp decline in public confidence in the spring of 2005, "as the promise of those elections remained unfulfilled."[71]

One reason for these illusory hopes is that most Americans knew very little about Afghanistan and Iraq. In 1898, President

William McKinley admitted being unsure about the location of the Philippines. A century later, in 2006, geographic knowledge remained patchy. After three years of U.S. fighting in Iraq, a survey found that nearly two-thirds of Americans ages eighteen to twenty-four could not find the country on a map.[72] Just 32 percent of Americans knew that the second major sect within Islam, along-side Shiite, was Sunni.[73]

Not everyone was overconfident about the war. Commander Edward W. Jewell, a doctor on the USNS *Comfort,* wrote in his journal in March 2003, "A surgeon buddy of mine Mike from Massachusetts thinks an attack on our ship is a near given, with a 50 percent chance of success. However, he is a proctologist and Red Sox fan and naturally pessimistic."[74]

Americans also set a high bar for success in nation-building, based on their ideals. People would only be certain that the outcome in Iraq was positive if the country somehow became a secure democracy resembling the United States. In a series of surveys in which Americans were asked to choose one metric for evaluating success in Iraq from a list, the top choices were these: when a stable and democratic Iraqi government was established, when Iraqis were able to provide for their own security, and when Iraqis led peaceful and normal lives.[75]

To be seen favorably, therefore, the operation needed to satisfy several different and potentially incompatible metrics. After all, the best means of creating short-term stability in Iraq might be to abandon democratic reforms. Furthermore, what we understand by "stable," "democratic," and "normal lives" is inevitably influenced by our own experiences living in a prosperous, free, and idealistic society. By contrast, few Americans selected metrics for success based on the original—and more easily achievable—premises for the war, such as preventing the Iraqi government from supporting terrorists or producing weapons of mass destruction.

As soon as the conflicts in Afghanistan and Iraq switched from interstate wars to nation-building, there was heightened sensitivity to violations of American ideals. We were no longer fighting for our principles in a righteous crusade against evil, excusing most sins. Now we were running the government and trying to live up to our ideals, highlighting our sins.

Critics increasingly pointed to the U.S. killing of noncombatants. Indeed, the American military sometimes failed to do everything it could to protect civilians in Iraq. Between May 2003 and the end of 2006, around 5,000 to 8,000 Iraqi civilians were killed by U.S. forces, mainly from air strikes or crossfire. But one recent study found that the U.S. military was more successful at minimizing noncombatant deaths than is often believed. The behavior of American troops in Iraq compares favorably to the conduct of the insurgents, as well as to the actions of other countries battling rebels, like the Russians in Chechnya. Noncombatant deaths in Iraq also pale in comparison to those in interstate wars like World War II. The United States killed more than ten times as many civilians in one night of firebombing in Tokyo in 1945 as it did during the first three and a half years of counterinsurgency in Iraq.[76]

The United States was also widely blamed for civilian deaths caused by Iraqi insurgents. In interstate wars, no one holds Washington responsible for massacres carried out by the enemy, such as Nazi killings in World War II. But in nation-building missions like Iraq, Washington is held culpable for these actions. By failing to plan for postwar reconstruction in Iraq, the administration deserves some responsibility for the anarchy that followed. However, a major part of the blame for the civil war there rests with Saddam's regime, which deepened divisions in Iraqi society. Furthermore, if an Al Qaeda recruit slips across the border into Iraq, marches to the first bus he can find, and blows himself up, the primary responsibility for the attack surely lies with the terrorist and his sponsors, not the United States.

It's really no surprise that Americans had unrealistic expectations and set a high bar for success in Afghanistan and Iraq, given President Bush's grandiose claims about building a beacon of freedom in the Middle East. In his 2007 State of the Union address, Bush established a tough standard for what victory would look like: "A democratic Iraq that upholds the rule of law, respects the rights of its people, provides them security, and is an ally in the war on terror."[77]

The Bush administration also encouraged Americans to believe that this outcome would be quickly achieved. Deputy Secretary of Defense Paul Wolfowitz announced shortly before the invasion, "Like the people of France in the 1940s [the Iraqis] view us as their hoped-for liberator."[78] Vice President Cheney told NBC's *Meet the Press,* "My belief is we will, in fact, be greeted as liberators."[79] In November 2003, Bush argued that in Iraq, "democracy will succeed, and that success will send forth the news, from Damascus to Tehran, that freedom can be the future of every nation. The establishment of a free Iraq at the heart of the Middle East will be a watershed event in the global democratic revolution."[80]

This was not just empty rhetoric for public consumption. The Bush administration genuinely believed that the overthrow of Saddam Hussein would be sufficient to implant democracy in Iraq. Penn Kemble, former acting director of the U.S. Information Agency, noted that "the distinction between liberation and democratization...was an idea never understood by the administration."[81] The U.S. wartime strategy in Iraq was based on overly optimistic assumptions about the stabilization of the country. In a fit of wishful thinking, Washington planned to reduce the number of U.S. troops to thirty thousand within six months of the invasion. According to General Tommy Franks, new technologies give "today's commanders the kind of Olympian perspective that Homer had given his Gods."[82] But the Greeks also invented another relevant concept: hubris.

The worst possible error a president can make in managing public expectations is to prematurely announce that victory is at hand. This was the mistake that U.S. officials made in 1900 regarding the Philippine insurgency and in the late 1920s concerning Augusto Sandino's rebellion in Nicaragua. On May 1, 2003, in a piece of carefully choreographed political theater, Bush landed on an aircraft carrier and declared an end to major combat operations in Iraq, while a banner behind him read MISSION ACCOMPLISHED. A month later, on June 5, 2003, Bush delivered a message to U.S. troops at Camp As Sayliyah: "America sent you on a mission to remove a grave threat and to liberate an oppressed people, and that mission has been accomplished."[83]

A few days after the May 1 "Mission Accomplished" speech, 41 percent of Americans thought that the war in Iraq was basically over. But by mid-September, that number had fallen to 10 percent.[84] Therefore, in large part because of presidential rhetoric, around one in three Americans had a jarring experience: a war they thought was finished had only just begun. In November 2003, ABC's "World News Tonight" included a shot of an American medic looking after wounded troops. The medic looked directly at the camera and said, "All major combat operations have ceased," before winking and adding sarcastically, *"Right."*[85]

One study of the 2007 "surge" policy found a lag before the American public recognized any real improvement in stability in Iraq. A major reason was that "a perceived record of distortion and manipulation on the part of an administration can prevent the public from accurately perceiving the reality of a conflict, even when that reality has actually shifted." Rather than cry wolf, it was cry success. Bush's "Mission Accomplished" speech "later reduced the persuasiveness of his assertions that the U.S. military was making progress in Iraq."[86]

Big Empire, Big Government

Many Americans, especially on the left, saw Bush's adventures in nation-building as a disastrous campaign of imperialism. The United States was following in the footsteps of the British colonialists in Afghanistan and Iraq. The American Empire Project inherited the mantle of the Anti-Imperialist League and opposed the sacrifice of ideals and the blood and treasure expended abroad. As the project put it, "Americans have long believed that the very notion of empire is an offense against our democratic heritage, yet in recent months, these two words—American empire—have been on everyone's lips."[87]

Meanwhile, Americans on the political right believed that prolonged nation-building in Afghanistan and Iraq violated another ideal: limited government. Lacking confidence in Washington's ability to solve complex social problems in the United States, conservatives were naturally skeptical about the value of drawn-out interventions abroad.

Among the strongest opponents of big-government nation-building was, ironically enough, the Bush administration itself. Senior officials were arch-crusaders. They wanted to employ the U.S. military as a rapier, toppling regimes with a single stab to the heart, before withdrawing and moving on to the next enemy of freedom. In October 2001, Bush claimed that he was against "using the military for nation-building. Once the job is done, our forces are not peacekeepers. We ought to put in place a UN protection and leave."[88]

Donald Rumsfeld's 2003 speech "Beyond Nation Building" justified a speedy exit from Iraq by contrasting the prolonged operations in Kosovo and the resulting "culture of dependence" with America's light footprint in Afghanistan. Well-intentioned missions like those in the Balkans had "adverse side effects," making it difficult for the target population to stand on their own two feet.[89] Faced with widespread looting and instability in Iraq, Rumsfeld stuck to his limited-government guns: "Freedom's untidy, and free people are free to make mistakes and commit crimes and do bad things. They're also free to live their lives and do wonderful things."[90]

Of course, the United States was drawn into precisely the kind of sustained reconstruction operations in Afghanistan and Iraq that Bush and his colleagues so despised. For some critics on the right, the nation-building missions became part of Bush's disastrous program of "big-government conservatism," along with bloated spending bills, deficits, and earmarks. Congressman Mike Pence argued that the Republican Party needed to return to traditional conservative values, opposing "any effort to use our military for nation-building or progressive social experimentation."[91]

The anti-imperialist left and the anti–big government right ended up making similar arguments. Neither group had much faith in the capacity of the U.S. government to reconstruct foreign societies. As one leading radical commented, "Three years after the [Kosovo] war the United Nations still runs Kosovo really by executive orders. They issue postage stamps, passports, driver's licenses and the like and decisions made by the local parliament are invalid without the signatures of the UN administrators." But this radical was not Noam Chomsky; it was Donald Rumsfeld. He wanted to transform the notion of U.S. intervention by tearing up the old nation-building playbook.[92]

Neither the left-wing nor the right-wing critique is wholly convincing. The charge of imperialism is tough to square with the Bush administration's desire to withdraw from Afghanistan and Iraq and hand the messy business of postwar stabilization over to allies and the United Nations. In many empires in history, Rumsfeld's skepticism about the wisdom of directly controlling subject populations would have identified him as a strong *anti-imperialist.*

The problem with the conservative critique is that big government is precisely what is needed in the aftermath of regime change. Large numbers of troops and a long-term commitment have the best shot at producing reasonably stable democracy.[93] In Iraq, the lack of U.S. forces, and the absence of planning for the postwar era, created a carnival atmosphere for thugs and extremists. The small U.S. footprint did produce a sense of freedom, but it was the freedom to loot, destroy, and kill.

Obama's Vietnam

Bush's favored analogy for Iraq was World War II. But once the campaign shifted to nation-building, a more worrying parallel became popular. Once again, the media was quick to draw analogies to the Vietnam War. During the first year of the intervention in Afghanistan, the *New York Times* ran 245 stories that mentioned Afghanistan and Vietnam. During the first year in Iraq, it ran 584 stories mentioning Iraq and Vietnam. As a point of comparison, the *Times* of London published less than half as many similar pieces: 113 for Afghanistan and 227 for Iraq.[94] Polls showed a steady rise in the number of Americans who thought that the Iraq War would "turn out to be another Vietnam," from 25 percent in 2004 to a plurality of 46 percent in 2007.[95]

Similarly, in early 2009, after President Barack Obama decided to send more troops to Afghanistan, *Newsweek*'s headline read, "Obama's Vietnam."[96] By October 2009, 52 percent of Americans thought that the conflict in Afghanistan had "turned into a situation like the United States faced in the Vietnam War."[97]

But the parallels between Afghanistan and Vietnam soon fall apart under examination. For a start, casualties in Vietnam were more than fifty times higher. In other words, comparing Afghanistan and Vietnam is like comparing a 2-story house with the 102-

story Empire State Building. Furthermore, the Taliban of 2010, with its hard core of ideologues allied with a loose coalition of warlords, is a world away from the tens of thousands of committed Vietcong fighters in Vietnam, backed to the hilt by Communist North Vietnam.[98]

Backlash

Just as in previous eras, perceptions of failure in Afghanistan and Iraq produced a backlash against nation-building. An "Iraq syndrome" emerged, which scholar Lawrence Freedman described as "the renewed, nagging and sometimes paralyzing belief that any large-scale U.S. military intervention abroad is doomed to practical failure and moral iniquity."[99] In the current climate, sending U.S. troops abroad for peacekeeping or counterinsurgency missions is a tough sell. The number of Americans who agreed that the United States should "mind its own business internationally and let other countries get along the best they can" rose from 30 percent in 2002, to 42 percent in 2006, to a plurality of 49 percent in 2009—the highest figure in more than forty years of asking that question.[100]

This is where we stand in 2010: in the backlash phase of the sixth cycle of American nation-building, waiting for a victory in interstate war to launch the United States on its next cycle.

The wars in Afghanistan and Iraq reveal the stark dangers that result when the crusade and quagmire traditions combine. The Bush administration was determined to overthrow the Taliban in Afghanistan but lacked the required commitment to rebuild the country. Indeed, officials were eager to launch another crusade as soon as the dust had settled in Kabul. Again, in 2002–2003, the administration was torn between a desire to change the Iraqi regime and an aversion to dealing with the consequences. Trying to reconcile these beliefs, officials cycled through the stages of grief.

First, before the war, there was *avoidance,* or a refusal to think about or plan for nation-building in Iraq. Second, after the fall of Saddam, there was *denial,* or a dismissal of the insurgency. In a November 2005 press conference, Secretary of Defense Donald Rumsfeld rejected the term "insurgents," favoring instead "enemies of the government." His colleague at the press conference, Chairman of the Joint Chiefs of Staff Peter Pace, kept slipping up and using the phrase "insurgents." Pace told reporters, "I have to use the word 'insurgent' because I can't think of a better word right now." Rumsfeld interjected, "Enemies of the legitimate Iraqi government—how's that?" A few seconds later, Pace again mentioned "the insurgents" and apologized to his boss: "Sorry, sir. I'm not trainable today."[101] This begs the question: how could the United States succeed in Iraq when it refused even to recognize its adversary?

Third, and finally, there was *acceptance,* as Bush committed additional U.S. forces to Iraq and shifted to a new counterinsurgency strategy. But a heavy price was paid, with fears of getting bogged down in a prolonged nation-building operation helping to create a real quagmire.

In 2010, the major concern about the quagmire tradition lies in Afghanistan. The stakes are high. A resurgent Taliban would destabilize the country and threaten neighboring Pakistan. At the same time, it appears that the likely costs and risks are worth bearing. By historical standards, U.S. deaths have been modest, and most Afghans back the international forces and reject the Taliban.

Fostering stability and development in Afghanistan is a long-term project that will require a committed strategy involving nongovernmental organizations, international donors, and U.S. and allied ground forces. Ultimately, of course, building the Afghan nation is a task for the Afghans, just as it was for the Germans, Japanese, and South Koreans. The United States is a facilitator, not a swaggering overlord.

Above all, this project needs patience, realistic expectations, and a willingness to live with suboptimal and morally ambiguous results. But in the United States, there is a growing sense that Afghanistan is an unwinnable quagmire. How much time has Obama got? Just as in southern Reconstruction, the clock is ticking.

CHAPTER 10

The Founding Tradition

The United States has embarked on interstate wars from Berlin to Baghdad. It has engaged in nation-building from South Carolina to South Vietnam. American beliefs about war have always varied widely according to gender, race, partisanship, and a hundred other factors. Over time, popular attitudes have shifted profoundly. War has become less romantic and ennobling. U.S. troops write fewer letters home about valor and chivalry. Campaigns of conquest and annexation are no longer acceptable. Meanwhile, the nature of combat has altered dramatically, with revolution after revolution in military affairs: from telegrams to the Internet, from cannon fire to daisy cutter bombs.

But for all this diversity and change, core elements in the nation's way of war have been remarkably stable over the past century and a half. We are addicted to regime change and allergic to nation-building. We see interstate wars as crusades: the stars burn brightly on America's banner; illuminated by their dazzling light, Americans fight ferociously for righteous goals against enemy countries. We see stabilization missions as quagmires: the vivid radiance of Old Glory casts our efforts to nation-build in dark shadows. What conceivable outcome in Somalia, Haiti, or Afghanistan would look impressive to an American idealist? War in its purest form is a grand campaign to topple tyrants and rid the world of evil. This is how we think about war. This is our way of war. This is how we fight.

Back to the Future

Where do we go from here? There's an obvious solution. We don't like limited interstate war, fought for objectives short of regime change. We disapprove of nation-building of any kind. Therefore, the United States should steer clear of these campaigns. Sticking to crusades against foreign countries will avoid politically unpopular conflicts and recapture the glory days of World War II.

The 1984 Weinberger-Powell Doctrine, for instance, eschewed limited wars and nation-building in favor of "all-or-nothing" campaigns, where massive force is employed to achieve clear goals with guaranteed public support. Similarly, Donald Rumsfeld sought to sharpen the U.S. military blade so that Washington could eliminate terrorists and overthrow tyrants with precision firepower and awe-inspiring technology, while avoiding prolonged stabilization missions.

But fighting only crusades is hardly a viable choice. The truth is that our addiction to regime change is dangerous. In the Spanish-American War, the pursuit of maximum objectives landed the United States in an avoidable conflict against Filipino nationalists. In the Korean War, the crusading spirit prompted a reckless march to the Yalu River in a bid to liberate North Korea and then, after Chinese intervention, encouraged many Americans to favor risky escalatory policies. In the Gulf War, the American public wanted to overthrow Saddam Hussein, even though this would have destroyed the U.S.-led coalition, produced an illegal war, and threatened U.S. interests.

In the current strategic environment, limited interstate war is an essential option in the military toolbox. Technology is becoming ever more destructive, and the political consequences of war are increasingly complex and difficult to predict. U.S. presidents must be able to fight for restricted objectives against foreign countries. They also need access to a brake pedal, so that if necessary, Washington can de-escalate the fighting midcourse and look for a way out.

Americans' allergy to nation-building is similarly hazardous. The tendency to view every stabilization mission as a debacle can become a self-fulfilling prophecy, where disillusionment undermines our commitment to the operation, leading to very real failure. Knee-jerk skepticism gifts our enemies with a playbook for defeating the United States: kill and destroy, and conjure up the image of a morass with no end in sight. Perceptions of failure also produce a skewed memory of the past, with southern Reconstruction and Somalia both falsely seen as terrible warnings from history.

In today's world, nation-building is both inevitable and essential. All roads, it seems, lead to nation-building, whether we are fighting wars of self-defense, as in Afghanistan; engaging in humanitarian interventions, as in Somalia; stabilizing conflict-prone societies, as in Bosnia and Kosovo; or trying to contain the proliferation of weapons of mass destruction, as in Iraq. Reconstruction and counterinsurgency operations are the future of combat.

The combination of our addiction to regime change and our allergy to nation-building is especially harmful. In Afghanistan and Iraq, the Bush administration was committed to overthrowing tyranny but loath to invest the time, troops, and treasure required to stabilize these societies. The result: five thousand dead Americans.

We need to rethink the crusade and quagmire traditions. This might seem implausible. Americans are not about to abandon their beliefs about war in favor of those of another country. For one thing, the culture of each society creates its own set of problems. The antimilitarism of Germany and Japan, for example, means that neither *punches its weight* in international affairs and neither *pulls its weight* in dealing with major international conflicts.

But we don't need to look abroad for a different perspective on war. Rather, we can turn our attention back through history, before the Civil War, to the time of the Founding Fathers. For sure, much of the early American thinking about war is irrelevant to the problems we face today. After all, the redcoats aren't about to appear on the horizon. And certain nineteenth-century beliefs should be actively rejected, especially the murderous and acquisitive attitude toward Native Americans.

But there is also much we can learn. The Founders didn't believe in the crusade and quagmire traditions. Instead, they adopted the opposite approach to war. We disdain limited wars and nation-building, but these were precisely the uses of force favored by the Founders. We celebrate grand crusades against enemy countries, but this was the type of campaign most feared by the Founders. I call this alternative view of war the *founding tradition*.

Faith of Our Fathers

The Founding Fathers were not pacifists. They recognized that conflict was inevitable because of man's ambition and love of power. Indeed, the United States was born in the crucible of violence and bloodshed. For a people lacking the social glue of monarchy or an ancient common heritage, memories of the Revolutionary War offered a critically important shared bond. The sword was a necessary tool of statecraft.

But interstate war should be an absolute last resort. Thomas Jefferson called war "as much a punishment to the punisher as to the sufferer."[1] The Founders feared that the United States could get bogged down in a dangerous military quagmire. Interestingly, however, the quicksand might emerge not in a nation-building mission, but in a war against a foreign country. Secretary of State John Quincy Adams announced in 1821 that America should not go "abroad in search of monsters to destroy." Battling the European great powers, even in a noble cause, could lead the United States to become involved, "beyond the power of extrication, in all the wars of interest and intrigue, of individual avarice, envy, and ambition, which assume the colors and usurp the standard of freedom."[2]

When interstate war did break out, it should be fought as a limited war rather than a crusade. The objectives were not unconditional surrender or regime change, but narrower and more specific goals. And instead of using *all* necessary force, the Founders favored *minimum* necessary force. As historian Reginald Stuart put it, "Americans recoiled from the kind of war where wanton destruction of property, the slaughter of innocents, and political obliteration of the enemy were commonplace."[3]

The Founders' caution about interstate war influenced the creation of the U.S. Constitution. Compared to the earlier Articles of Confederation, the Constitution strengthened the nation in foreign policy by empowering the federal government. But the Founders also deliberately divided the power to make war between the president and Congress, so that conflicts would be harder to start than to end. The president was commander in chief, but Congress had the right to initiate war, sustain or end war through the power of the purse, and play a critical role in negotiating peace by approving treaties. As Jefferson argued, "We have already given, in example, one effectual check to the Dog of War by transferring the power of letting him loose from the Executive to the Legislative body, from those who are to spend to those who are to pay."[4]

Yes, the separation of powers threatened political gridlock. But this had its advantages with a dangerous issue like war by impeding hasty actions and letting cooler heads prevail. James Wilson, one of the architects of the U.S. Constitution, believed that the need for support from a diverse Congress meant that "nothing but our national interest can draw us into a war."[5]

The Founders' preference for limited war was put into practice when the United States locked horns with Britain in 1812 and Mexico in 1846. After the outbreak of the Civil War in 1861, Americans *always* favored maximum objectives, including regime change, when the United States fought against another country. Before 1861, Americans *never* favored this war aim.[6]

A Complicated and Transcendent Injustice

In 1812, the United States was a supporting actor on the fringes of the international stage as the main drama, Napoleon's bid for French hegemony, played out in Europe. Britain's campaign of economic warfare against Napoleon systematically encroached on America's rights as a neutral country to trade with continental Europe. Another U.S. grievance was impressment: London's efforts to forcibly enlist British sailors working on U.S. ships often scooped American citizens up in the net. And there was a deeper, more fundamental complaint: Britain didn't give the United States its due respect and had never truly accepted American independence. President James Madison decided that redress could come only through force.

Upon the outbreak of fighting with Britain, there were hints of crusading sentiment among Americans. Especially in parts of the West and the South, the bugle rang out, with cries of mission and revenge and demands for the annexation of Canada. General William Hull declared to Canadians, "You will be emancipated from tyranny and oppression, and restored to the dignified station of freemen."[7] Representative William King announced, "We shall take Canada. Yes, sir, by force; by valor."[8] Andrew Jackson exclaimed that the "hour of national vengeance is now at hand."[9]

But the War of 1812 was not a crusade. It was a classic limited war. The United States fought for narrow objectives: to protect its neutral rights and stop the impressment of American sailors by the Royal Navy. Madison favored the seizure of Canadian territory, but in large part as a bargaining chip to be traded for maritime concessions.[10] When the military situation deteriorated in 1814, Washington looked to end the fighting and negotiated a compromise peace deal with Britain based on a return to the prewar status quo.

Some of the combat was savage. The scalping knives of the Kentucky militia were not just for show. But it was far from a campaign of all necessary force. The American troops that invaded Canada were a pale imitation of Sherman's Civil War army. U.S. soldiers burned flour mills and civilian homes in the village of Dover, Ontario, but as one enlistee noted, "Every possible respect was paid to the women and children, and the best part of the furniture in the houses which were destroyed, was even carried out by the troops previous to their being set on fire."[11] The U.S. officer responsible for torching civilian dwellings was officially reprimanded—a very rare instance of an attack on noncombatants being controversial in an interstate war.

Compared to subsequent crusades against foreign countries, in 1812 there was little sense of a zealous struggle. President Madison explained that British attacks on U.S. rights were a "complicated and transcendent injustice."[12] As a clarion call, it fell short of "a date which will live in infamy." When Congress held a lengthy debate on war, the tone was measured and defensive, not ideological and righteous. The vote to initiate hostilities was the closest of any declaration of war in U.S. history (79 to 49 in the House, 19 to 13 in the Senate). Congress called for a day of fasting and prayer because Americans had been "compelled to resort to arms, for the maintenance and protection of those rights which have been achieved by the blood of their fathers."[13]

Later Americans often chafed against the restrictions of limited war, demanding more escalation. But critics of the War of 1812 argued that the campaign was not limited enough. In the Northeast, rather than a wave of crusading fervor, there were threats of secession. Political leaders in New England worked systematically to prevent further U.S. offensives into Canada and to push for a rapid peace treaty. Encouraged by domestic sentiment, Madison accepted a negotiated settlement with London, averting a dangerously expanded war against an adversary that was no longer distracted by fighting Napoleon.[14]

An Army of Reformers

In 1846, the United States engaged in another limited interstate war, this time against Mexico. The quarrel was over the status of Texas, which had broken away from Mexico a decade before and been admitted to the Union in 1845. The Mexican government refused to recognize the secession of this rebellious province and disputed the Texan claim that the boundary with Mexico was the Rio Grande, as opposed to the Nueces River, farther north. American leaders sought to defend Texas, but they also had one eye, and in some cases both eyes, on other low-hanging fruit in northern Mexico, especially California. When U.S. forces were attacked near the Rio Grande, President James Polk claimed that American blood had been shed on American soil and successfully pushed for a declaration of war.

The Mexican War was a struggle that bridged the founding tradition and the crusade tradition. The idealistic fervor, moralistic retribution, and yearning for grand objectives so familiar to later Americans were all evident. The public responded enthusiastically to the outbreak of hostilities, as a romantic and patriotic spirit gripped the nation. Herman Melville wrote from Lansingburgh, New York, "People here are all in a state of delirium about the Mexican War. . . . Nothing is talked of but the 'Halls of the Montezumas.' "[15]

There was a strong sense of missionary idealism. Mexico was viewed as the opposite of America: Catholic, Hispanic, ignorant, and superstitious. The war would bring progress to a backward land. U.S. Army captain William Seaton Henry wrote that the Rio Grande valley could be saved if the "Anglo American race" governed the territory according to "republican simplicity and justice."[16] The Boston newspaper *Uncle Sam* published a new song after the war began:

> *An army of reformers, we —*
> *March on to glorious victory;*
> *And on the highest peak of Ande,*
> *Unfurl our banners to the wind,*
> *Whose stars shall light the land anew,*
> *And shed rich blessings like the dew.*[17]

The "All of Mexico" movement campaigned for maximum war aims and the annexation of the entire country. Mexicans and Americans alike would benefit from U.S. rule and newfound commercial opportunities.

But the Mexican War was fundamentally a limited war. The objective was territorial gain, not regime change. The All of Mexico movement never attained wide appeal, partly because of racial fears about absorbing millions of Mexicans into the United States. In the 1848 Treaty of Guadalupe Hidalgo, the United States paid Mexico $15 million and assumed several million dollars of Mexican debt, in exchange for the cession of 525,000 square miles of territory in California and today's American Southwest, as well as

Mexico's recognition that the border with Texas was the Rio Grande.

Even though the United States won almost all the battles, the campaign was unpopular with many Americans. As in 1812, critics of the Mexican War did not seek escalation. Instead, they claimed that Washington had too readily grasped the sword. Crusading beliefs competed with an older and more measured view of war. Several leading opponents of the campaign, like Daniel Webster, were in the winter of their lives—men from another age.

Quakers opposed the conflict on pacifist grounds. Northern Whigs and abolitionists saw it as a plot by the southern slave states to add new territory for the expansion of slavery. Abolitionist William Lloyd Garrison described the campaign as one "of aggression, of invasion, of conquest, and rapine—marked by ruffianism, perfidy, and every other feature of national depravity."[18] Henry David Thoreau refused to pay a poll tax in protest of the war and spent a night in the Concord, Massachusetts, jail. The New England Conference of the Methodist Church repeatedly condemned the Mexican War—a striking attitude, given the later ubiquitous presence of Methodists in the crusading vanguard.[19]

Abraham Lincoln also was skeptical. At first, he said, President Polk had dazzled Americans "by fixing the public's gaze upon the exceeding brightness of military glory—that attractive rainbow that rises in showers of blood." But then Polk had "swept, *on* and *on,* till, disappointed in his calculation of the ease with which Mexico might be subdued, he now finds himself, he knows not where."[20] In January 1848, the House of Representatives passed a resolution claiming that hostilities had been "unnecessarily and unconstitutionally begun by the President of the United States."[21]

By 1848, with the Mexican army destroyed and the enemy's capital in American hands, the United States could have demanded even more than half a million square miles of territory. But Polk

An antiwar cartoon from the Mexican-American War depicting U.S. general Zachary Taylor in full dress uniform sitting atop a mountain of skulls

settled for fewer gains than were militarily possible because of domestic opposition to expanded war aims. Once again, elite and public opinion acted as a brake upon escalation.[22]

Ralph Waldo Emerson captured the ambivalence of many Americans when he concluded that although the Mexican War was unjust, it was also a catalyst by which the United States could realize its manifest destiny, by expanding to the Pacific: "Most of the great results of history are brought about by discreditable means."[23]

A Fragile Vessel

Why did the Founders favor limited wars against foreign countries? With the United States weak and internally divided, crusading was not a realistic option. The youthful nation was dangerously exposed to adversaries, including the Spanish, British, and French. Many Europeans predicted a short life span for the independent United States. Some thought that a vengeful Britain or an avaricious France would strangle the new republic at birth. Others, like Frederick the Great of Prussia, held that the Union would quickly unravel, with each of the former colonies begging London for forgiveness.[24]

And even if, in wartime, Americans could steel themselves against foreign powers, freedom might still die at the hands of the enemy within. The earliest Americans were deeply imbued with the liberal creed. But rather than seek to spread their values by wielding the sword, the Founders wanted to protect liberalism at home from the corrupting effects of conflict. War was less an opportunity than a contagion. To go to war, or to escalate a war, was to gamble with the best hope for liberty in the world.

Freedom hung by a thread. Influenced by Calvinist ideas about the inherent imperfection and sinfulness of man, the Founders thought that Americans were perfectly capable of destroying their own experiment in liberty. Jefferson believed that war undermined freedom by fueling debt, concentrating power in the executive, and building up large standing armies. Alexander Hamilton remarked that "the violent destruction of life and property incident to war, the continual effort and alarm attendant on a state of continual danger, will compel nations the most attached to liberty to resort for repose and security to institutions which have a tendency to destroy their civil and political rights."[25]

The Founders' historical memory also encouraged restraint.

We see the Civil War and World War II as models for how to fight. But the founding generation recalled a very different set of conflicts: the catastrophic losses and sectarian tone of the religious wars of the 1600s, and the ideological and brutal French revolutionary and Napoleonic wars of their own time.

To understand how an interstate war could escalate dangerously, drawing warriors and civilians into the martial vortex, the Founders simply had to look across the Atlantic. In 1793, the revolutionary regime in Paris enacted the *levée en masse,* which mobilized the entire people for war. The young men would fight. The married men would forge weapons. The women would make clothes and serve in hospitals. Even the old men would be carried to public squares, where they could issue thundering speeches imparting a hatred of kings. Soon the French had a million men in the field, and warfare was transformed into a contest of nation against nation. The awful horror of Napoleon's Grand Army cutting a swath through Russia in 1812 and then wasting away on its pitiful retreat was a model for the kind of conflict that the United States should never fight.

A New Appetite

What happened to the founding tradition? During the nineteenth century, a profound force was injected into the petri dish of America's experiment in liberty: *power.* The country's growing economic and demographic strength led people to abandon their preference for limited war and favor crusades instead. When the cub became a lion, it roared, and in time it forgot the wisdom of the weak.

Power gave free rein to Americans' underlying sense of idealism and vengeance. The United States now had the option to follow its sacred principles to their ultimate conclusion, by fighting to redeem its enemies and all mankind. The temptation to pursue righteous warfare proved irresistible. Limited victories might once have been acceptable, but increasingly they seemed unworthy. Intoxicated by the sense of military possibility, fears abated about the effects of conflict on liberty at home. The priority in wartime was no longer to protect the city on the hill from unrestrained combat, but to crusade for regime change.

Each new steel mill and coal mine, and each new tank and stealth bomber, chipped away at the inhibitions against grand ambition and made the country the crusader state it was born to be. The escalation of the Civil War into a remorseless revolutionary struggle was motivated by idealism and wrath, but it was permitted by northern industrial and demographic might. Similarly, during the Spanish-American War, Professor Hermann E. Von Holst wrote, "The unparalleled, bewildering rate at which our power has grown and the proud consciousness that the future development of our boundless resources baffles imagination itself have taught us to deem feasible whatever we choose to will."[26]

Today, more than a century later, with American primacy unchallenged, power continues to permit a crusading approach to war. According to political scientist Robert Jervis, "The forceful and unilateral exercise of U.S. power is not simply the by-product of September 11.... It is the logical outcome of the current unrivaled U.S. position in the international system."[27] In the wake of 9/11, the United States had the capacity to spread liberty and bring its adversaries to justice. Why should it voluntarily stay its hand?

The Founders' belief in limited war is now almost forgotten. Most people have only the dimmest recollection of the War of 1812—perhaps some vague memory of the composition of "The Star-Spangled Banner." Despite vastly expanding the nation's territory, the Mexican War is also rarely recalled, and went largely uncelebrated on its centennial in 1946, in part because it was uncomfortably acquisitive. There are no monuments to these conflicts on the Mall.

Can we learn anything from the Founders about interstate war? Obviously, there is much that we can ignore. We certainly don't need a repeat of the covetous campaign against Mexico. But we can profit from the Founders' belief in restraint and their use of interstate war as a tool to attain narrow political goals. Early Americans feared escalation because they were weak. We should fear escalation because of the complexity of the modern world and the devastating power of technology. The Founders lived in an era of muskets and cannons. We inhabit a world of ICBMs and biological weapons. The escalation of conflict in 1812 meant marching a few thousand men across the Canadian border. Today it means risking the lives of thousands or millions.

Whereas the Founders sought to protect their neutral rights in a limited war against Britain in 1812, we may need to defend the freedom of the seas around Taiwan in a restricted military operation against China. Whereas the Founders looked to wind down the campaign against Britain in 1814, a president today must be able to de-escalate a war midcourse without being vilified. Leadership is not just about striving for ultimate victory in the manner of Lincoln and FDR. It's also about averting disaster by declining to do what is within one's power to do.

Implements of the American Soldier

The Founders also supported the military's involvement in nation-building. The job of soldiers was not just to destroy but also to build—right here in the United States. American troops formed what historian Michael Tate called a "multipurpose army," engaging in roles that blurred the lines between military and civilian duties.[28]

In the early Republic, troops cut down trees and farmed. They built forts, schools, chapels, hospitals, and roads—fully nineteen hundred miles by 1830. They dug canals, erected bridges, and dredged harbors. They constructed everything from the Minots Ledge Lighthouse in Boston harbor to the Washington Aqueduct. In 1820 Colonel Zachary Taylor, "Old Rough and Ready," remarked, "The ax, pick, saw & trowel, has become more the implement of the American soldier than the cannon, musket or sword."[29] As one enlisted man noted, "We had lived more like pioneers than soldiers."[30]

U.S. troops helped to survey and map the West. In the most famous expedition, from 1804 to 1806, Captain Meriwether Lewis and Second Lieutenant William Clark led a party of nearly thirty men to the Pacific Ocean. The U.S. Army Corps of Topographical Engineers, or "topogs," became a major locus of American science, producing a bounty of maps and zoological and other scientific data. Troops operated a telegraph service, delivered the mail, aided travelers heading west, and offered relief to the destitute. The frontier was often a lawless place without regular courts or police. Soldiers helped to fill the judicial void by incarcerating suspected criminals.[31]

The United States Military Academy at West Point was a great foundry of American nation-building. Established by President Thomas Jefferson in 1802, the academy became a seminary of science, and for decades it provided the best engineering education in the United States. The first superintendent was Jonathan Williams, a mathematician and former research assistant to Benjamin Franklin, whose military experience amounted to brief service with the Pennsylvania militia and the translation of a French article on artillery.[32]

Fully 71 percent of the classroom time at West Point was spent on engineering, mathematics, and natural philosophy, and only 29 percent on everything else, including military studies. The top graduates headed straight for the U.S. Army Corps of Engineers and the Corps of Topographical Engineers. In the words of one cadet in 1848, "The engineers were a species of gods, next to which came the 'topogs'—only a grade below the first, but still a grade—they were but demigods."[33]

West Pointers spread out to imprint their scientific and engineering mark on America. One commentator likened West Point to "the great city clock by which all the smaller clocks and watches are regulated."[34] When Harvard and Yale set up schools of engineering, they chose West Point graduates to head those institutions. In 1850, the president of Brown University claimed that "although there are more than 120 colleges in the United States, the West Point Academy has done more to build up the system of internal improvements in the United States than all the colleges combined."[35]

There were concerns that these nation-building activities would dull the U.S. military's rapier edge and erode its fighting ability. As an inspector touring frontier positions in 1826 noted, "Ask an officer at one of those posts what his place is in the event of alarms, and his answer will be, I don't know.... We never have alarms."[36] Some soldiers grew frustrated. One private signed up "because I preferred military duty to hard work." But he found that "I am deceived....I enlisted to avoid work, and here I am, compelled to perform three or four times the amount of labor I did before my enlistment."[37] In the late 1850s, another private refused an order to look after a sow and her litter of pigs: "To hell mit der piggins, I'm no swiney doctor."[38]

Jefferson and the other Founders saw the value in broadening the functions of the military beyond preparing for interstate war. If the United States had to have a standing army, it should at least be useful. According to Michael Tate, "The majority of Americans championed, and even came to routinely expect, the other diverse roles performed by the army."[39] Historian Francis Paul Prucha wrote, "The army consciously considered itself a force for national development, and if its military preparations had beneficial economic and social effects, the men who directed the activities of the army were delighted."[40]

Why didn't the Founders see nation-building as a violation of their ideals? Modern-day Americans, for instance, sometimes fear that nation-building will turn the United States into an empire. But for the earliest U.S. citizens, deploying the military in small units on the frontier made a standing army more tolerable and reduced fears that a Caesar would arise to overthrow the Republic.

Similarly, today Americans often see nation-building as a form of welfare, undermining the ideals of limited government. But in the early nineteenth century, the belief in limited government sharply restricted the state's resources, forcing it to rely on the army to perform a wide range of functions. Nation-building allowed the military to be as economical and productive as possible.

Over time, the American view of the military's proper role began to narrow. People focused on external threats and the crushing of enemy tyrants. In turn, our great crusading victories introduced the country to a new activity: nation-building in foreign lands. Americans found the reconstruction of conquered territory to be a gloomy business indeed. The result was the emergence of a new school of thought: the quagmire tradition.

Can we learn anything here from the Founders? Major differences between the eras might seem to render moot any useful lessons. Modern-day nation-building in Kosovo or Afghanistan is far removed from the experience of Jefferson and company. Furthermore, the benefits of nineteenth-century nation-building were more immediate because these activities occurred within the United States.

But in our globalized and interconnected world, events in Iraq can have as profound an impact on the lives of most Americans as did the situation on the Northwest frontier in the early nineteenth century. And at the very least, the beliefs of the founding generation demonstrate that there is nothing inherently "un-American" in developing a military designed for a diverse range of tasks.

In the modern world, we need our own multipurpose army: a Swiss Army knife rather than a rapier. Whereas from 1816 to 1820 U.S. soldiers constructed a road from Tennessee to Louisiana, American forces today can build roads that bind Afghanistan together. Whereas West Point supplied a nation-builder's education in the nineteenth century, the academy today can prepare cadets for twenty-first-century nation-building, with a greater focus on foreign languages and culture. Whereas U.S. troops helped destitute pioneers heading west by repairing wagons and providing food, soldiers today can give humanitarian aid to those suffering from famine, war, or natural disasters.

This is not a call for endless nation-building. Indeed, if the United States is more cautious about crusading, there may be fewer regime changes and fewer nation-building missions. What we need instead is a sober, humble, and committed approach to these operations.

Sober because nation-building should begin only after a careful appraisal of the likely costs and benefits to our interests and values. We also need to avoid illusions about the probable speed of transformation.

Humble because interventions are not about imperial control, but about empowering local actors to build their own country. One of the principal challenges is to align the mission with the forces of nationalism rather than provoke a patriotic backlash. We spectacularly failed to achieve this in Vietnam, but we had some success in the Philippines, Kosovo, and Afghanistan.

Committed because when we do begin nation-building, we should typically see it through, employing sufficient force to over-awe adversaries, establish law and order, and secure the population. Winning an interstate war is only half the battle; we need to win the peace as well.

Knowledge Will Forever Govern Ignorance

For all its sins and failings, the United States remains one of the best hopes for expanding the reach of freedom and democracy around the world. But to achieve America's promise, we need to reflect on our beliefs about that most critical of events: war.

All three of our traditions are useful. The crusade tradition helps Americans mobilize for large-scale wars against foreign countries. The quagmire tradition makes us sensitive to the very real risks and costs of nation-building. The founding tradition highlights the wisdom of restraint during interstate war and promotes the military's involvement in a range of duties beyond conventional fighting.

But while all the traditions are valuable, it is the founding tradition that needs to be heard more loudly in today's marketplace of ideas. Americans must be willing to employ the full range of military alternatives—nation-building, limited interstate war, crusading interstate war—rather than just the most extreme and destructive option.

As we sit on the steps of the Lincoln Memorial, the inspiration to reflect on our national view of war lies, conveniently, in front of us. For over on the right is a memorial to Thomas Jefferson. And behind the Capitol, out of view on Independence Avenue, is a building dedicated to James Madison, who led the United States in the limited war against Britain in 1812 and was the last Founding Father to die. The building is part of the Library of Congress, and on one of its exterior walls is engraved a quotation from Madison: "Knowledge will forever govern ignorance: and a people who mean to be their own governours, must arm themselves with the power which knowledge gives."

ACKNOWLEDGMENTS

I take great pleasure in highlighting my many debts.

I would like to thank a number of Swarthmore College students for skillful research assistance, including Julian Chender, Isaac Hock, Alex Imas, Jason Lissy, Jeffrey Merkle, JeeYoung Oh, Michael Pollack, Mara Revkin, and Manoli Strecker.

My colleagues offered incisive comments, and I am grateful to Adam Berinsky, Steve Casey, Kelly Greenhill, Gena Hamshaw, James Hayman, Geoffrey Herrera, Michael Horowitz, Bruce Jentleson, Dominic Johnson, David Kennedy, Jim Kurth, Douglas Macdonald, Walter McDougall, Richard Rosecrance, Adam Smith, Harry S. Stout, and David Traxel. Amy Oakes deserves particular gratitude for her consistent support, wise counsel, and superb ideas.

Much of this book was written while I was a research fellow at the Harvard Kennedy School. I would like to thank Sean Lynn-Jones, Steven Miller, Stephen Walt, and the other fellows at the Belfer Center for making my year at Harvard both productive and stimulating. Special mention must go to Teresa Cravo, Kate Hayman, and Lee Seymour for their wonderful friendship and hospitality toward a traveling Brit. I am especially grateful to Swarthmore College and the James Michener Faculty Fellowship for funding my sabbatical year.

I would also like to thank the expert librarians at Swarthmore

College and the Widener Library at Harvard for facilitating my hundreds of book requests with great efficiency and professionalism.

I was very fortunate to work with the best agent in New York City, Will Lippincott, who ably guided the project from its earliest days. Many thanks go to my editor, Junie Dahn, who did a wonderful job improving the manuscript and provided invaluable advice at critical moments. Copyeditors rarely receive the recognition they deserve. Barbara Jatkola's eagle eye and incredible skill had a major positive impact on the book. I am grateful indeed for her dedicated work.

My final and most important debt is offered to my family: the Tierneys, the Tracys, the Smiths, the McMillens, the Kelas, and the Lyfords. Without their support, this book would not have appeared.

NOTES

Epigraph

1. Pearlman, *Warmaking and American Democracy,* 7.
2. Donald Rumsfeld, press conference, July 24, 2003, available at http://www .defense.gov/transcripts/transcript.aspx?transcriptid=2894.

Chapter 1. Introduction

1. "A Day of Terror," *New York Times,* September 12, 2001.
2. "U.S. Official Resigns over Afghan War," *Washington Post,* October 27, 2009. The full letter is available at http://www.washingtonpost.com/wp-srv/hp/ssi/ wpc/ResignationLetter.pdf.
3. George Will, "Time to Get Out of Afghanistan," *Washington Post,* September 1, 2009.
4. Barack Obama, speech at West Point, December 1, 2009, available at http:// www.whitehouse.gov/the-press-office/remarks-president-address-nation- way-forward-afghanistan-and-pakistan.
5. "The Second Gore Bush Presidential Debate," October 11, 2000, available at http://www.debates.org/index.php?page=October-11-2000-debate-transcript.
6. Mead, *Special Providence.*
7. McDougall, *Promised Land, Crusader State.*
8. There are other differences of structure, argument, and emphasis. The crusade tradition overlaps to some extent with Mead's Wilsonian tradition and Jacksonian tradition, and we both agree that a strain of American culture seeks to export our values and gain revenge in wartime. Unlike Mead, I focus on wars rather than foreign policy more generally, adopt a chronological rather than a purely thematic approach, systematically distinguish perceptions of interstate wars from perceptions of nation-building, and suggest that Americans should recognize the potential as well as the pitfalls of nation-building. Like McDougall, I see the United States evolving into a crusader state, but I suggest that the process began in earnest during the Civil War rather than the Spanish-American War, and my argument is more positive about nation-building.

9. Weigley, *The American Way of War*. See also Mahnken, "The American Way of War in the Twenty-first Century"; Gray, "The American Way of War"; Kurth, "Variations on the American Way of War."

Chapter 2. For Liberty and Vengeance

1. Abraham Lincoln, "Speech at the Dedication of the National Cemetery at Gettysburg," November 19, 1863, in Lincoln, et al., *Life and Works of Abraham Lincoln*, 5:182–83.
2. For a discussion of the Civil War as a de facto interstate war, see chapter 4. Interstate wars are defined as requiring ground troops, so purely air campaigns, such as the bombing of Libya in 1986 and the rocket strikes against Afghanistan and Sudan in 1998, are excluded. The use of ground troops signals to Americans *This is a war,* while firing a handful of missiles at Sudan is far more ambiguous.
3. The only partial exception is the Spanish-American War, in which it was physically impossible for the United States to remove the government in Madrid, and Americans instead backed regime change for virtually the entire Spanish Empire: Cuba, the Philippines, Guam, and Puerto Rico. In the Korean War, the U.S. government and the American public originally favored regime change in North Korea but later moderated this goal. In the Gulf War, Washington did not follow through on the popular wish to march on Baghdad.
4. For a discussion, see Mueller, *War, Presidents and Public Opinion;* Lacquement, "The Casualty-Aversion Myth."
5. Roberts and Olson, *John Wayne, American,* 581.
6. Dallek, *The American Style of Foreign Policy,* 95.
7. Tocqueville, *Democracy in America,* 764.
8. Tocqueville's explanation for this behavior, focusing on the organization of the military and the attraction of martial careers, is different from the argument presented in this book. Ibid., 755.
9. Twain, *A Connecticut Yankee in King Arthur's Court,* 437.
10. Ibid., 427.
11. Ibid., 434.
12. Between 1816 and 2003, the United States was responsible for five out of the eighteen cases in which one country intentionally or indiscriminately killed more than fifty thousand enemy civilians in interstate war. Prussia/Germany was responsible for three episodes of mass killing, and Britain and Russia were responsible for two each. Data from Downes, *Targeting Civilians in War,* 44–47.
13. Armstrong, *Unconditional Surrender,* 14. Since 1945, the same pattern has held true. In the Korean War, London tended to be warier than Washington about escalating the war. In the Falklands War (1982), Britain aimed to recapture the Falkland Islands from Argentina and restore the prewar status quo. There was no question of regime change as an objective. But if the United States had fought a similar campaign, Americans would have expected the Argentine military junta to be overthrown. In the Gulf War, Britain was among the most

hawkish U.S. allies. But only 27 percent of the British public wanted to march on Baghdad and topple Saddam Hussein's regime, compared to more than 70 percent of Americans. Freedman and Karsh, *The Gulf Conflict,* 412.

14. Sheehan, *Where Have All the Soldiers Gone?* 180; Berger, "Norms, Identity, and National Security in Germany and Japan."

15. When a Japanese civilian police inspector was killed on a peacekeeping mission in Cambodia in 1993, it prompted considerable national debate.

16. Scholars known as realists argue that states usually act according to power politics and strategic interests. But in many cases they have depicted the United States as an exception that—unfortunately from their point of view—is too often driven by moralism and emotion. Kennan, *American Diplomacy;* Morgenthau, *American Foreign Policy.*

17. "Andrew Jackson Proclaims War as a Crusade, 1812," in Chambers and Piehler, *Major Problems in American Military History,* 107. Italics in original. See also Locke, *Two Treatises of Government;* Huntington, "American Ideals Versus American Institutions"; Hartz, *The Liberal Tradition in America.*

18. Tocqueville, *Democracy in America,* 297–98.

19. Robert Kagan, "Neocon Nation: Neoconservatives, c. 1776," *World Affairs,* spring 2009, http://www.worldaffairsjournal.org/articles/2008-spring/full-neocon.html.

20. Hartz, *The Liberal Tradition in America,* 9; Huntington, *The Soldier and the State,* 144; Myrdal, *An American Dilemma;* Abbott, "Still Louis Hartz After All These Years."

21. McCartney, *Power and Progress,* 64–65.

22. Mead, *Special Providence;* McDougall, *Promised Land, Crusader State;* Tuveson, *Redeemer Nation;* Jewett, *The Captain America Complex,* chap. 2; Monten, "The Roots of the Bush Doctrine," 120–21; Preston, "Bridging the Gap Between the Sacred and the Secular"; McCartney, *Power and Progress,* 29; Gamble, *The War for Righteousness;* Noll and Harlow, *Religion and American Politics.*

23. Kohut and Stokes, *America Against the World,* 103.

24. Tocqueville, *Democracy in America,* xxix.

25. Gallup polls, 1958–2007. This figure has fallen from 77 percent rejecting an atheist candidate in 1958 to 48 percent in 2007. But during the same period, the willingness to vote for qualified blacks increased more dramatically. Data from http://www.pollingreport.com.

26. Tocqueville, *Democracy in America,* 343.

27. Smith, *America's Mission,* 9.

28. Holsti, "Promotion of Democracy as Popular Demand?" 152–80.

29. One systematic study found that "in Britain, World War II evokes far more negative memories than in the United States," with many British people remembering the conflict as tragic or pointless. Scott and Zac, "Collective Memories in Britain and the United States," 329.

30. Downes, *Targeting Civilians in War;* Valentino, Huth, and Croco, "Bear Any Burden?"

31. Liberman, "An Eye for an Eye," 692; Liberman, "Punitiveness and U.S. Elite Support for the 1991 Persian Gulf War"; Liberman and Skitka, "Just Deserts in Iraq."

32. Euripides, *Medea,* 75; Frijda, "The Lex Talionis."
33. Singer et al., "Empathic Neural Responses Are Modulated by the Perceived Fairness of Others"; Quervain et al., "The Neural Basis of Altruistic Punishment."
34. Quervain et al., "The Neural Basis of Altruistic Punishment"; Frijda, "The Lex Talionis."
35. Kohut and Stokes, *America Against the World,* 110–11; Brown, *No Duty to Retreat;* Mead, *Special Providence,* 236.
36. Lipset, *American Exceptionalism,* 63.
37. Nisbett, *The Geography of Thought,* chap. 5; Kohut and Stokes, *America Against the World,* 54, 210.
38. Grasmick et al., "Protestant Fundamentalism and the Retributive Doctrine of Punishment." Fundamentalists and evangelicals are not a monolithic punitive group. Indeed one study found that non-southern fundamentalists were actually *less* supportive of capital punishment than other non-southerners, apparently because they were influenced by biblical injunctions to show compassion and forgiveness. Unnever and Cullen, "Christian Fundamentalism and Support for Capital Punishment," 187. Those who oppose the death penalty in the United States are more likely than supporters to explain their belief by reference to their faith. Kohut and Stokes, *America Against the World,* 105–12.
39. Nisbett and Cohen, *Culture of Honor;* Mead, *Special Providence,* 227.
40. Liberman, "An Eye for an Eye," 692.
41. Carroll, *War Letters,* 308.
42. Mead, *Special Providence.*
43. Kennan, *American Diplomacy,* 66.
44. Brontë, *Jane Eyre,* 45.

Chapter 3. Through a Glass, Darkly

1. *Webster's New Collegiate Dictionary.* Boston: Houghton Mifflin, 2008, 926.
2. Mark Twain, "Mark Twain, the Greatest American Humorist, Returning Home," *New York World,* October 6, 1900.
3. Halberstam, *The Making of a Quagmire.*
4. "Avoid a Bosnian Quagmire," *New York Times,* September 2, 1993.
5. Isaacs, *Vietnam Shadows,* 96.
6. "Peacekeeping Operations in Kosovo Resolution," House of Representatives, March 11, 1999, transcript available at http://thomas.loc.gov/cgi-bin/query/F?r106:1:./temp/~r1063DTMGY:e406720.
7. Jimmy Carter, interview, *Today,* NBC, September 30, 2004, available at http://today.msnbc.msn.com/id/6138962/.
8. Bob Herbert, "The Afghan Quagmire," *New York Times,* January 5, 2009.
9. Jentleson and Britton, "Still Pretty Prudent"; Oneal, Lian, and Joyner, "Are the American People 'Pretty Prudent'?" In 2004, the public was asked to rank America's top nineteen foreign policy priorities. Three of the four *least* popular

choices were core tasks of nation-building: "promote human rights abroad" (number 16), "promote democracy abroad" (number 18), and, in last position, "improve living standards in poor nations" (number 19). Number 17 was "solve Israeli/Palestinian conflict." The most popular choices were defending against terrorist attacks and protecting jobs. Kohut and Stokes, *America Against the World,* 47–48.

10. Daalder, "Knowing When to Say No," 41; Bacevich, *American Empire,* 135.
11. Gelpi, Feaver, and Reifler, "Success Matters"; Tierney, "America's Quagmire Mentality." One poll found that most Americans would support an intervention, assuming that it successfully ended ethnic cleansing—suggesting that it's the perception of failure that makes Americans disapprove of these operations. Kull and Destler, *Misreading the Public,* 102–3.
12. The most famous music inspired by a nation-building mission is, revealingly, the anti–Vietnam War protest songs.
13. The public is *four times* more sensitive to casualties in nation-building missions than in interstate wars. In other words, there is the same drop in support if one hundred Americans die in nation-building or if four hundred Americans die fighting against another country. Sullivan, "Sustaining the Fight."
14. U.S. atrocities only became a major public issue during campaigns in the Philippines, Latin America (in the 1920s), Vietnam, and Iraq—all of which were nation-building missions.
15. German Marshall Fund of the United States and the Chicago Council on Foreign Relations, "Worldviews 2002," available at http://www.thechicago council.org/past_pos.php.
16. Ferguson, *Colossus,* 238.
17. Central Research Services poll, July 20–30, 1995, available from the Roper Center's Japanese Data Archive http://www.ropercenter.uconn.edu/jpoll/ home.html. See also Sondhaus, *Strategic Culture and Ways of War,* 105–13; Midford, *Japanese Public Opinion and the War on Terrorism.*
18. A poll in October 1999 found that 82 percent of the Australian public supported the deployment of forces to East Timor. Coleman, *International Organizations and Peace Enforcement,* 257.
19. Martin and Fortmann, "Support for International Involvement in Canadian Public Opinion After the Cold War"; "Accentuating the Positive," *Economist,* March 3, 2007, 46.
20. Vought, "Preparing for the Wrong War."
21. Krepinevich, *The Army and Vietnam;* Krepinevich, "How to Win in Iraq."
22. Dobbins et al., *America's Role in Nation-Building,* 153. According to the Department of Defense, between 1980 and 2008, 24,048 service members were killed in accidents, while 6,270 died in suicides, for an average of 1,045 deaths per year, or 2.86 per day. U.S. Census Bureau, http://www.census.gov/compendia/ statab/2010/tables/10s0504.xls.
23. Mueller, "The Banality of 'Ethnic War' "; Sadowski, *The Myth of Global Chaos.*
24. Frijda, "The Lex Talionis," 267.

25. Peter Schneider, "Across a Great Divide," *New York Times,* March 13, 2004. One 1994 study asked people in the United States, Canada, and Europe basic factual questions about international affairs, such as "Who is the President of Russia?" The Americans scored lower on the test than anyone except the Spanish. Of the five questions asked, more than half of the Americans got none or one right, while more than half of the Germans got four or five right. Dimock and Popkin, "Political Knowledge in Comparative Perspective."

26. Stephanson, *Manifest Destiny,* 90.

27. Zinn, *A People's History of the United States;* Chomsky, *Hegemony or Survival;* Kinzer, *Overthrow.*

28. In 2002–2003, the United States spent about $51 per person on development assistance, compared to Norway's $381 per person. Of the world's top twenty-two national donors, the United States gives the smallest amount of foreign aid relative to gross domestic product (GDP). Steven Radelet, "Think Again: U.S. Foreign Aid," *Foreign Policy*, March 1, 2005, available at http://www.foreignpolicy.com/articles/2005/02/28/think_again_us_foreign_aid; Kull, Destler, and Ramsay, *The Foreign Policy Gap;* Kohut and Stokes, *America Against the World,* 188–89.

29. Donald Rumsfeld, "Beyond Nation Building," February 14, 2003, available at http://www.defenselink.mil/speeches/speech.aspx?speechid=337.

30. There are alternative explanations for the quagmire tradition, but none is convincing. Could it be that we're skeptical about nation-building because U.S. interests are not engaged in places such as Somalia and because these countries don't pose a significant threat? The problem with this argument is that since the Civil War, Americans have been consistently gloomy about nation-building, whether the involvement of U.S. interests has been low (Somalia), moderate (the Balkans), or high (the ex-Confederacy, Afghanistan, Iraq). For instance, the direction that Iraq follows in the years ahead, in terms of its internal stability and foreign policy decisions, is of enormous consequence for U.S. interests. American troops in Iraq are arguably having a more profound impact on the U.S. strategic position than their fellow soldiers anywhere else in the world. But the scale of these interests has not prevented the public from perceiving the operation as a failed quagmire. Alternatively, is it possible that Americans favor interstate wars because in these cases in the past, the United States was attacked, while nation-building has been a war of choice? Historically, however, Americans have been comfortable with interstate war and have followed the crusader template both when the United States has been attacked (World War II, the overthrow of the Taliban in Afghanistan) and in wars of choice (the Spanish-American War, Grenada, Panama, Iraq). Similarly, Americans have been disillusioned by nation-building missions that were campaigns of choice (Somalia, Bosnia, Kosovo, Iraq), as well as by operations that were the consequence of being attacked (southern Reconstruction, Afghanistan).

31. U.S. Department of the Army, *The U.S. Army/Marine Corps Counterinsurgency Field Manual,* foreword.

32. Dobbins et al., *America's Role in Nation-Building,* 164.
33. Blechman and Wittes, "Defining Moment," 5.
34. DiPrizio, *Armed Humanitarians,* 71, 148–49; Power, *"A Problem from Hell,"* 366.
35. U.S. Department of Defense, *Quadrennial Defense Review,* 36.
36. More than one million Americans have died in interstate wars since 1861 (mostly in the Civil War and World War II). Around ten thousand Americans have been killed while nation-building (mostly in the Philippines and Iraq). The Vietnam War is excluded because it was both an interstate war and a nation-building mission (see chapter 7). If all the U.S. deaths in Vietnam were counted as nation-building deaths, the ratio would still be 15:1.
37. In *Plan of Attack* (150), Bob Woodward quotes Colin Powell employing the Pottery Barn rule in 2002. Powell has since denied using this phrasing, and the term may originate with journalist Thomas Friedman. Ironically, the rule is a misnomer: if you break something by accident in a Pottery Barn store, it is writ ten off as a loss.

Chapter 4. Birth of a Nation

1. Paludan, *"A People's Contest,"* 351.
2. Twain and Rachels, *Mark Twain's Civil War,* 90; Fischer, *Liberty and Freedom,* 331; Bernard, *Lincoln and the Music of the Civil War,* 51.
3. Tuveson, *Redeemer Nation,* 198–99; Fahs, *The Imagined Civil War,* 78–79; Wilson, *Patriotic Gore,* 92.
4. Carroll, *War Letters,* 102–3.
5. As with interstate war more generally, the United States' primary mission was to defeat the adversary's army on the battlefield and conquer territory. The North treated southern soldiers as if they were POWs, not rebels. Washington blockaded southern ports, which under international law implied a war between sovereign nations. When Abraham Lincoln entered the Confederate White House in Richmond in 1865, he sat at the executive desk and talked as if the adversary was another state: "This must have been President Davis's chair." Stout, *Upon the Altar of the Nation,* 438.
6. Ibid., 11–12.
7. Ibid., 35.
8. Ibid., 28.
9. McPherson, *For Cause and Comrades,* 16–17.
10. Paludan, *"A People's Contest,"* 68.
11. Detzer, *Donnybrook,* 352–53.
12. Whitman and Warner, *The Portable Walt Whitman,* 483.
13. Melville, "The March into Virginia Ending in the First Manassas."
14. McPherson, *What They Fought For,* 56.
15. Manning, *What This Cruel War Was Over,* 45.
16. Hess, *Liberty, Virtue, and Progress,* 97.

17. McPherson, *What They Fought For,* 64.

18. Frank and Duteau, "Measuring the Political Articulateness of United States Civil War Soldiers."

19. Carroll, *War Letters,* 64.

20. Maslowski, "To the Edge of Greatness," 240.

21. Stout, *Upon the Altar of the Nation,* 177.

22. Frank and Duteau, "Measuring the Political Articulateness of United States Civil War Soldiers," 63.

23. McPherson, "Lincoln and the Strategy of Unconditional Surrender," 40; Neely, *The Last Best Hope of Earth;* Goodwin, *Team of Rivals.*

24. Carroll, *War Letters,* 77.

25. Ibid., 82.

26. McPherson, "From Limited War to Total War in America," 299.

27. "Letter to Cuthbert Bullitt," July 28, 1862, Lincoln et al., *Life and Works of Abraham Lincoln,* 7:98; Stout, *Upon the Altar of the Nation,* 139.

28. Frank and Duteau, "Measuring the Political Articulateness of United States Civil War Soldiers."

29. McPherson, *Battle Cry of Freedom,* 619; McPherson, "Was It More Restrained Than You Think?"; Janda, "Shutting the Gates of Mercy."

30. McPherson, *Battle Cry of Freedom,* 822; Simon, "Grant, Lincoln, and Unconditional Surrender," 196–98.

31. Stout, *Upon the Altar of the Nation,* 26.

32. In the Revolutionary War, perhaps 20 percent of southern whites were Loyalists, and around 30 percent were uncommitted, while in the Civil War, only about 10 percent of southern whites were Unionists. The Confederacy mobilized an incredible 80 percent of its draft-age white males for the military. Mitchell, "The Perseverance of the Soldiers," 112; Gallagher, *The Confederate War,* 28.

33. McPherson, "Lincoln and the Strategy of Unconditional Surrender," 58; Gallagher, *The Confederate War,* chap. 1.

34. Frank and Duteau, "Measuring the Political Articulateness of United States Civil War Soldiers," 71.

35. Silber, *Daughters of the Union;* McDougall, *Throes of Democracy,* 451–52; Gallagher, *The Confederate War,* 75–80.

36. Stout, *Upon the Altar of the Nation,* 113.

37. Hess, *Liberty, Virtue, and Progress,* 100.

38. Parish, "The War for the Union as a Just War," 90; McPherson, "Lincoln and the Strategy of Unconditional Surrender," 54–55.

39. Paludan, *"A People's Contest,"* 10.

40. Abraham Lincoln, "Annual Message to Congress," December 1, 1862, in Lincoln et al., *Life and Works of Abraham Lincoln,* 6:81.

41. McPherson, *For Cause and Comrades,* 114; McPherson, *What They Fought For,* 35; Hess, *The Union Soldier in Battle;* Hess, *Liberty, Virtue, and Progress.*

42. McPherson, *Drawn with the Sword*, 211.

43. McPherson, *What They Fought For*, 30.

44. Stout, *Upon the Altar of the Nation*, 174–75.

45. Hess, *Liberty, Virtue, and Progress*, 34–35.

46. Stout, *Upon the Altar of the Nation*, 184–85.

47. Redkey, *A Grand Army of Black Men*, 210.

48. McPherson, *For Cause and Comrades*, 71. Italics in original.

49. Morone, *Hellfire Nation*, 213; Tuveson, *Redeemer Nation*, 53; McPherson, *For Cause and Comrades*, 63–64; McCartney, *Power and Progress*, 12–13; Parish, "From Necessary Evil to National Blessing," 65; Jewett and Lawrence, *Captain America and the Crusade Against Evil*, 62.

50. Parish, "From Necessary Evil to National Blessing," 86–88; Moorehead, *American Apocalypse*.

51. McPherson, *For Cause and Comrades*, 13.

52. McPherson, *What They Fought For*, 43.

53. Manning, *What This Cruel War Was Over*, 153.

54. McPherson, *For Cause and Comrades*, 99.

55. Schama, *The American Future*, 94.

56. Parish, "The War for the Union as a Just War," 92.

57. Abraham Lincoln, "Speech at the Dedication of the National Cemetery at Gettysburg," November 19, 1863, in Lincoln et al., *Life and Works of Abraham Lincoln*, 5:183; Pillar, "Ending Limited War," 256–58.

58. Manning, *What This Cruel War Was Over*, 153.

59. Pearlman, *Warmaking and American Democracy*, 33.

60. Fischer, *Liberty and Freedom*, 329; McPherson, *For Cause and Comrades*, 20; Manning, *What This Cruel War Was Over*, 32; http://history.sandiego.edu/gen/snd/bonnieblueflag.html.

61. Nelson and Sheriff, *A People at War*, 69; Rubin, *A Shattered Nation*.

62. Nelson and Sheriff, *A People at War*, 63.

63. McPherson, *For Cause and Comrades*, 98.

64. Abraham Lincoln, "Second Inaugural Address," March 4, 1865, in Lincoln et al., *Life and Works of Abraham Lincoln*, 5:224.

65. Small, *Democracy and Diplomacy*, 122.

66. McPherson, "Was It More Restrained Than You Think?" 43.

67. McPherson, *For Cause and Comrades*, 153.

68. Ibid., 154.

69. Woodworth, *While God Is Marching On*, 261.

70. Stewart, *Holy Warriors*, 206.

71. "General William T. Sherman, U.S.A., Justifies Taking War to Civilians, 1864," in Chambers and Piehler, *Major Problems in American Military History*, 167.

72. Janda, "Shutting the Gates of Mercy," 16.

73. McPherson, *For Cause and Comrades*, 149.

74. Ibid., 150.

75. Ibid.

76. Gallagher, *The Confederate War,* 105.

77. Finseth, *The American Civil War,* 539.

78. Stout, *Upon the Altar of the Nation,* 456.

79. Warren, *The Legacy of the Civil War,* 59–64.

80. Nelson and Sheriff, *A People at War,* 107; Leonard, *Above the Battle,* 9–24; Paludan, *"A People's Contest,"* 325–26.

81. Dray, *Capitol Men,* 169, 361–62.

82. Gillette, *Retreat from Reconstruction,* 180.

83. Foner, *Reconstruction,* 499.

84. Gillette, *Retreat from Reconstruction,* 230.

85. Fitzgerald, *Splendid Failure,* 118; Simpson, *The Reconstruction Presidents,* 174–84.

86. Trefousse, *Carl Schurz,* 104.

87. Slap, *The Doom of Reconstruction,* 206; Beisner, *Twelve Against Empire,* 19; Richardson, *The Death of Reconstruction,* 18.

88. Slap, *The Doom of Reconstruction,* 206.

89. Gillette, *Retreat from Reconstruction,* 184. Italics in original.

90. Ibid., 242, 256; McPherson, *Ordeal by Fire,* 594.

91. Gillette, *Retreat from Reconstruction,* 238–39.

92. Foner, *Forever Free,* 162.

93. Ibid., 159; Woodward, "The Political Legacy of Reconstruction," 527.

94. Fitzgerald, *Splendid Failure,* 151; McPherson, *Ordeal by Fire,* 574; Marty, *Righteous Empire,* 137; Foner, *Reconstruction,* 366; Keller, *Affairs of State,* 216; Mayers, *Wars and Peace,* 20; McDougall, *Throes of Democracy,* 541.

95. The Tweed Ring Scandal centered on William Tweed, who was a New York state senator, and ran the Democratic Party political machine in New York City. Tweed and his associates brazenly embezzled between $40 million and $200 million from taxpayers, a sum that would be worth billions of dollars in today's money. Fitzgerald, *Splendid Failure,* 117; Slap, *The Doom of Reconstruction,* 206; Current, *Those Terrible Carpetbaggers.*

96. Ibid., 22.

97. Foner, *Reconstruction,* 278.

98. Richardson, *The Death of Reconstruction,* 80.

99. Foner, *Reconstruction,* 497.

100. Gillette, *Retreat from Reconstruction,* 230.

101. McPherson, *Ordeal by Fire,* 543–44.

102. Perman, *The Road to Redemption,* 169–72.

103. Lane, *The Day Freedom Died,* 10–20; Lemann, *Redemption,* 17–20.

104. Lemann, *Redemption,* 26; Richard Rubin, "The Colfax Riot," *Atlantic Monthly,* July/August 2003, available at http://www.theatlantic.com/issues/2003/07/rubin.htm.

105. Fitzgerald, *Splendid Failure,* 191.

106. Gillette, *Retreat from Reconstruction*, 164.

107. McPherson, *Ordeal by Fire*, 593.

108. Hess, *Liberty, Virtue, and Progress*, 113. Italics in original.

109. Gillette, *Retreat from Reconstruction*, 310.

110. Richardson, *The Death of Reconstruction*, 137.

111. Fitzgerald, *Splendid Failure*, 183.

112. The Paris Commune was a radical leftist government that took power in Paris for a few weeks in 1871, before it was brutally repressed. Richardson, *The Death of Reconstruction*.

113. Slap, *The Doom of Reconstruction*, 209.

114. Ibid., 211.

115. Ibid.

116. Ibid., 83.

117. McPherson, *Ordeal by Fire*, 604.

118. Fitzgerald, *Splendid Failure*, 194.

119. Budiansky, *The Bloody Shirt*, 73.

120. Foner, *Reconstruction*, 410.

121. In 1876, Republican candidate Rutherford B. Hayes and Democratic candidate Samuel J. Tilden both claimed to have received the most votes in Florida, Louisiana, and South Carolina, and therefore to have won the election. Eventually, the Democrats acquiesced in the victory of Hayes. The quid pro quo was the termination of the nation-building mission in the South. Zuczek, *State of Rebellion*, chap. 9; Foner, *Reconstruction*, 582.

122. DuBois, *Black Reconstruction in America*, 30.

123. Kennedy, *Profiles in Courage*, chap. 7.

124. Foner, *Forever Free*, 231.

Chapter 5. Heel of Achilles

1. Dunne, *Mr. Dooley in Peace and in War*, 44.

2. Bouvier, "Imaging a Nation," 94; Rourke, *Presidential Wars and American Democracy*, 77.

3. Kagan, *Dangerous Nation*, 399.

4. Karnow, *In Our Image*, 94; McCartney, *Power and Progress*, 99.

5. May, *Imperial Democracy*, 142. For a skeptical take on the relationship between the sinking of the *Maine* and the decision to attack Cuba, see Pérez, "The Meaning of the Maine."

6. Wilkerson, *Public Opinion and the Spanish-American War*, 117.

7. Jewett, *The Captain America Complex*, 44.

8. Miller, *"Benevolent Assimilation,"* 11.

9. Pratt, *Expansionists of 1898*, 282–83; Hamilton, *President McKinley, War and Empire*, 156, 196; Gleijeses, "1898," 685.

10. Gould, *The Presidency of William McKinley*, 85.

11. Silbey, *A War of Frontier and Empire,* 37.

12. Barrett, *Admiral George Dewey,* 59.

13. Hoganson, *Fighting for American Manhood,* 142.

14. McCartney, *Power and Progress,* 184–85.

15. Walker, "Last of the Rough Riders," 47.

16. McCartney, *Power and Progress,* 129.

17. May, *Imperial Democracy,* 245.

18. Gleijeses, "1898," 705; Love, *Race over Empire,* 160–61.

19. Dunne, *Mr. Dooley in Peace and in War,* 43.

20. May, *American Imperialism,* 188–89; May, *Imperial Democracy,* 255.

21. May, *Imperial Democracy,* 259; Dallek, *The American Style of Foreign Policy,* 23–24; Smith, "William McKinley's Enduring Legacy," 209, 236.

22. Ninkovich, *The United States and Imperialism,* 35; Smith, *The Spanish-American War,* 203.

23. Offner, *An Unwanted War,* 198–204, 213; May, *Imperial Democracy,* 246; McCartney, *Power and Progress,* 207–19; Smith, "William McKinley's Enduring Legacy," 226; Karnow, *In Our Image,* 127; Love, *Race over Empire,* 174–75.

24. The $20 million price tag seems expensive compared to earlier territorial deals in American history. After all, Manhattan Island was purchased in 1626 for $24, and the value of the land had appreciated astronomically, to around $120 billion, in 2008. But if the same $24 had been invested at 6 percent compound annual interest, it would have been worth nearly $204 billion in 2008 — almost enough for two Manhattans. By contrast, if the $20 million paid to Spain had been invested at 6 percent in 1899, it would have amounted to a mere $14 billion in 2008. This calculation assumes a 6 percent interest rate, with interest compounded every month at one-twelfth the yearly rate. See also William D. Nordhaus, "The Question of Global Warming: An Exchange," *New York Review of Books,* September 25, 2008, 93.

25. Smith, *The Spanish-American War,* 199.

26. McCartney, *Power and Progress,* 249–51.

27. Osgood, *Ideals and Self-Interest in America's Foreign Relations,* 35; Stephanson, *Manifest Destiny,* 84–87.

28. McDougall, *Promised Land, Crusader State,* 112.

29. May, *Imperial Democracy,* 259.

30. McCartney, *Power and Progress,* 227.

31. Jewett and Lawrence, *Captain America and the Crusade Against Evil,* 71.

32. Pratt, *Expansionists of 1898,* 314; McCartney, *Power and Progress,* 148.

33. McCartney, *Power and Progress,* 75–76; McDougall, *Promised Land, Crusader State,* 112.

34. Ninkovich, *The United States and Imperialism,* 39.

35. Olcott, *The Life of William McKinley,* 109–11.

36. Dunne, *Mr. Dooley Remembers,* 305.

37. Jewett, *Mission and Menace,* 149.

38. McCartney, *Power and Progress*, 162.
39. Ibid., 168–69.
40. Linderman, *The Mirror of War*, 92–93.
41. McCartney, *Power and Progress*, 152.
42. Mayers, *Wars and Peace*, 25.
43. McCartney, *Power and Progress*, 80; Beisner, *Twelve Against Empire*, xiv.
44. McCartney, *Power and Progress*, 187.
45. Holsinger, ed., *War and American Popular Culture*, 188.
46. McClure and Morris, *The Authentic Life of William McKinley*, 229.
47. Walker, "Last of the Rough Riders," 43–44.
48. McCartney, *Power and Progress*, 221–22.
49. Mayers, *Wars and Peace*, 30; May, *Imperial Democracy*, 253–54; Love, *Race over Empire*, 167–68.
50. Kaplan, "George Dewey," 165
51. Hoganson, *Fighting for American Manhood*, 110–11.
52. Linderman, *The Mirror of War*, 175.
53. Hoganson, *Fighting for American Manhood*, 86.
54. Hubbell and Beaty. *An Introduction to Poetry*, 92–4; Brantlinger, "Kipling's 'The White Man's Burden' and Its Afterlives," 172.
55. Linn, *The Philippine War*, 325.
56. Boot, *The Savage Wars of Peace*, 128.
57. May, "Why the United States Won the Philippine-American War," 365; Linn, *The Philippine War*, 322.
58. Miller, *"Benevolent Assimilation,"* 167; Tierney, *Chasing Ghosts*, 130–34.
59. Hoganson, *Fighting for American Manhood*, 7; Barnet, *The Rockets' Red Glare*, 137.
60. Linn, *The Echo of Battle*, 83.
61. Silbey, *A War of Frontier and Empire*, 195.
62. Boot, *The Savage Wars of Peace*, 100–102.
63. McCartney, *Power and Progress*, 261–62; Miller, *"Benevolent Assimilation,"* 114–15, 250; Rystad, *Ambiguous Imperialism*, 201; Hoganson, *Fighting for American Manhood*, 145; Welch, *Response to Imperialism*, 94.
64. Miller, *"Benevolent Assimilation,"* 115–17; Welch, *Response to Imperialism*, 61, 119; Rystad, *Ambiguous Imperialism*, chap. 4; Beisner, *Twelve Against Empire*, 165.
65. Mark Twain, "Mark Twain, the Greatest American Humorist, Returning Home," *New York World*, October 6, 1900; Welch, *Response to Imperialism*, 124–25.
66. The poem was first published in the *New York Times*, February 15, 1899. Several other versions were published elsewhere.
67. Trefousse, *Carl Schurz*, 285, 288.
68. Rystad, *Ambiguous Imperialism*, chaps. 8, 9.
69. Miller, *"Benevolent Assimilation,"* 152; McDougall, *Promised Land, Crusader State*, 114.

70. Brands, *Bound to Empire*, 84.
71. Mayers, *Dissenting Voices in America's Rise to Power*, 193; Karnow, *In Our Image*, 150–51.
72. Osgood, *Ideals and Self-Interest in America's Foreign Relations*, 53.
73. Brands, *Bound to Empire*, 84; Osgood, *Ideals and Self-Interest in America's Foreign Relations*, 53; Karnow, *In Our Image*, 80; McDougall, *Promised Land, Crusader State*, 114; Love, *Race over Empire*, 196.
74. Bender, *A Nation Among Nations*, 239; Dallek, *The American Style of Foreign Policy*, 29; Love, *Race over Empire*, 197; May, *American Imperialism*, 218.
75. Karnow, *In Our Image*, 197.
76. Ninkovich, *The United States and Imperialism*, 68; Smith, *America's Mission*, chap. 2; Karnow, *In Our Image*, 197; Stanley, *A Nation in the Making*, 103, 106.
77. Silbey, *A War of Frontier and Empire*, 211.
78. May, *Social Engineering in the Philippines*, 95.
79. Ibid., 71–72; Karnow, *In Our Image*, 238; Brands, *Bound to Empire*, 146, 153.
80. Boot, *The Savage Wars of Peace*, 125.
81. Tompkins, *Anti-imperialism in the United States*, 274.
82. Brands, *Bound to Empire*, 104.
83. Ibid., 163.
84. Kramer, *The Blood of Government*, 424.
85. Smith, "William McKinley's Enduring Legacy," 210–12.
86. See, for example, Schirmer, *Republic or Empire*.
87. Linn, *The Philippine War;* Boot, *The Savage Wars of Peace;* Gates, *Schoolbooks and Krags*.
88. Welch, *Response to Imperialism*, 24; Miller, "*Benevolent Assimilation*," 179.
89. Miller, "*Benevolent Assimilation*," 153.
90. Kinzer, *Overthrow*, 54; Miller, "*Benevolent Assimilation*," 208.
91. Buckley, *American Patriots*, 153.
92. Ninkovich, *The United States and Imperialism*, 39; Kramer, *The Blood of Government*.
93. Miller, "*Benevolent Assimilation*," 102.
94. Asprey, *War in the Shadows*, 129; Tierney, *Chasing Ghosts*, 127; Karnow, *In Our Image*, 147.
95. Gates, *Schoolbooks and Krags*, 112.
96. Karnow, *In Our Image*, 207–8.
97. Kennan, *American Diplomacy*, 16.
98. Rystad, *Ambiguous Imperialism*, 235.
99. Painter, *Standing at Armageddon*, 159.
100. Mayers, *Wars and Peace*, 33.
101. Miller, "*Benevolent Assimilation*," 122.
102. Beisner, *Twelve Against Empire*, 77; Fry, *Dixie Looks Abroad*, 118, 129.
103. Hixson, *The Myth of American Diplomacy*, 105; Markowitz, *American Anti-imperialism*, 177.

104. Love, *Race over Empire*, 14.
105. Miller, *"Benevolent Assimilation,"* 37.

Chapter 6. To End All War

1. "Over There—and Gone Forever," *New York Times,* November 12, 2007.
2. Harries and Harries, *The Last Days of Innocence,* 65.
3. Rochester, *American Liberal Disillusionment,* 37; Fleming, *The Illusion of Victory,* 94; LeShan, *The Psychology of War,* 67.
4. Dawley, *Changing the World,* 145.
5. Jewett, *The Captain America Complex,* 48; Traxel, *Crusader Nation,* 277.
6. "President Wilson's Address to the United States Senate, on Essential Terms of Peace in Europe," January 22, 1917, Wilson, *President Wilson's State Papers and Addresses,* 352.
7. Ibid., 372–83.
8. Ibid., 418.
9. Ambrosius, *Wilsonian Statecraft,* 103.
10. "Wilson's Address to Congress, Stating the War Aims and Peace Terms of the United States," January 8, 1918, Wilson, *President Wilson's State Papers and Addresses,* 464–72; Gale, *Americanism,* 94–100; Calhoun, *Power and Principle,* 174–75.
11. "The President's Triumph," *New York Times,* January 11, 1918; "The President Speaks," *New York Times,* September 28, 1918; Knock, *To End All Wars,* 146, 164; Osgood, *Ideals and Self-Interest in America's Foreign Relations,* 258, 274–78.
12. Mayers, *Dissenting Voices in America's Rise to Power,* 239; Cooper, *The Vanity of Power,* 206; Chatfield, "World War I and the Liberal Pacifists in the United States," 1931.
13. Mayers, *Dissenting Voices in America's Rise to Power,* 240–41; Kennedy, *Over Here,* 49–50; Chatfield, "World War I and the Liberal Pacifists in the United States"; Traxel, *Crusader Nation,* 336.
14. Meigs, *Optimism at Armageddon,* 14; Gamble, *The War for Righteousness,* 151.
15. Owen and Lewis, *The Collected Poems of Wilfred Owen,* 191.
16. I use "Allies" here as shorthand for Britain, France, Italy, Russia, the United States, and other aligned countries. Technically, Britain, France, and Russia were known as the Triple Entente, and the United States was an "associated power" rather than a formal ally.
17. Ferrell, *Woodrow Wilson and World War I,* 81.
18. Freidel, *Over There,* 274–75.
19. Tiebout, *A History of the 305th Infantry,* 157–58.
20. Carroll, *War Letters,* 144.
21. Kennedy, *Over Here,* 212–13.
22. Farwell, *Over There,* 19.
23. Kennedy, *Over Here,* 184–85.
24. Endy, "Just War, Holy War," 25.

NOTES

25. Harries and Harries, *The Last Days of Innocence*, 193.
26. Hart, *Selected Addresses and Public Papers of Woodrow Wilson*, 266–69.
27. Armstrong, *Unconditional Surrender*, 15.
28. Kennedy, *The Will to Believe*, 150–52.
29. Cooper, *The Warrior and the Priest*, 327.
30. Fleming, *The Illusion of Victory*, 278; Livermore, *Politics Is Adjourned*, 210–23.
31. Mead, *The Doughboys*, 328.
32. Rochester, *American Liberal Disillusionment*, 48.
33. Kennedy, *The Will to Believe*, 166.
34. Fleming, *The Illusion of Victory*, 285–89; Harries and Harries, *The Last Days of Innocence*, 407.
35. "Wilson's Address to Congress Advising that Germany's Course Be Declared War Against the United States," April 2, 1917, Wilson, *President Wilson's State Papers and Addresses*, 372–83.
36. Downes, *Targeting Civilians in War*, 87; Gilbert, *The First World War*, 541.
37. "Germany Not Far from Collapse," *New York Times*, March 3, 1918.
38. Fleming, *The Illusion of Victory*, 194–95.
39. Capozzola, *Uncle Sam Wants You*, 208.
40. Esposito, *The Legacy of Woodrow Wilson*, 127.
41. Wilson and Link, *The Papers of Woodrow Wilson*, 441; Widenor, *Henry Cabot Lodge*, 272–73.
42. Kane, *Between Virtue and Power*, 167.
43. Heffner, *A Documentary History of the United States*, 291; Ambrosius, *Woodrow Wilson and the American Diplomatic Tradition*, chaps. 2, 3.
44. Dallek, *The American Style of Foreign Policy*, 64–65.
45. "President Wilson's Address to Congress, Analyzing German and Austrian Peace Utterances," February 11, 1918, Wilson, *President Wilson's State Papers and Addresses*, 474; Pearlman, *Warmaking and American Democracy*, 31.
46. Nordholt, *Woodrow Wilson*, 258–59.
47. Kennedy, *Over Here*, 207.
48. Linenthal, *Changing Images of the Warrior Hero in America*, 98–104.
49. Carroll, *War Letters*, 129.
50. Wilson and Link, *The Papers of Woodrow Wilson*, 558.
51. Cooper, *The Warrior and the Priest*, 327.
52. Leonard, *Above the Battle*, 132.
53. Karp, *The Politics of War*, 320; Chatfield, "World War I and the Liberal Pacifists in the United States," 1926; Gamble, *The War for Righteousness*, 195.
54. Cooper, *The Vanity of Power*, 194–95; Stephanson, *Manifest Destiny*, 114–15; Bacevich, *The New American Militarism*, 11; Calhoun, *Power and Principle*, 19.
55. Unger, *Fighting Bob La Follette*, 271.
56. Jewett and Lawrence, *Captain America and the Crusade Against Evil*, 73; Dawley, *Changing the World*, 128–30; Farwell, *Over There*, 129; Gamble, *The War for Righteousness*.

57. Osgood, *Ideals and Self-Interest in America's Foreign Relations*, 277–78.
58. Nordholt, *Woodrow Wilson*, 235.
59. Traxel, *Crusader Nation*, 286–87.
60. Gamble, *The War for Righteousness*, 179.
61. Thompson, "Progressive Publicists and the First World War," 381; Kennedy, *Over Here*, 50.
62. Putnam, *Theodore Roosevelt*, 277.
63. Gamble, *The War for Righteousness*, 157, 172.
64. Dawley, *Changing the World*, 145; Gamble, *The War for Righteousness*, 174.
65. Widenor, *Henry Cabot Lodge*, 284–85.
66. Ibid., 276; Fry, *Dixie Looks Abroad*, 162.
67. "Wilson's Address to Congress Advising that Germany's Course Be Declared War Against the United States," April 2, 1917, Wilson, *President Wilson's State Papers and Addresses*, 372–83.
68. Gamble, *The War for Righteousness*, 162.
69. Thompson, *Woodrow Wilson*, 175.
70. Knock, *To End All Wars*, 174.
71. Kennedy, *The Will to Believe*, 158.
72. Barnet, *The Rockets' Red Glare*, 146.
73. Kennedy, *Over Here*, 68.
74. Nordholt, *Woodrow Wilson*, 270.
75. Mead, *The Doughboys*, 397–99.
76. Ferrell, *Woodrow Wilson and World War I*, 133.
77. Gallup, *The Gallup Polls*, 54–65, 253.
78. Osgood, *Ideals and Self-Interest in America's Foreign Relations*, 299.
79. Divine, *Perpetual War for Perpetual Peace*, 22.
80. The National World War I Museum at Liberty Memorial is in Kansas City, Missouri.
81. McDougall, *Promised Land, Crusader State*, 131.
82. Blassingame, "The Press and American Intervention in Haiti and the Dominican Republic," 35.
83. Boot, *The Savage Wars of Peace*, 156; Rotberg, *Haiti*, 138.
84. Blassingame, "The Press and American Intervention in Haiti and the Dominican Republic," 29.
85. Schoultz, *Beneath the United States*, 255.
86. Schmitz, *Henry L. Stimson*, 47.
87. Gobat, *Confronting the American Dream*, 235–38.
88. Langley, *The Banana Wars*, 195.
89. Tierney, *Chasing Ghosts*, 192–93; Blassingame, "The Press and American Intervention in Haiti and the Dominican Republic."
90. Roosevelt, "Our Foreign Policy," 584; Pike, *FDR's Good Neighbor Policy*, 130–32.
91. Smith, *America's Mission*, 120–21.

92. Musicant, *The Banana Wars*, 234.
93. Calder, *The Impact of Intervention*, 251.
94. Healy, *Drive to Hegemony*, 289.
95. Langley, *The United States and the Caribbean in the Twentieth Century*, 92; Musicant, *The Banana Wars*, chap. 5; Tierney, *Chasing Ghosts*, 178; Schmidt, *The United States Occupation of Haiti*, 186–87.
96. Boot, *The Savage Wars of Peace*, 251.
97. Wood, *The Making of the Good Neighbor Policy*, 155.
98. LaFeber, *Inevitable Revolutions*, 69.
99. Wood, *The Making of the Good Neighbor Policy*, 152.
100. Schoultz, *Beneath the United States*, 268.
101. Healy, *Drive to Hegemony*, 288; Wood, *The Making of the Good Neighbor Policy*, 26.
102. Schmitz, *Thank God They're on Our Side*, 28.
103. Schmidt, *The United States Occupation of Haiti*, 155.
104. Boot, *The Savage Wars of Peace*, 161–62.
105. Woodiwiss, *Organized Crime and American Power*, 190.
106. Ninkovich, *The United States and Imperialism*, 137.
107. McPherson, "Americanism Against American Empire," 181.
108. Healy, *Drive to Hegemony*, 228.
109. Tierney, *Chasing Ghosts*, 184; Schoultz, *Beneath the United States*, 265.
110. Pike, *FDR's Good Neighbor Policy*, 167.
111. Schoultz, *Beneath the United States*, 267.
112. Schmidt, *The United States Occupation of Haiti*, 214.
113. Pike, *FDR's Good Neighbor Policy*, 134.
114. McPherson, "Americanism Against American Empire," 180.
115. Ninkovich, *The United States and Imperialism*, 136.
116. Gobat, *Confronting the American Dream*, 270.
117. Blassingame, "The Press and American Intervention in Haiti and the Dominican Republic," 39; Dawley, *Changing the World*, 103.
118. Millett, *The Politics of Intervention*, 252.

Chapter 7. When the Saints Go Marching In

1. Carroll, *War Letters*, 189.
2. Gardner, *The Last of the Hitlers*.
3. Barnet, *The Rockets' Red Glare*, 187; Casey, *Cautious Crusade*, 24–30.
4. http://www.history.navy.mil/faqs/faq66-1.htm.
5. Linenthal, *Changing Images of the Warrior Hero in America*, 116; Rose, *Myth and the Greatest Generation*, 70; O'Neill, *A Democracy at War*, 130. The verses are part of "An Ode of Dedication," by Hermann Hagedorn, which was originally read before the Harvard Chapter of Phi Beta Kappa in June 1917.
6. Schroeder, "Alliances," 254.

7. Franklin Roosevelt, "Address to Congress Requesting a Declaration of War with Japan," December 8, 1941, http://www.presidency.ucsb.edu/ws/index.php?pid=16053; Jewett and Lawrence, *Captain America and the Crusade Against Evil*, 76.
8. Casey, *Cautious Crusade*, 110.
9. Larson, *Casualties and Consensus*, 16; Casey, *Cautious Crusade*, 119, 208; Armstrong, *Unconditional Surrender*.
10. McDougall, *Promised Land, Crusader State*, 152.
11. Divine, *Second Chance*, 69, 134; Leigh, *Mobilizing Consent*, 115; Sobel, *The Impact of Public Opinion on U.S. Foreign Policy Since Vietnam*, 28; Dallek, *The American Style of Foreign Policy*, 132.
12. Rose, *Myth and the Greatest Generation*, 65.
13. Berinsky, *In Time of War*, chaps. 3, 6; Casey, *Cautious Crusade*, 151.
14. Randall Jarrell, "Losses" (1948), available in Goldensohn, *American War Poetry*, 208.
15. Downes, *Targeting Civilians in War*, 1–2, 116.
16. Rose, *Myth and the Greatest Generation*, 218–19.
17. Buley, *The New American Way of War*, 25; Downes, *Targeting Civilians in War*, 136; Hopkins, "Bombing and the American Conscience During World War II."
18. Armstrong, *Unconditional Surrender*, 17.
19. Fussell, *Wartime*, 167.
20. Leigh, *Mobilizing Consent*, 80.
21. Dallek, *The American Style of Foreign Policy*, 136–38; Leigh, *Mobilizing Consent*, 79–80; Blum, *V Was for Victory*, 29.
22. Fischer, *Liberty and Freedom*, 556–58.
23. Carroll, *War Letters*, 188.
24. Jewett and Lawrence, *Captain America and the Crusade Against Evil*, 76.
25. Sittser, *A Cautious Patriotism*, 99, 122.
26. Divine, *Second Chance*, 161; Sittser, *A Cautious Patriotism*, 236–37; Abrams, *Preachers Present Arms*, 272.
27. Dallek, *The American Style of Foreign Policy*, 134. A Gallup poll on December 12–17, 1941, revealed that only 21 percent of Americans thought that U.S. entry into World War I in 1917 was a mistake—down from 39 percent in a Gallup poll on January 24-29, 1941. All polling data, for the remainder of the book, is from the Roper Center for Public Opinion Research (http://www.ropercenter.uconn.edu/) or http://www.pollingreport.com, unless otherwise specified.
28. Divine, *Second Chance*, 169–71.
29. Stouffer et al., *The American Soldier*; Westbrook, "Fighting for the American Family"; Rose, *Myth and the Greatest Generation*, 62, 280.
30. Richler, *Writers on World War II*, 365.
31. Rose, *Myth and the Greatest Generation*, 42.
32. Ibid., 109.
33. Fussell, *Wartime*, 132; Rose, *Myth and the Greatest Generation*, 68.
34. Steinbeck, *Once There Was a War*, 13.

35. Sittser, *A Cautious Patriotism,* 17.
36. Rose, *Myth and the Greatest Generation,* 77; Stouffer et al., *The American Soldier;* Barnet, *The Rockets' Red Glare,* 225.
37. Abzug, *Inside the Vicious Heart,* 30.
38. Rose, *Myth and the Greatest Generation,* 212.
39. Liberman and Skitka, "Just Deserts in Iraq," 6.
40. Roosevelt, "Address to Congress Requesting a Declaration of War with Japan"; Blum, *V Was for Victory,* 4.
41. Dower, *War Without Mercy,* 48.
42. Casey, *Cautious Crusade,* 47.
43. Rose, *Myth and the Greatest Generation,* 13; Dallek, *The American Style of Foreign Policy,* 148.
44. Sittser, *A Cautious Patriotism,* 217.
45. McCullough, *Truman,* 554. See also Schaffer, *Wings of Judgment.*
46. Mueller, "Fifteen Propositions About American Foreign Policy," 8.
47. Dower, *War Without Mercy,* 53.
48. Overy, *Why the Allies Won,* 294; Berinsky, *In Time of War,* chap. 3.
49. Dower, *War Without Mercy,* 55.
50. Fischer, *Liberty and Freedom,* 517.
51. Jewett, *The Captain America Complex,* 53.
52. Mead, *Special Providence,* 257.
53. Barnet, *The Rockets' Red Glare,* 253; Holsti, *Public Opinion and American Foreign Policy,* 29–30; Almond, *The American People and Foreign Policy,* 73–76.
54. Terkel, *"The Good War"*; Brokaw, *The Greatest Generation;* Ambrose, *Citizen Soldiers.* The Vietnam generation was more likely than the World War II generation to remember World War II as the good war, where people united to fight for freedom. Schuman and Scott, "Generations and Collective Memories," 374.
55. Davies, *No Simple Victory,* 25.
56. Sittser, *A Cautious Patriotism,* 178.
57. Sherry, *In the Shadow of War,* 96.
58. Glad and Rosenberg, "Bargaining Under Fire," 188.
59. Berinsky, *In Time of War,* chap. 1; Dallek, *The American Style of Foreign Policy,* 183; Gelpi, Feaver, and Reifler, *Paying the Human Costs of War,* 25.
60. Carroll, *War Letters,* 336.
61. Sherry, *In the Shadow of War,* 181; Mead, *Special Providence,* 219; Wiltz, "The Korean War and American Society," 122.
62. Berinsky, *In Time of War,* chap. 1.
63. Lienesch, *Redeeming America,* 202.
64. Linenthal, *Changing Images of the Warrior Hero in America,* 141; Foot, *A Substitute for Victory,* 138–39.
65. Whitfield, "Korea, the Cold War, and American Democracy," 220.
66. "General Douglas MacArthur's Address to Congress," April 19, 1951, in Ford, *Issues of War and Peace,* 248–50.

67. Mueller, *War, Presidents and Public Opinion*, 103–5; Glad and Rosenberg, "Bargaining Under Fire," 186–87; Fry, *Dixie Looks Abroad*, 232.

68. Glad and Rosenberg, "Bargaining Under Fire," 189–90; Dallek, *Lone Star Rising*, 398; Casey, *Selling the Korean War*, 235.

69. Carroll, *War Letters*, 353.

70. Small, *Democracy and Diplomacy*, 95.

71. Another important factor that took the wind out of America's crusading sails was the dovishness of U.S. allies, who were eager to end the war with a negotiated settlement. Fearing potential escalation, the allies resisted U.S. efforts to pass a UN resolution branding China an aggressor. The effect was to confuse the American people and challenge the popular image of the war as good against evil. According to the State Department in January 1951, "The UN debate on the aggressor resolution tended to detract from the unequivocal moral position of the UN." The effect was to encourage Americans to seek an exit strategy short of absolute victory. Casey, *Selling the Korean War*, 212–14, 263; Larson, *Casualties and Consensus*, 58; Mueller, *Policy and Opinion in the Gulf War*, 100.

72. Huebner, *The Warrior Image*, 126.

73. Buchanan, *Vietnam Zippos;* John F. Kennedy, "Inaugural Address," January 20, 1961 http://www.presidency.ucsb.edu/ws/index.php?pid=8032.

74. Fry, *Dixie Looks Abroad*, 267.

75. Record, *The Wrong War*, 24; Khong, *Analogies at War*, chap. 5.

76. Ferguson, *Colossus*, 97. Even among Vietnam War hawks, memories of Chinese intervention in Korea tended to induce caution about invading North Vietnam.

77. Harris survey, February 1965.

78. Larson, *Casualties and Consensus*, 24, 61-63; Huebner, *The Warrior Image*, 172; Lunch and Sperlich, "Public Opinion and the War in Vietnam"; Mueller, *War, Presidents and Public Opinion*, chap. 4.

79. Lyrics available at http://www.lyricstime.com.

80. Mueller, *War, Presidents and Public Opinion*, 86.

81. Huebner, *The Warrior Image*, 203.

82. Hunt, *Pacification*, 141–43; Huebner, *The Warrior Image*, 204.

83. Olson and Roberts, *Where the Domino Fell*, 187.

84. Gelpi, Feaver, and Reifler, *Paying the Human Costs of War*, 30; Mueller, *War, Presidents and Public Opinion*, 106.

85. Rottinghaus, "Following the 'Mail Hawks,'" 375.

86. Carroll, *War Letters*, 413.

87. Ibid., 425.

88. Franklin, *Vietnam and Other American Fantasies*, 140–48. The presentation of war in *Star Trek* was subtle and ambiguous, and several early episodes, such as "Errand of Mercy" (1967), suggest doubts about the military strategy in the Cold War.

89. Schneider, "'Rambo' and Reality," 54; Mueller, *Policy and Opinion in the Gulf War*, 111.

90. Summers, *On Strategy,* 184; Hoffman, *Decisive Force,* 23.

91. Ronald Reagan, "Address to the Veterans of Foreign Wars Convention," August 18, 1980.

92. Ronald Reagan, "Remarks on Presenting the Medal of Honor," February 24, 1981; Bacevich, *The New American Militarism,* 107.

93. Gallup poll, May 17–22, 1946; National Opinion Research Center poll, December 1946.

94. Harris poll, October 1965; Chicago Council on Foreign Relations poll, December 6–14, 1974; Mueller, "Changes in American Public Attitudes Toward International Involvement," 329–37.

95. Kaiser, *American Tragedy,* 427.

96. Vertzberger, *The World in Their Minds,* 272–73; Krepinevich, *The Army and Vietnam;* Shafer, *Deadly Paradigms.*

97. Dobbins et al., *After the War,* xiii, chap. 3. Critics rightly point out that other factors played a crucial role in the transition of these societies to democratic prosperity, including the preexisting level of social development, the experience of total defeat, and the Cold War context. But in a counterfactual scenario *without* U.S. nation-building in the former Axis states, far less favorable outcomes are easily imaginable. Furthermore, there is a basic inconsistency. Critics often dilute the credit given to the United States for the outcome in Germany and Japan because broader forces help to explain success. But these same critics rarely look at other, more problematic cases of nation-building and dilute their censure of the United States on the grounds that broader forces explain failure. For skeptics, success in nation-building has a thousand causal fathers, while failure has just one — the United States.

98. Brazinksy, *Nation Building in South Korea.*

99. Karabell, *Architects of Intervention,* chaps. 7, 8; Little, "His Finest Hour?"

100. Crandall, *Gunboat Diplomacy,* 92; Palmer, *Intervention in the Caribbean,* 160; Smith, *America's Mission,* 228–32; Lowenthal, *The Dominican Intervention.*

101. Dower, *War Without Mercy,* 13.

102. Powers, *The War at Home,* 177.

103. Sherry, *In the Shadow of War,* 319.

104. Macdonald, *Adventures in Chaos.*

105. Greene, *The Quiet American.*

106. Johnson, *Overconfidence and War,* chap. 6; Baritz, *Backfire,* chap. 1; McDougall, *Promised Land, Crusader State,* 188.

107. Sherry, *In the Shadow of War,* 285; Jordan, Taylor, and Mazarr, *American National Security,* 245; Krepinevich, *The Army and Vietnam.*

108. Powell, *My American Journey,* 84.

109. Huebner, *The Warrior Image,* 110, 188.

110. Dower, *War Without Mercy,* 64.

111. In 2001, it was revealed that Senator Bob Kerrey took part in a military operation during the Vietnam War in which civilians were killed. (Whether they

died mistakenly or because of deliberate actions is disputed.) Kerrey noted that if the incident had happened during World War II rather than Vietnam, it wouldn't have produced the same media criticism. Adams, *Echoes of War,* 197.

112. Logevall, *Choosing War,* 386–87; Macdonald, *Adventures in Chaos,* 23–24.
113. Summers, *On Strategy,* 171.
114. Gillette, *Retreat from Reconstruction,* 310.
115. Fry, *Dixie Looks Abroad,* 232.
116. Ibid., 252.
117. Fite, *Richard B. Russell,* 219, 350, 355, 393.
118. Russell, Logue, and Freshley, *Voice of Georgia,* 281.
119. Woods, "Dixie's Dove," 153–66; Fry, *Dixie Looks Abroad,* 236, 276.
120. Ferguson, *Colossus,* 101.
121. Buley, *The New American Way of War,* 74.
122. Gelpi, Feaver, and Reifler, *Paying the Human Costs of War,* 33–37.
123. Handel, *Masters of War,* Appendix B, 234–47.
124. Entman, *Projections of Power,* 55.
125. Wittkopf, Jones, and Kegley, *American Foreign Policy,* 278.
126. Entman, *Projections of Power,* 66, 69; Hoffman, *Decisive Force,* chap. 4; Gelpi, Feaver, and Reifler, *Paying the Human Costs of War,* 37.
127. Gillen, "Captain America, Post-Traumatic Stress Syndrome, and the Vietnam Era," 112; Wright, *Comic Book Nation.*

Chapter 8. Black Gold and Black Hawks

1. Mueller, "American Public Opinion and the Gulf War," 211; "Pregnant Troops Leave the War; Central Command Not Counting," *Washington Times,* June 15, 2004; "36 Women Pregnant Aboard a Navy Ship That Served in Gulf," *New York Times,* April 30, 1991.
2. Mueller, *Policy and Opinion in the Gulf War,* xiii; Hoffman, *Decisive Force,* 78.
3. Lyrics available at http://www.allthelyrics.com.
4. Mueller, *Policy and Opinion in the Gulf War,* 18; Simpson, *From the House of War,* 18.
5. Mueller, *Policy and Opinion in the Gulf War,* 55; Biddle, *Military Power,* 1; Sobel, *The Impact of Public Opinion on U.S. Foreign Policy Since Vietnam,* 146–50; Allen et al., "The Media and the Gulf War," 256–57.
6. Rozell, "Media Coverage of the Persian Gulf War," 164; Hallin, "Images of the Vietnam and the Persian Gulf Wars in U.S. Television"; Allen et al., "The Media and the Gulf War."
7. Rozell, "Media Coverage of the Persian Gulf War," 167.
8. Hallin and Gitlin, "The Gulf War as Popular Culture and Television Drama," 158.
9. Adams, *The Best War Ever,* 5.
10. Sobel, *The Impact of Public Opinion on U.S. Foreign Policy Since Vietnam,* 152; Holsti, *Public Opinion and American Foreign Policy,* 61; Mueller, *Policy and Opinion in the Gulf War,* 72.

11. "Hill Democrats Mute Criticism of Bush Actions; Reluctance to Question President Said to Be a Result of Political, Historical Factors," *Washington Post*, February 21, 1991; Dauber, "The Shots Seen 'Round the World," 659.

12. Small, *Democracy and Diplomacy*, 160; Freedman and Karsh, *The Gulf Conflict*, 285.

13. Gacek, *The Logic of Force*, 2.

14. Hoffman, *Decisive Force*, 89.

15. Snow and Drew, *From Lexington to Desert Storm*, 312.

16. Gallup poll, January 23–26, 1991. The following month, 53 percent favored the use of tactical nuclear weapons if Iraq employed chemical or biological weapons. NBC News/*Wall Street Journal* poll, February 26–27, 1991. See also Downes, *Targeting Civilians in War*, 223; Freedman and Karsh, *The Gulf Conflict*, 329; Mueller, *Policy and Opinion in the Gulf War*, 79, 122. For a discussion of gender differences in the willingness to kill Iraqi civilians, see Conover and Sapiro, "Gender, Feminist Consciousness, and War."

17. Freedman and Karsh, *The Gulf Conflict*, 413; Bush and Scowcroft, *A World Transformed*. Although it was the correct strategic decision to avoid escalating the war, Washington could have demanded more Iraqi concessions in exchange for a cease-fire, including a prohibition on the use of helicopters, which would later be employed by Saddam to repress southern Iraqi Shiites who rose up in revolt.

18. Overall backing for the war and for removing Saddam was strong, but there was variation. As usual, men and whites were the most committed supporters of the campaign. Jews also joined the crusading vanguard, in part because Saddam was an old enemy of Israel. Meanwhile, women and blacks were more cautious about both the war itself and marching on Baghdad. Mueller, *Policy and Opinion in the Gulf War*, 78; Mueller, "American Public Opinion and the Gulf War," 204; Conover and Sapiro, "Gender, Feminist Consciousness, and War"; Jelen, "Religion and Foreign Policy Attitudes," 390; Bacevich, *The New American Militarism*, 143; "Holy War Doctrines," *U.S. News and World Report*, February 11, 1991; Liberman, "An Eye for an Eye," 703. See also Gallup polls, October 18–19 and December 6–7, 1990; *USA Today* polls, December 29–30, 1990, and January 16, 1991.

19. *New York Times* poll, February 28, 1991; Mueller, *Policy and Opinion in the Gulf War*, 78; Mueller, "American Public Opinion and the Gulf War," 215.

20. Freedman and Karsh, *The Gulf Conflict*, 412.

21. Gallup poll, April 4–5, 1991.

22. Liberman, "An Eye for an Eye," 697; Elshtain, "Just War as Politics," 49. For the lack of public support for a war to protect oil supplies, see Rourke, *Presidential Wars and American Democracy*, 43.

23. "Bush's Holy War: The Crusader's Cloak Can Grow Heavy on the Shoulders," *New York Times*, February 3, 1991.

24. Mueller, "American Public Opinion and the Gulf War," 213.

25. Bennett, "The Persian Gulf War's Impact on Americans' Political Information," 185.

26. Sherry, *In the Shadow of War,* 472.
27. Elshtain, "Just War as Politics," 49.
28. Hallin and Gitlin, "The Gulf War as Popular Culture and Television Drama," 160.
29. Mueller, "American Public Opinion and the Gulf War," 203.
30. Krebs and Lobasz, "Fixing the Meaning of 9/11," 442.
31. Dumbrell, "The US Congress and the Gulf War," 60.
32. Liberman, "An Eye for an Eye"; Liberman, "Punitiveness and U.S. Elite Support for the 1991 Persian Gulf War," 4–5.
33. Hoffman, *Decisive Force,* 88; Foyle, *Counting the Public In,* 214; Schuman and Rieger, "Historical Analogies, Generational Effects, and Attitudes Toward War," 316–17; Liberman, "Punitiveness and U.S. Elite Support for the 1991 Persian Gulf War," 11.
34. Liberman, "An Eye for an Eye," 698.
35. Schuman and Rieger, "Historical Analogies, Generational Effects, and Attitudes Toward War."
36. Martel, *Victory in War,* 193.
37. Liberman, "Punitiveness and U.S. Elite Support for the 1991 Persian Gulf War," 4, 20–26.
38. Mueller, "American Public Opinion and the Gulf War," 213.
39. LeShan, *The Psychology of War,* 96.
40. Sobel, *The Impact of Public Opinion on U.S. Foreign Policy Since Vietnam,* 156; Mueller, *Policy and Opinion in the Gulf War,* 88.
41. Gallup poll, July 31–August 2, 1992; Mueller, *Policy and Opinion in the Gulf War,* 88; Sobel, *The Impact of Public Opinion on U.S. Foreign Policy Since Vietnam,* 157.
42. Carroll, *War Letters,* 462.
43. Mueller, *Policy and Opinion in the Gulf War,* 104.
44. Hoffman, *Decisive Force,* xii.
45. Mueller, *Policy and Opinion in the Gulf War,* 52.
46. Tierney, "America's Quagmire Mentality."
47. Debate in the House of Representatives, October 5, 1993, available at http://thomas.loc.gov/.
48. Weiss, *Military-Civilian Interactions,* 66–69; DiPrizio, *Armed Humanitarians,* 47, 190; Woods, "U.S. Government Decisionmaking Processes During Humanitarian Operations in Somalia," 159; Dobbins et al., *America's Role in Nation-Building,* 64; Seybolt, *Humanitarian Military Intervention,* 55–57; Wheeler, *Saving Strangers,* 189; Mueller, *The Remnants of War,* 127.
49. "Somalia 1992: Picking Up Pieces as Famine Subsides," *New York Times,* December 31, 1992.
50. Johnson and Tierney, *Failing to Win,* 226.
51. Dobbins et al., *America's Role in Nation-Building,* 55–70; Seybolt, *Humanitarian Military Intervention,* 57–60.
52. Crocker, "The Lessons of Somalia," 3.

NOTES

53. Larson and Savych, *American Public Support for U.S. Military Operations*, xx.

54. Johnson and Tierney, *Failing to Win*, chap. 8.

55. "A Common Cry Across the U.S.: It's Time to Exit," *New York Times*, October 9, 1993.

56. Gallup poll, October 5, 1993.

57. Peceny, *Democracy at the Point of Bayonets*, 151; DiPrizio, *Armed Humanitarians*, 93; Weiss, *Military-Civilian Interactions*, 124–25; Dobbins et al., *America's Role in Nation-Building*, 80; Mueller, *The Remnants of War*, 130.

58. "Summary of U.S. Government Policy on Bosnia," released by the U.S. Department of State, Bureau of European and Canadian Affairs, July 16, 1998, http://www.state.gov/www/regions/eur/fs_980716_bosqanda.html; DiPrizio, *Armed Humanitarians*, chap. 6.

59. "Muslims Resurrect a Village," *New York Times*, January 19, 1996.

60. Carroll, *War Letters*, 472.

61. Program on International Policy Attitudes poll, February 13–April 20, 1998; Kull and Ramsay, "U.S. Public Opinion on Intervention in Bosnia," 80.

62. Clark, *Waging Modern War*, 151–52.

63. Curt Tarnoff, "Kosovo: Reconstruction and Development Assistance," Congressional Research Service Report for Congress, June 7, 2001, available at http://www.au.af.mil/au/awc/awcgate/crs/rl30453.pdf; Freedman, "Victims and Victors"; Dobbins et al., *America's Role in Nation-Building*, chap. 7; Totten, "The (Really) Moderate Muslims of Kosovo."

64. Entman, *Projections of Power*, 98–99.

65. Pew Research Center poll, March 15–19, 2000.

66. von Hippel, *Democracy by Force*, 181.

67. According to Department of Defense data, between 1980 and 2008, 24,048 service members were killed in accidents, while 6,270 died in suicides, for an average of 1,045 fatalities per year, or 2.86 per day. U.S. Census Bureau, http://www.census.gov/compendia/statab/2010/tables/10s0504.xls.

68. Gelpi, Feaver, and Reifler, *Paying the Human Costs of War*, 38; Gallup poll, October 8–10, 1993.

69. Gelpi, Feaver, and Reifler, *Paying the Human Costs of War*, 5.

70. Sewall, "Multilateral Peace Operations," 205, 222.

71. Shawcross, *Deliver Us from Evil*, 31, 406.

72. Dempsey, "Fool's Errands," 80.

73. James L. Payne, "Deconstructing Nation Building," *American Conservative*, October 24, 2005, available at http://www.amconmag.com/article/2005/oct/24/00013/.

74. The wider tendency to adopt tough metrics is suggested by two polling questions on Haiti, which were posed to the same group of Americans. A plurality of 43 percent felt that Clinton was doing a "good job" rather than a "poor job" in Haiti. But surprisingly, a plurality of 40 percent also thought that Clinton's policies in Haiti were a "failure." These seem like the same question, but there's a subtle dif-

ference. On the one hand, asking if Clinton was doing a "good job" cued people to think about the difficult nature of the mission, prompting them to be a little more generous in their judgments. On the other hand, inquiring whether the operation was a "success" encouraged Americans to think about whether the outcome in Haiti matched up with their ideals of democracy and stability and to be more skeptical in their evaluations. *Time*/CNN poll, March 29–30, 1995.

75. Larson and Savych, *American Public Support for U.S. Military Operations,* 30.
76. Bill Clinton, "Remarks to Operation Allied Force Troops at Aviano Air Base in Italy," June 22, 1999, http://www.presidency.ucsb.edu/ws/index.php?pid=57773.
77. Noam Chomsky, "Humanitarian Imperialism: The New Doctrine of Imperial Right," *Monthly Review,* September 2008, http://www.chomsky.info/articles/200809--.htm; Chomsky, *The New Military Humanism;* Chomsky, *Hegemony or Survival.*
78. Totten, "The (Really) Moderate Muslims of Kosovo."
79. Bill Clinton, "State of the Union Address," January 23, 1996.
80. "Nation-Building Exposes GOP's House Divided," *Los Angeles Times,* March 21, 2004.
81. Mandelbaum, "Foreign Policy as Social Work."
82. Michael R. Gordon, "Bush Would Stop U.S. Peacekeeping in Balkan Fights," *New York Times,* October 21, 2000; Rice, "Promoting the National Interest."
83. Goodnight and Olson, "Shared Power, Foreign Policy, and Haiti," 613–14.
84. Data from http://www.lexisnexis.com and http://www.newsbank.com.
85. NBC News/*Washington Post* poll, October 22–26, 1993.
86. Gacek, *The Logic of Force,* 290.
87. Fox News poll, April 21–22, 1999.
88. Contrast, for example, the following polls on Somalia: ABC News/*Washington Post* poll, December 11–14, 1992; NBC News/*Wall Street Journal* poll, December 12–15, 1992; Harris poll, December 4–8, 1992.
89. Goodnight and Olson, "Shared Power, Foreign Policy, and Haiti," 616, 623.
90. Buley, *The New American Way of War,* 75.
91. Osama bin Laden, "Declaration of War Against the Americans Occupying the Land of the Two Holy Places," August 23, 1996, http://www.pbs.org/newshour/terrorism/international/fatwa_1996.html.
92. Porter, "Good Anthropology, Bad History," 46.
93. Kull and Ramsay, "U.S. Public Opinion on Intervention in Bosnia," 74. Virginia Page Fortna published a book called *Does Peacekeeping Work?* The answer: "a clear and resounding yes." Even though peacekeeping missions are often deployed in the most difficult and intractable cases of ethnic conflict, they nevertheless reduce the odds of war breaking out again by 55 to 85 percent, by alleviating fear and mistrust and by providing incentives for insurgents to lay down their arms. Fortna, *Does Peacekeeping Work?* 173.
94. Seybolt, *Humanitarian Military Intervention,* 21; DiPrizio, *Armed Humanitarians,* 71, 148–49; Power, *"A Problem from Hell,"* 366.

95. Federation of American Scientists, http://www.fas.org/irp/offdocs/pdd25.htm.
96. "The Second Gore-Bush Presidential Debate," October 11, 2000 http://www.debates.org/index.php?page=october-11-2000-debate-transcript.
97. Gordon and Trainor, *Cobra II*, 14; Dueck, *Reluctant Crusaders*, 149.

Chapter 9. The Bush Warriors

1. *Der Spiegel*, February 18 and March 18, 2002; Spike Harley, "Mr. America," *Sydney Morning Herald*, March 21, 2002; Jewett and Lawrence, *Captain America and the Crusade Against Evil*, 43.
2. Amis, *The Second Plane*, 3.
3. Carroll, *Operation Homecoming*, 3.
4. On March 11, 2004, a series of bombs struck the train system of Madrid, killing 191 people. The following year, on July 7, 2005, four bombs exploded in London, killing 52 people in addition to the bombers.
5. Lustick, *Trapped in the War on Terror*, 16–18; Larson and Savych, *American Public Support for U.S. Military Operations*, 97, 124; Holsti, *Public Opinion and American Foreign Policy*, 275.
6. Entman, *Projections of Power*, 1.
7. "Tillman Set for What Lies Ahead," *New York Times*, February 1, 2003; "A Son's Death, a Mother's Agony, a Country's Shame," *New York Times*, May 8, 2008.
8. O'Hanlon, "A Flawed Masterpiece."
9. A *USA Today*/Gallup poll, November 8–11, 2001, found that 89 percent of Americans believed that the United States did not make a mistake by using force in Afghanistan.
10. George W. Bush, State of the Union address, January 29, 2002, http://www.presidency.ucsb.edu/ws/index.php?pid=29644.
11. Robert Kagan and William Kristol, "Remember the Bush Doctrine," *Weekly Standard*, April 15, 2002, http://www.newamericancentury.org/Editorial-041202.pdf.
12. Larson and Savych, *American Public Support for U.S. Military Operations*, xxiii; Gelpi, Feaver, and Reifler, *Paying the Human Costs of War*, 126–27.
13. "The Second Gore-Bush Presidential Debate."
14. Liberman and Skitka, "Just Deserts in Iraq," 4. The Iraqi Intelligence Service reportedly orchestrated a failed 1993 plot to kill George H. W. Bush with a car bomb during a visit to Kuwait.
15. Everts and Isernia, "The Polls-Trends," 266–71; Holsti, "American Public Opinion on the War in Iraq," 33.
16. Carroll, *Operation Homecoming*, 25.
17. Boot, "The New American Way of War," 44.
18. Franks and McConnell, *American Soldier*, 854.
19. Holsti, "American Public Opinion on the War in Iraq," 4; Larson and Savych, *American Public Support for U.S. Military Operations*, 159.
20. Kohut and Stokes, *America Against the World*, 117; "Different Faiths, Different Messages," Pew Research Center for the People and the Press, March 19, 2003;

"Public Confidence in War Effort Falters," Pew Research Center for the People and the Press, March 25, 2003; Gelpi, Feaver, and Reifler, *Paying the Human Costs of War,* chaps. 5–7.

21. Zogby poll, February 6–8, 2003.

22. Downes, *Targeting Civilians in War,* 2, 233; NBC News/*Wall Street Journal* poll, April 12–13, 2003.

23. On September 26, 2002, thirty-three international relations scholars, including many prominent realists, took out an advertisement in the *New York Times* titled "War with Iraq Is Not in America's National Interest." See also Brent Scowcroft, "Don't Attack Saddam: It Would Undermine Our Antiterror Efforts," *Wall Street Journal,* August 15, 2002.

24. Liberman and Skitka, "Just Deserts in Iraq," 7–8; Everts and Isernia, "The Polls-Trends," 265.

25. Liberman and Skitka, "Just Deserts in Iraq," 4; Boettcher and Cobb, "Echoes of Vietnam?" 839, 843.

26. Monten, "The Roots of the Bush Doctrine," 140–55.

27. Woodward, *Plan of Attack,* 88; Monten, "The Roots of the Bush Doctrine," 140–55. Italics in original.

28. George W. Bush, "Remarks on Coalition Activities in Iraq," Washington, DC, July 23, 2003, http://www.presidency.ucsb.edu/ws/index.php?pid=64466.

29. "Different Faiths, Different Messages."

30. Carroll, *Operation Homecoming,* 245.

31. "A New Crusade Within the GOP," *Los Angeles Times,* March 25, 2007; Marsden, *For God's Sake,* chap. 7; "Different Faiths, Different Messages."

32. George W. Bush, "Address Before a Joint Session of the Congress on the United States Response to the Terrorist Attacks of September 11," September 20, 2001, http://www.presidency.ucsb.edu/ws/index.php?pid=64731.

33. George W. Bush, "Address to the Nation on the Anniversary of the Terrorist Attacks of September 11," September 11, 2002, http://www.presidency.ucsb.edu/ws/index.php?pid=62948.

34. George W. Bush, "Address to the Nation on Iraq from the U.S.S. *Abraham Lincoln,*" May 1, 2003, http://www.presidency.ucsb.edu/ws/index.php?pid=68675.

35. Fayazmanesh, *The United States and Iran,* 119.

36. Bush, "Address to the Nation on Iraq from the U.S.S. *Abraham Lincoln.*"

37. Woodward, *Plan of Attack,* 88–89.

38. See, for example, George W. Bush, "Remarks in a Discussion in Nashua, New Hampshire," August 30, 2004, http://www.presidency.ucsb.edu/ws/index.php?pid=63410.

39. Singer, *The President of Good and Evil,* 2.

40. George W. Bush, "National Day of Prayer and Remembrance for the Victims of the Terrorist Attacks on September 11, 2001," September 13, 2001, http://www.presidency.ucsb.edu/ws/index.php?pid=61759.

41. Liberman and Skitka, "Just Deserts in Iraq," 12.

42. Willman, *Rednecks and Bluenecks;* "Middle America's Soul," *Economist,* December 23, 2006, 45–47; "The Country of Country," *New York Times,* May 11, 2003.

43. "Country Anthem Plays a Drumbeat for War," *USA Today,* February 26, 2003.

44. Liberman and Skitka, "Just Deserts in Iraq," 15.

45. George W. Bush, "Commencement Address at the United States Naval Academy in Annapolis, Maryland," May 27, 2005, http://www.presidency.ucsb.edu/ws/index.php?pid=63919.

46. Dick Cheney, "Remarks by the Vice President to the Council on Foreign Relations," February 15, 2002, http://www.presidency.ucsb.edu/ws/index.php?pid=85613.

47. *Der Spiegel,* October 27, 2008.

48. ABC News/*Washington Post* poll, October 2–6, 2002.

49. Goodson, "Lessons of Nation-Building in Afghanistan"; Mueller, *The Remnants of War,* 134–36; Weiss, *Military-Civilian Interactions,* 167.

50. ABC News/*Washington Post* poll, December 11–14, 2008. In 2003, 76 percent of people perceived the mission as going "very well" or "somewhat well," but by the end of 2008, this figure had fallen to just 27 percent. CBS News polls, March 20–24, 2003, and December 4–7, 2008.

51. "Tillman's Parents Are Critical of Army," *Washington Post,* May 23, 2005; "The Dead-End Inquiry on Tillman," *New York Times,* news blog, July 14, 2008.

52. Brookings Institution, "Afghanistan Index," available at http://www.brookings.edu/foreign-policy/afghanistan-index.aspx.

53. Dobbins et al., *After the War,* 90–103.

54. From 1650 to 1700, adult male literacy rates in rural America were around 55 percent, and in urban areas they were 77 percent. Grubb, "Growth of Literacy in Colonial America," 453-54.

55. Michael O'Hanlon and Bruce Riedel, "What's Right with Afghanistan," *Wall Street Journal,* September 1, 2009; Robert B. Zoellick, "What We Can Achieve in Afghanistan," *Washington Post,* October 30, 2009; Brookings Institution, "Afghanistan Index"; ABC News/BBC/Association for Rural Development poll, December 11–23, 2009.

56. Carroll, *Operation Homecoming,* 70.

57. Johnson and Tierney, *Failing to Win,* 69.

58. Everts and Isernia, "The Polls-Trends," 269–71.

59. Willman, *Rednecks and Bluenecks,* chap. 4; http://www.cowboylyrics.com.

60. Turner, "What Every Soldier Should Know," 9.

61. Ricks, *Fiasco;* Gordon and Trainor, *Cobra II;* Dobbins, "Preparing for Nation-Building," 27; Krepinevich, "How to Win in Iraq."

62. Carroll, *Operation Homecoming,* 299.

63. "Heartfelt Words from Lost Soldiers Reveals Hopes, Fears," *USA Today,* October 25, 2005.

64. Nicholas D. Kristof, "Winners of the Iraq Poetry Contest," *New York Times,* June 10, 2007, http://kristof.blogs.nytimes.com/2007/06/10/winners-of-the-

iraq-poetry-contest/; "Injured in Iraq, a Soldier Is Shattered at Home," *New York Times*, April 5, 2007.

65. Mirra, *Soldiers and Citizens,* 116–21.

66. Dobbins et al., *After the War,* 104–27. See also the data available at the Brookings Institution, http://www.brookings.org/saban/iraq-index.aspx.

67. CBS polls, September 14–16, 2007, and March 12–16, 2009.

68. CBS News/*New York Times* poll, September 19–23, 2009.

69. Liberman, "An Eye for an Eye."

70. Fox News/Opinion Dynamics poll, March 25–26, 2003; CNN/*USA Today*/Gallup poll, March 29–30, 2003.

71. Gelpi, Feaver, and Reifler, *Paying the Human Costs of War,* 63.

72. Susan Jacoby, "Best Is the New Worst," *New York Times,* May 30, 2008.

73. Pew Research Center, "Public Knowledge of Current Affairs Little Changed by News and Information Revolution," April 15, 2007. Ignorance may also produce more favorable views. In 2008, as the situation stabilized in Iraq, the share of news coverage devoted to the Iraq War plummeted. One result was that Americans became less aware of the number of U.S. deaths in Iraq (with only 28 percent correctly identifying the figure of four thousand fatalities). Here, respondents tended to underestimate rather than overestimate the figure. "Awareness of Iraq War Fatalities Plummets," Pew Research Center for the People and the Press, March 12, 2008.

74. Carroll, *Operation Homecoming,* 51.

75. Gelpi, Feaver, and Reifler, "Success Matters," 42; Cobb, Boettcher, and Willingham, "Defining Victory in Iraq."

76. Kahl, "In the Crossfire or the Crosshairs?" 11.

77. George W. Bush, "Address Before a Joint Session of the Congress on the State of the Union," January 23, 2007, http://www.presidency.ucsb.edu/ws/index.php?pid=24446.

78. Paul Wolfowitz, "Veterans of Foreign Wars Remarks," March 11, 2003, http://www.defense.gov/speeches/speech.aspx?speechid=359.

79. Dick Cheney, interview, *Meet the Press,* NBC, March 16, 2003, http://www.mtholyoke.edu/acad/intrel/bush/cheneymeetthepress.htm.

80. George W. Bush, "Remarks on the 20th Anniversary of the National Endowment for Democracy," November 6, 2003, http://www.presidency.ucsb.edu/ws/index.php?pid=844.

81. Monten, "The Roots of the Bush Doctrine," 145.

82. Buley, *The New American Way of War,* 120.

83. George W. Bush, "Remarks to the Troops at Camp As Sayliyah," June 5, 2003, http://www.presidency.ucsb.edu/ws/index.php?pid=64952.

84. Gallup polls, May 5–7 and September 19–21, 2003.

85. "Pfc. Jessica Lynch Isn't Rambo Anymore," *New York Times,* November 9, 2003.

86. Baum and Groeling, "Reality Asserts Itself."

87. American Empire Project, http://www.americanempireproject.com; Bacevich, *The Limits of Power.*

88. Dobbins et al., *After the War,* 91.

89. Donald Rumsfeld, "Beyond Nation Building," February 14, 2003, http://www.defenselink.mil/speeches/speech.aspx?speechid=337.

90. Donald Rumsfeld, press conference, April 11, 2003, http://www.defense.gov/transcripts/transcript.aspx?transcriptid=2367.

91. Mike Pence, "The Republican Future: Big-Government Approach Has Failed," *Washington Times,* December 8, 2008.

92. Rumsfeld, "Beyond Nation Building."

93. Dobbins et al., *After the War;* Dobbins et al., *America's Role in Nation-Building.*

94. Data from http://www.lexisnexis.com and http://www.newsbank.com.

95. Pew polls, 2004–2007; Schuman and Corning, "Comparing Iraq to Vietnam."

96. "Obama's Vietnam," *Newsweek,* February 9, 2009.

97. CNN poll, October 16–18, 2009.

98. Another bias shaping perceptions of success is partisanship. The quagmire tradition became especially pronounced among Democrats, while being resisted by Republicans. One 2004 poll asked people to evaluate their confidence that the United States would succeed in Iraq on a scale from 0 to 10. The average score for Republicans was 7.0 and for Democrats 3.3. Misperceptions abounded on both sides of the aisle. Years after the overthrow of Saddam, many Republicans continued to believe that Iraq possessed weapons of mass destruction (WMD) and the Iraqi dictator was involved in 9/11. Meanwhile, as Democrats grew disillusioned with the war, many of them forgot that they had originally backed the invasion, thinking that Saddam had WMD. Democrats were also slow to acknowledge that the "surge" policy had succeeded in diminishing violence in Iraq. Program on International Policy Attitudes poll, October 2004; Gaines et al., "Same Facts, Different Interpretations"; Schuman and Corning, "Comparing Iraq to Vietnam"; Jacobson, "Perception, Memory, and the Partisan Polarization of Opinion on the Iraq War"; Berinsky, *In Time of War.*

99. Lawrence Freedman, "Rumsfeld's Legacy: The Iraq Syndrome?" *Washington Post,* January 9, 2005; Mueller, "The Iraq Syndrome"; Steel, "An Iraq Syndrome?"

100. "America's Place in the World," Pew Research Center and the Council on Foreign Relations, December 2009, http://people-press.org/report/569/americas-place-in-the-world.

101. Donald Rumsfeld and Peter Pace, press conference, November 29, 2005, http://www.defense.gov/transcripts/transcript.aspx?transcriptid=1492.

Chapter 10. The Founding Tradition

1. Jefferson, *Memoir, Correspondence, and Miscellanies,* 304.

2. Hunt, *Ideology and U.S. Foreign Policy,* 195.

3. Stuart, *War and American Thought,* 91.

4. Stuart, *The Half-way Pacifist*, 13–14; Rourke, *Presidential Wars and American Democracy*, 9.
5. Silverstone, *Divided Union*, 32–36.
6. The United States also engaged in hostilities against France in 1798 and the Barbary pirates and their North African patrons during the early nineteenth century, but these were essentially naval campaigns. Both conflicts were also limited military operations, with goals short of regime change.
7. Hickey, *The War of 1812*, 75.
8. Mayers, *Dissenting Voices in America's Rise to Power*, 37.
9. Stuart, *War and American Thought*, 138.
10. For a discussion, see Silverstone, *Divided Union*, 95–96.
11. Bellesiles, "Experiencing the War of 1812," 226.
12. James Madison, "War Message," June 1, 1812, http://millercenter.org/scripps/archive/speeches/detail/3614; Bellesiles, "Experiencing the War of 1812."
13. Stuart, *War and American Thought*, 129; Bellesiles, "Experiencing the War of 1812."
14. Hickey, *The War of 1812*, 53, 255; Bellesiles, "Experiencing the War of 1812"; Silverstone, *Divided Union*, 100.
15. Cunliffe, *Soldiers and Civilians*, 69–70.
16. Johannsen, *To the Halls of the Montezumas*, 291; McCaffrey, *Army of Manifest Destiny*, 205; Winders, *Mr. Polk's Army*, 183; McDougall, *Promised Land, Crusader State*, 94–95.
17. Johannsen, *To the Halls of the Montezumas*, 300.
18. Ibid., 275.
19. Connor and Faulk, *North America Divided*, 149.
20. Lincoln, *Speeches and Writings*, 168.
21. Small, *Democracy and Diplomacy*, 18.
22. Silverstone, *Divided Union*, 179–201.
23. Emerson, *The Prose Works of Ralph Waldo Emerson*, 452.
24. Kluger, *Seizing Destiny*, 214.
25. Hamilton et al., *The Federalist*, 42; Monten, "The Roots of the Bush Doctrine"; Mead, *Special Providence*, 186–90.
26. McCartney, *Power and Progress*, 233.
27. Jervis, "The Compulsive Empire," 82.
28. Tate, *The Frontier Army in the Settlement of the West*, x.
29. Prucha, *Broadax and Bayonet*, 104; Coffman, *The Old Army*, 44.
30. Coffman, *The Old Army*, 167.
31. Prucha, *Broadax and Bayonet*.
32. Schama, *The American Future*, 52–54.
33. Morrison, "Educating the Civil War Generals," 108; Huntington, "New Contingencies, Old Roles," 39; Crackel, *Mr. Jefferson's Army*.
34. Cunliffe, *Soldiers and Civilians*, 171.
35. Wagoner and McDonald, "Mr. Jefferson's Academy," 146; Cunliffe, *Soldiers and Civilians*, 170.

36. Coffman, *The Old Army,* 101.
37. Prucha, *Broadax and Bayonet,* 105.
38. Coffman, *The Old Army,* 171.
39. Tate, *The Frontier Army in the Settlement of the West,* 306.
40. Prucha, *The Sword of the Republic,* 192.

BIBLIOGRAPHY

Abbott, Phillip. "Still Louis Hartz After All These Years. A Defense of the Liberal Society Thesis." *Perspectives on Politics* 3, no. 1 (March 2005): 93–110.

Abrams, Ray H. *Preachers Present Arms: The Role of the American Churches and Clergy in World Wars I and II, with some Observations on the War in Vietnam.* Scottdale, PA: Herald Press, 1969.

Abzug, Robert H. *Inside the Vicious Heart: Americans and the Liberation of Nazi Concentration Camps.* New York: Oxford University Press, 1985.

Adams, David K., and Cornelis A. van Minnen, eds. *Aspects of War in American History.* Keele, Eng.: Keele University Press, 1997.

Adams, Michael C. C. *The Best War Ever: America and World War II.* Baltimore: Johns Hopkins University Press, 1994.

———. *Echoes of War: A Thousand Years of Military History in Popular Culture.* Lexington: University Press of Kentucky, 2002.

Allen, Barbara, Paula O'Loughlin, Amy Jasperson, and John L. Sullivan. "The Media and the Gulf War: Framing, Priming, and the Spiral of Silence." *Polity* 27, no. 2 (Winter 1994): 255–84.

Almond, Gabriel A. *The American People and Foreign Policy.* New York: Praeger, 1960.

Ambrose, Stephen E. *Citizen Soldiers: The U.S. Army from the Normandy Beaches to the Bulge to the Surrender of Germany, June 7, 1944–May 7, 1945.* New York: Simon & Schuster, 1997.

Ambrosius, Lloyd E. *Wilsonian Statecraft: Theory and Practice of Liberal Internationalism During World War I.* Wilmington, DE: SR Books, 1991.

———. *Woodrow Wilson and the American Diplomatic Tradition: The Treaty Fight in Perspective.* New York: Cambridge University Press, 1987.

Amis, Martin. *The Second Plane: September 11, Terror and Boredom.* New York: Vintage, 2009.

Anderson, Terry H. "American Popular Music and the War in Vietnam." *Peace and Change* 11, no. 2 (February 1986): 51–65.

Armstrong, Anne. *Unconditional Surrender: The Impact of the Casablanca Policy upon World War II.* New Brunswick, NJ: Rutgers University Press, 1961.

Asprey, Robert B. *War in the Shadows: The Guerrilla in History*, Vol. 1. New York: William Morrow, 1994.

Bacevich, Andrew J. *American Empire: The Realities and Consequences of U.S. Diplomacy*. Cambridge: Harvard University Press, 2002.

————. *The Limits of Power: The End of American Exceptionalism*. New York: Henry Holt, 2008.

————. *The New American Militarism: How Americans Are Seduced by War*. New York: Oxford University Press, 2005.

Baritz, Loren. *Backfire: A History of How American Culture Led Us into Vietnam and Made Us Fight the Way We Did*. New York: William Morrow, 1985.

Barnet, Richard J. *The Rockets' Red Glare: When America Goes to War; The Presidents and the People*. New York: Simon & Schuster, 1990.

Barrett, John. *Admiral George Dewey: A Sketch of the Man*. New York: Harper, 1899.

Baum, Matthew A., and Tim Groeling. "Reality Asserts Itself: Public Opinion on Iraq and the Elasticity of Reality." Paper presented at the American Political Science Association Conference, Boston, 2008.

Beisner, Robert L. *Twelve Against Empire: The Anti-Imperialists, 1898–1900*. New York: McGraw-Hill, 1968.

Bellesiles, Michael. "Experiencing the War of 1812." In *Britain and America Go to War: The Impact of War and Warfare in Anglo-America, 1754–1815,* edited by Julie Flavell and Stephen Conway, 205–40. Gainesville: University Press of Florida, 2004.

Bender, Thomas A. *A Nation Among Nations: America's Place in World History*. New York: Hill & Wang, 2006.

Bennett, Stephen Earl. "The Persian Gulf War's Impact on Americans' Political Information." *Political Behavior* 16, no. 2 (June 1994): 179–201.

Berger, Thomas U. "Norms, Identity, and National Security in Germany and Japan." In *The Culture of National Security: Norms and Identity in World Politics,* edited by Peter J. Katzenstein, 317–56. New York: Columbia University Press, 1996.

Berinsky, Adam J. *In Time of War: Understanding Public Opinion from World War II to Iraq*. Chicago: University of Chicago Press, 2009.

Bernard, Kenneth. *Lincoln and the Music of the Civil War*. Caldwell, ID: Caxton, 1966.

Biddle, Stephen D. *Military Power: Explaining Victory and Defeat in Modern Battle*. Princeton, NJ: Princeton University Press, 2004.

Blassingame, John W. "The Press and American Intervention in Haiti and the Dominican Republic, 1904–1920." *Caribbean Studies* 9, no. 2 (July 1969): 27–43.

Blechman, Barry M., and Tamara Cofman Wittes. "Defining Moment: The Threat and Use of Force in American Foreign Policy." *Political Science Quarterly* 114, no. 1 (Spring 1999): 1–30.

Blum, John Morton. *V Was for Victory: Politics and American Culture During World War II*. New York: Harcourt Brace Jovanovich, 1976.

Boettcher, William A., and Michael D. Cobb. "Echoes of Vietnam? Casualty Framing and Perceptions of Success and Failure in Iraq." *Journal of Conflict Resolution* 50, no. 6 (December 2006): 831–54.

Boot, Max. "The New American Way of War." *Foreign Affairs* 82, no. 4 (July/August 2003): 41–58.

———. *The Savage Wars of Peace: Small Wars and the Rise of American Power.* New York: Basic Books, 2002.

Bouvier, Virginia M. "Imaging a Nation: U.S. Political Cartoons and the War of 1898." In *Whose America? The War of 1898 and the Battle to Define the Nation,* edited by Virginia M. Bouvier, 91–122. Westport, CT: Praeger, 2001.

Brands, H. W. *Bound to Empire: The United States and the Philippines.* New York: Oxford University Press, 1992.

Brantlinger, Patrick. "Kipling's 'The White Man's Burden' and Its Afterlives." *English Literature in Translation* 50, no. 2 (March 2007): 172–91.

Brazinksy, Gregg. *Nation Building in South Korea: Koreans, Americans, and the Making of a Democracy.* Chapel Hill, NC: University of North Carolina Press, 2007.

Brokaw, Tom. *The Greatest Generation.* New York: Random House, 1994.

Brontë, Charlotte. *Jane Eyre.* New York: Courier Dover, 2003.

Brown, Richard Maxwell. *No Duty to Retreat: Violence and Values in American History and Society.* New York: Oxford University Press, 1991.

Buchanan, Sherry. *Vietnam Zippos.* London: Thames & Hudson, 2007.

Buckley, Gail Lumet. *American Patriots: The Story of Blacks in the Military from the Revolution to Desert Storm.* New York: Random House, 2001.

Budiansky, Stephen. *The Bloody Shirt: Terror After Appomattox.* New York: Viking, 2008.

Buley, Benjamin. *The New American Way of War: Military Culture and the Political Utility of Force.* New York: Routledge, 2008.

Bush, George, and Brent Scowcroft. *A World Transformed.* New York: Knopf, 1998.

Calder, Bruce J. *The Impact of Intervention: The Dominican Republic During the U.S. Occupation of 1916–1924.* Austin: University of Texas Press, 1984.

Calhoun, Frederick S. *Power and Principle: Armed Intervention in Wilsonian Foreign Policy.* Kent, OH: Kent State University Press, 1986.

Capozzola, Christopher. *Uncle Sam Wants You: World War I and the Making of the Modern American Citizen.* New York: Oxford University Press, 2008.

Carroll, Andrew, ed. *Operation Homecoming: Iraq, Afghanistan, and the Home Front, in the Words of U.S. Troops and Their Families.* New York: Random House, 2006.

———. *War Letters: Extraordinary Correspondence from American Wars.* New York: Scribner, 2001.

Casey, Steven. *Cautious Crusade: Franklin D. Roosevelt, American Public Opinion, and the War Against Nazi Germany.* New York: Oxford University Press, 2001.

———. *Selling the Korean War: Propaganda, Politics, and Public Opinion in the United States, 1950–1953.* Oxford: Oxford University Press, 2008.

Chambers, John Whiteclay II, and G. Kurt Piehler, eds. *Major Problems in American Military History*. New York: Houghton Mifflin, 1999.

Chatfield, Charles. "World War I and the Liberal Pacifists in the United States." *American Historical Review* 75, no. 7 (December 1970): 1920–37.

Chomsky, Noam. *Hegemony or Survival: America's Quest for Global Dominance*. New York: Owl Books, 2004.

———. *The New Military Humanism: Lessons from Kosovo*. Monroe, ME: Common Courage Press, 1999.

Clark, Wesley K. *Waging Modern War: Bosnia, Kosovo, and the Future of Combat*. New York: PublicAffairs, 2002.

Cobb, Michael D., William A. Boettcher III, and John Willingham. "Defining Victory in Iraq: Measuring Public Perceptions of Prospective Success and Failure in a Counterinsurgency Campaign." Paper presented at the International Studies Association Convention, San Francisco, 2008.

Coffman, Edward M. *The Old Army: A Portrait of the American Army in Peacetime, 1784–1898*. New York: Oxford University Press, 1986.

Coleman, Katharina Pichler. *International Organizations and Peace Enforcement: The Politics of International Legitimacy*. Cambridge: Cambridge University Press, 2007.

Connor, Seymour V., and Odie B. Faulk. *North America Divided: The Mexican War, 1846–1848*. New York: Oxford University Press, 1971.

Conover, Pamela Johnston, and Virginia Sapiro. "Gender, Feminist Consciousness, and War." *American Journal of Political Science* 37, no. 4 (November 1993): 1079–99.

Cooper, John Milton, Jr. *The Vanity of Power: American Isolationism and the First World War, 1914–1917*. Westport, CT: Greenwood, 1969.

———. *The Warrior and the Priest: Woodrow Wilson and Theodore Roosevelt*. Cambridge: Harvard University Press, 1983.

Crackel, Theodore J. *Mr. Jefferson's Army: Political and Social Reform of the Military Establishment, 1801–1809*. New York: New York University Press, 1987.

Crandall, Russell. *Gunboat Diplomacy: U.S. Interventions in the Dominican Republic, Grenada, and Panama*. New York: Rowman & Littlefield, 2006.

Crocker, Chester A. "The Lessons of Somalia: Not Everything Went Wrong." *Foreign Affairs* 74, no. 3 (May/June 1995): 2–8.

Cunliffe, Marcus. *Soldiers and Civilians: The Martial Spirit in America, 1775–1865*. Brookfield, VT: Ashgate, 1993.

Current, Richard Nelson. *Those Terrible Carpetbaggers: A Reinterpretation*. New York: Oxford University Press, 1988.

Daalder, Ivo H. "Knowing When to Say No: The Development of US Policy for Peacekeeping." In *UN Peacekeeping, American Politics, and the Uncivil Wars of the 1990s*, edited by William J. Durch, 35–67. New York: St. Martin's Press, 1996.

Dallek, Robert. *The American Style of Foreign Policy: Cultural Politics and Foreign Affairs*. New York: Oxford University Press, 1983.

————. *Lone Star Rising: Lyndon Johnson and His Times, 1908–1960.* New York: Oxford University Press, 1991.

Dauber, Cori. "The Shots Seen 'Round the World: The Impact of the Images of Mogadishu on American Military Operations." *Rhetoric and Public Affairs* 4, no. 4 (November 2001): 653–87.

Davies, Norman. *No Simple Victory: World War II in Europe, 1939–1945.* New York: Viking, 2006.

Dawley, Alan. *Changing the World: American Progressives in War and Revolution.* Princeton, NJ: Princeton University Press, 2003.

Demchak, Chris C. *Military Organizations, Complex Machines: Modernization in the U.S. Armed Services.* Ithaca, NY: Cornell University Press, 1991.

Dempsey, Gary T. "Fool's Errands: America's Recent Encounters with Nation Building." *Mediterranean Quarterly* 12, no. 1 (Winter 2001): 57–80.

Detzer, David. *Donnybrook: The Battle of Bull Run, 1861.* Orlando, FL: Harcourt, 2005.

Dimock, Michael A., and Samuel L. Popkin. "Political Knowledge in Comparative Perspective." In *Do the Media Govern? Politicians, Voters, and Reporters in America,* edited by Shanto Iyengar and Richard Reeves, 217-24. Thousand Oaks, CA: Sage Publications, 1997.

DiPrizio, Robert C. *Armed Humanitarians: U.S. Interventions from Northern Iraq to Kosovo.* Baltimore: Johns Hopkins University Press, 2002.

Divine, Robert A. *Perpetual War for Perpetual Peace.* College Station: Texas A&M University Press, 2000.

————. *Second Chance: The Triumph of Internationalism in America During World War II.* New York: Atheneum, 1967.

Dobbins, James. "Preparing for Nation-Building." *Survival* 48, no. 3 (Autumn 2006): 27–40.

Dobbins, James, et al. *After the War: Nation-Building from FDR to George W. Bush.* Santa Monica, CA: Rand, 2008.

————. *America's Role in Nation-Building: From Germany to Iraq.* Santa Monica, CA: Rand, 2003.

Dower, John W. *War Without Mercy: Race and Power in the Pacific War.* New York: Pantheon, 1993.

Downes, Alexander B. *Targeting Civilians in War.* Ithaca, NY: Cornell University Press, 2008.

Dray, Philip. *Capitol Men: The Epic Story of Reconstruction Through the Lives of the First Black Congressmen.* Boston: Houghton Mifflin, 2008.

DuBois, W. E. B. *Black Reconstruction in America.* New York: Atheneum, 1935.

Dueck, Colin. *Reluctant Crusaders: Power, Culture, and Change in American Grand Strategy.* Princeton, NJ: Princeton University Press, 2006.

Dumbrell, John. "The US Congress and the Gulf War." In *The Gulf War Did Not Happen: Politics, Culture and Warfare Post-Vietnam,* edited by Jeffrey Walsh, 49–62. Brookfield, VT: Ashgate, 1995.

Dunne, Finley Peter. *Mr. Dooley: In the Hearts of His Countrymen.* Charleston, SC: BiblioBazaar, 2007.

———. *Mr. Dooley in Peace and in War.* Boston: Small, Maynard, 1898.

———. *Mr. Dooley Remembers: The Informal Memoirs of Finley Peter Dunne.* Boston: Little, Brown, 1963.

Elshtain, Jean Bethke. "Just War as Politics: What the Gulf War Told Us About Contemporary American Life." In *But Was it Just? Reflections on the Morality of the Persian Gulf War,* edited by David E. Decosse, 43–60. New York: Doubleday, 1992.

Emerson, Ralph Waldo. *The Prose Works of Ralph Waldo Emerson.* Vol. 2. Boston: Fields, Osgood, 1870.

Endy, Melvin B., Jr. "Just War, Holy War, and Millennialism in Revolutionary America," *William and Mary Quarterly* 42, no. 1 (January 1985): 3–25.

Entman, Robert M. *Projections of Power: Framing News, Public Opinion, and U.S. Foreign Policy.* Chicago: University of Chicago Press, 2004.

Esposito, David M. *The Legacy of Woodrow Wilson: American War Aims in World War I.* Westport, CT: Praeger, 1996.

Euripides. *Medea and Other Plays.* Translated by Philip Vellacott. New York: Penguin Classics, 1963.

Everts, Philip, and Pierangelo Isernia. "The Polls-Trends: The War in Iraq." *Public Opinion Quarterly* 69, no. 2 (Summer 2005): 264–323.

Fahs, Alice. *The Imagined Civil War: Popular Literature of the North and South, 1861–1865.* Chapel Hill: University of North Carolina Press, 2001.

Farwell, Byron. *Over There: The United States in the Great War.* New York: W. W. Norton, 1999.

Fayazmanesh, Sasan. *The United States and Iran: Sanctions, Wars and the Policy of Dual Containment.* New York: Routledge, 2008.

Ferguson, Niall. *Colossus: The Price of America's Empire.* New York: Penguin, 2004.

Ferrell, Robert H. *Woodrow Wilson and World War I, 1917–1921.* New York: Harper & Row, 1985.

Finseth, Ian Frederick. *The American Civil War: An Anthology of Essential Writings.* New York: Routledge, 2006.

Fischer, David Hackett. *Liberty and Freedom.* New York: Oxford University Press, 2005.

Fite, Gilbert. *Richard B. Russell, Jr., Senator from Georgia.* Chapel Hill: University of North Carolina Press, 1991.

Fitzgerald, Michael W. *Splendid Failure: Postwar Reconstruction in the American South.* Chicago: Ivan R. Dee, 2007.

Fleming, Thomas. *The Illusion of Victory: America in World War I.* New York: Basic Books, 2003.

Foner, Eric. *Forever Free: The Story of Emancipation and Reconstruction.* New York: Knopf, 2005.

———. *Reconstruction: America's Unfinished Revolution, 1863–1877.* New York: Harper & Row, 1988.

Foot, Rosemary. *A Substitute for Victory: The Politics of Peacemaking at the Korean Armistice Talks.* Ithaca, NY: Cornell University Press, 1990.

Ford, Nancy Gentile. *Issues of War and Peace.* Westport, CT: Greenwood, 2002.

Fortna, Virginia Page. *Does Peacekeeping Work? Shaping Belligerents' Choices After Civil War.* Princeton, NJ: Princeton University Press, 2008.

Foyle, Douglas C. *Counting the Public In: Presidents, Public Opinion, and Foreign Policy.* New York: Columbia University Press, 1999.

Frank, Joseph Allan, and Barbara Duteau. "Measuring the Political Articulateness of United States Civil War Soldiers: The Wisconsin Militia." *Journal of Military History* 64, no. 1 (January 2000): 53–77.

Franklin, H. Bruce. *Vietnam and Other American Fantasies.* Amherst: University of Massachusetts Press, 2000.

Franks, Tommy R., and Malcolm McConnell. *American Soldier.* New York: HarperCollins, 2004.

Freedman, Lawrence. "Victims and Victors: Reflections on the Kosovo War." *Review of International Studies* 26, no. 3 (April 2000): 335–58.

Freedman, Lawrence, and Efraim Karsh. *The Gulf Conflict, 1990–1991: Diplomacy and War in the New World Order.* Princeton, NJ: Princeton University Press, 1993.

Freidel, Frank Burt. *Over There: The Story of America's First Great Overseas Crusade.* Boston: Little, Brown, 1964.

Friend, Theodore. *Between Two Empires: The Ordeal of the Philippines, 1929–1946.* New Haven, CT: Yale University Press, 1965.

Frijda, Nico H. "The Lex Talionis: On Vengeance." In *Emotions: Essays on Emotion Theory,* edited by Stephanie H. M. Van Goozen, Nanne E. Van de Poll, and Joseph A. Sergent, 263–89. Hillsdale, NJ: Lawrence Erlbaum, 1994.

Fry, Joseph A. *Dixie Looks Abroad: The South and U.S. Foreign Relations, 1789–1973.* Baton Rouge: Louisiana State University Press, 2002.

Fussell, Paul. *Wartime: Understanding and Behavior in the Second World War.* New York: Oxford University Press, 1989.

Gacek, Christopher M. *The Logic of Force: The Dilemma of Limited War in American Foreign Policy.* New York: Columbia University Press, 1994.

Gaines, Brian J., et al. "Same Facts, Different Interpretations: Partisan Motivation and Opinion on Iraq." *Journal of Politics* 69, no. 4 (November 2007): 957–74.

Gale, Oliver Marble. *Americanism: Woodrow Wilson's Speeches on the War, Why He Made Them, and What They Have Done.* Chicago: Baldwin Syndicate, 1918.

Gallagher, Gary W. *The Confederate War.* Cambridge: Harvard University Press, 1999.

Gallup, George. *The Gallup Polls: Public Opinion, 1935–1971.* New York: Random House, 1972.

Gamble, Richard M. *The War for Righteousness: Progressive Christianity, the Great War, and the Rise of the Messianic Nation.* Wilmington, DE: ISI Books, 2003.

Gardner, David. *The Last of the Hitlers.* Worcester, UK: BMM, 2001.

Gates, John Morgan. *Schoolbooks and Krags: The United States Army in the Philippines, 1898–1902.* Westport, CT: Greenwood, 1973.

Gelpi, Christopher, Peter D. Feaver, and Jason Reifler. *Paying the Human Costs of War: American Public Opinion and Casualties in Military Conflicts.* Princeton, NJ: Princeton University Press, 2009.

———. "Success Matters: Casualty Sensitivity and the War in Iraq." *International Security* 30, no. 3 (Winter 2005/2006): 7–46.

Gilbert, Martin. *The First World War.* New York: Macmillan, 2004.

Gillen, Shawn. "Captain America, Post-Traumatic Stress Syndrome, and the Vietnam Era." In *Captain America and the Struggle of the Superhero: Critical Essays,* edited by Robert G. Weiner, 104–15. Jefferson, NC: McFarland, 2009.

Gillette, William. *Retreat from Reconstruction, 1869–1879.* Baton Rouge: Louisiana State University Press, 1979.

Glad, Betty, and J. Philipp Rosenberg. "Bargaining Under Fire: Limit Setting and Maintenance During the Korean War." In *Psychological Dimensions of War,* edited by Betty Glad, 181–200. Newbury Park, CA: Sage, 1990.

Gleijeses, Piero. "1898: The Opposition to the Spanish-American War." *Journal of Latin American Studies* 35, no. 4 (November 2003): 681–719.

Gobat, Michael. *Confronting the American Dream: Nicaragua Under U.S. Imperial Rule.* Durham, NC: Duke University Press, 2005.

Goldensohn, Lorrie. *American War Poetry: An Anthology.* New York: Columbia University Press, 2006.

Goodnight, G. Thomas, and Kathryn M. Olson. "Shared Power, Foreign Policy, and Haiti, 1994: Public Memories of War and Race." *Rhetoric and Public Affairs* 9, no. 4 (December 2006): 601–34.

Goodson, Larry P. "Lessons of Nation-Building in Afghanistan." In *Nation-Building: Beyond Afghanistan and Iraq,* edited by Francis Fukuyama, 145–69. Baltimore: Johns Hopkins University Press, 2006.

Goodwin, Doris Kearns. *Team of Rivals: The Political Genius of Abraham Lincoln.* New York: Simon & Schuster, 2005.

Gordon, Michael R., and General Bernard E. Trainor. *Cobra II: The Inside Story of the Invasion and Occupation of Iraq.* New York: Pantheon, 2006.

Gould, Lewis L. *The Presidency of William McKinley.* Lawrence: Regents Press of Kansas, 1980.

Grasmick, Harold G., et al. "Protestant Fundamentalism and the Retributive Doctrine of Punishment." *Criminology* 30, no. 1 (February 1992): 21–45.

Gray, Colin S. "The American Way of War: Critique and Implications." In *Rethinking the Principles of War,* edited by Anthony D. McIvor, 13–40. Annapolis, MD: Naval Institute Press, 2005.

Greene, Graham. *The Quiet American.* New York: Viking, 1955.

Grubb, F. W. "Growth of Literacy in Colonial America: Longitudinal Patterns, Economic Models, and the Direction of Future Research." *Social Science History* 14, no. 4 (Winter 1990): 451-482.

Halberstam, David. *The Making of a Quagmire: America and Vietnam During the Kennedy Era.* Lanham, MD: Rowman & Littlefield, 2008.

Hallin, Daniel C. "Images of the Vietnam and the Persian Gulf Wars in U.S. Television." In *Seeing Through the Media: The Persian Gulf War,* edited by Susan Jeffords and Lauren Rabinovitz, 45–58. New Brunswick, NJ: Rutgers University Press, 1994.

Hallin, Daniel C., and Todd Gitlin. "The Gulf War as Popular Culture and Television Drama." In *Taken by Storm: The Media, Public Opinion, and U.S. Foreign Policy in the Gulf War,* edited by W. Lance Bennett and David L. Paletz, 149–63. Chicago: University of Chicago Press, 1994.

Hamilton, Alexander, et al. *The Federalist: A Commentary on the Constitution of the United States.* New York: Modern Library, 2001.

Hamilton, Richard F. *President McKinley, War and Empire.* Vol. 1: *President McKinley and the Coming of War, 1898.* New Brunswick, NJ: Transaction, 2006

Handel, Michael I. *Masters of War: Classical Strategic Thought.* 3rd ed. London: Frank Cass, 2001.

Harries, Meirion, and Susie Harries. *The Last Days of Innocence: America at War, 1917–1918.* New York: Random House, 1997.

Hart, Albert Bushnell, ed. *Selected Addresses and Public Papers of Woodrow Wilson.* New York: Boni & Liveright, 1918.

Hartz, Louis. *The Liberal Tradition in America: An Interpretation of American Political Thought Since the Revolution.* New York: Harcourt, Brace, 1955.

Healy, David. *Drive to Hegemony: The United States in the Caribbean, 1898–1917.* Madison: University of Wisconsin Press, 1988.

Heffner, Richard D. *A Documentary History of the United States.* New York: Signet, 2002.

Heinl, Robert Debs, Nancy Gordon Heinl, and Michael Heinl. *Written in Blood: The Story of the Haitian People, 1492–1995.* New York: University Press of America, 1996.

Hess, Earl J. *Liberty, Virtue, and Progress: Northerners and Their War for the Union.* New York: Fordham University Press, 1997.

———. *The Union Soldier in Battle: Enduring the Ordeal of Combat.* Lawrence: University Press of Kansas, 1997.

Hickey, Donald R. *The War of 1812: A Forgotten Conflict.* Urbana: University of Illinois Press, 1989.

Hixson, Walter L. *The Myth of American Diplomacy: National Identity and U.S. Foreign Policy.* New Haven, CT: Yale University Press, 2008.

Hoffman, F. G. *Decisive Force: The New American Way of War.* Westport, CT: Praeger, 1996.

Hoganson, Kristin L. *Fighting for American Manhood: How Gender Politics Provoked the Spanish-American and Philippine-American Wars.* New Haven, CT: Yale University Press, 1998.

Holsinger, M. Paul, ed. *War and American Popular Culture: A Historical Encyclopedia.* Westport, CT: Greenwood, 1999.

Holsti, Ole R. "American Public Opinion on the War in Iraq." Paper presented at the American Political Science Association Conference, Boston, 2008.

——. "Promotion of Democracy as Popular Demand?" In *American Democracy Promotion: Impulses, Strategies, and Impacts,* edited by Michael Cox, G. John Ikenberry, and Takashi Inoguchi, 152–80. Oxford: Oxford University Press, 2000.

——. *Public Opinion and American Foreign Policy.* Ann Arbor: University of Michigan Press, 2004.

Hopkins, George E. "Bombing and the American Conscience During World War II." *Historian* 28, no. 3 (May 1966): 451–73.

Hubbell, Jay B., and John Owen Beaty. *An Introduction to Poetry.* New York: Macmillan, 1922.

Huebner, Andrew J. *The Warrior Image: Soldiers in American Culture from the Second World War to the Vietnam Era.* Chapel Hill: University of North Carolina Press, 2008.

Hunt, Michael H. *Ideology and U.S. Foreign Policy.* New Haven, CT: Yale University Press, 2009.

Hunt, Richard A. *Pacification: The American Struggle for Vietnam's Hearts and Minds.* Boulder, CO: Westview Press, 1995.

Huntington, Samuel P. "American Ideals Versus American Institutions." *Political Science Quarterly* 97, no. 1 (Spring 1982): 1–37.

——. "New Contingencies, Old Roles." *Joint Forces Quarterly,* no. 2. (Autumn 1993): 38–43.

——. *The Soldier and the State: The Theory and Politics of Civil-Military Relations.* Cambridge: Harvard University Press, 1957.

Isaacs, Arnold R. *Vietnam Shadows: The War, Its Ghosts, and Its Legacy.* Baltimore: Johns Hopkins University Press, 1997.

Jacobson, Gary C. "Perception, Memory, and the Partisan Polarization of Opinion on the Iraq War." Paper presented at the American Political Science Association Conference, Boston, 2008.

Jacoby, Susan. *Wild Justice: The Evolution of Revenge.* Santa Cruz: University of California Press, 1983.

Janda, Lance. "Shutting the Gates of Mercy: The American Origins of Total War, 1860–1880." *Journal of Military History* 59, no. 1 (January 1995): 7–26.

Jefferson, Thomas. *Memoir, Correspondence, and Miscellanies, from the Papers of Thomas Jefferson.* Vol. 3. Boston: Gray & Bowen, 1830.

Jelen, Ted G. "Religion and Foreign Policy Attitudes: Exploring the Effects of Denomination and Doctrine." *American Politics Quarterly* 22, no. 3 (July 1994): 382–400.

Jentleson Bruce W., and Rebecca Britton. "Still Pretty Prudent: Post–Cold War American Public Opinion on the Use of Military Force." *Journal of Conflict Resolution* 42, no. 4 (August 1998): 395–417.

Jervis, Robert. "The Compulsive Empire." *Foreign Policy,* no. 137 (July/August 2003): 82–87.

Jewett, Robert. *The Captain America Complex: The Dilemma of Zealous Nationalism.* Philadelphia: Westminster Press, 1973.

————. *Mission and Menace: Four Centuries of American Religious Zeal.* Minneapolis: Fortress Press, 2008.

Jewett, Robert, and John Shelton Lawrence. *Captain America and the Crusade Against Evil: The Dilemma of Zealous Nationalism.* Grand Rapids, MI: William B. Eerdmans, 2004.

Johannsen, Robert W. *To the Halls of the Montezumas: The Mexican War in the American Imagination.* New York: Oxford University Press, 1985.

Johnson, Chalmers. *The Sorrows of Empire: Militarism, Secrecy, and the End of the Republic.* New York: Henry Holt, 2004.

Johnson, Dominic. *Overconfidence and War: The Havoc and Glory of Positive Illusions.* Cambridge: Harvard University Press, 2004.

Johnson, Dominic, and Dominic Tierney. *Failing to Win: Perceptions of Victory and Defeat in International Politics.* Cambridge: Harvard University Press, 2006.

Jordan, Amos A., William J. Taylor, Jr., and Michael J. Mazarr. *American National Security.* 5th ed. Baltimore: Johns Hopkins University Press, 1999.

Kagan, Robert. *Dangerous Nation.* New York: Knopf, 2006.

————. *Of Paradise and Power: America and Europe in the New World Order.* New York: Vintage, 2004.

Kahl, Colin H. "In the Crossfire or the Crosshairs? Norms, Civilian Casualties, and U.S. Conduct in Iraq." *International Security* 32, no. 1 (Summer 2007): 7–46.

Kaiser, David. *American Tragedy: Kennedy, Johnson, and the Origins of the Vietnam War.* Cambridge: Harvard University Press, 2000.

Kane, John. *Between Virtue and Power: The Persistent Moral Dilemma of U.S. Foreign Policy.* New Haven, CT: Yale University Press, 2008.

Kaplan, Justin. "George Dewey: Naval Hero and Political Disaster." In *Forgotten Heroes: Inspiring American Portraits from Our Leading Historians,* edited by Susan Ware, 161–68. New York: Free Press, 1998.

Karabell, Zachary. *Architects of Intervention: The United States, the Third World, and the Cold War, 1946–1962.* Baton Rouge: Louisiana State University Press, 1999.

Karnow, Stanley. *In Our Image: America's Empire in the Philippines.* New York: Ballantine, 1990.

Karp, Walter. *The Politics of War: The Story of Two Wars Which Altered Forever the Political Life of the American Republic.* New York: Harper & Row, 1979.

Kekatos, Kirk J. "Edward H. Amet and the Spanish-American War Film." *Film History* 14, no. 3/4 (September 2002): 405–17.

Keller, Morton. *Affairs of State: Public Life in Late Nineteenth Century America.* Cambridge: Harvard University Press, 1977.

Kennan, George F. *American Diplomacy.* Chicago: University of Chicago Press, 1984.

————. *Realities of American Foreign Policy.* New York: W. W. Norton, 1966.

Kennedy, David M. *Over Here: The First World War and American Society.* New York: Oxford University Press, 1980.

Kennedy, John F. *Profiles in Courage.* New York: Harper, 1956.

Kennedy, Paul. *The Rise and Fall of the Great Powers: Economic Change and Military Conflict from 1500 to 2000.* New York: Vintage, 1989.

Kennedy, Ross A. *The Will to Believe: Woodrow Wilson, World War I, and America's Strategy for Peace and Security.* Kent, OH: Kent State University Press, 2009.

Khong, Yuen Foong. *Analogies at War: Korea, Munich, Dien Bien Phu, and the Vietnam Decisions of 1965.* Princeton, NJ: Princeton University Press, 1992.

Kimball, Warren. *The Juggler: Franklin Roosevelt as Wartime Statesman.* Princeton, NJ: Princeton University Press, 1991.

King, David C., and Zachary Karabell. *The Generation of Trust: Public Confidence in the U.S. Military Since Vietnam.* Washington, DC: AEI Press, 2002.

Kinzer, Stephen. *Overthrow: America's Century of Regime Change from Hawaii to Iraq.* New York: Henry Holt, 2006.

Kluger, Richard. *Seizing Destiny: How America Grew from Sea to Shining Sea.* New York: Vintage Books, 2007.

Knock, Thomas J. *To End All Wars: Woodrow Wilson and the Quest for a New World Order.* New York: Oxford University Press, 1992.

Kohut, Andrew, and Bruce Stokes. *America Against the World: How We Are Different and Why We Are Disliked.* New York: Holt, 2007.

Kramer, Paul A. *The Blood of Government: Race, Empire, the United States, and the Philippines.* Chapel Hill: University of North Carolina Press, 2006.

Krebs, Ronald R., and Jennifer K. Lobasz. "Fixing the Meaning of 9/11: Hegemony, Coercion, and the Road to War in Iraq." *Security Studies* 16, no. 3 (July–September 2007): 409–51.

Krepinevich, Andrew F., Jr. *The Army and Vietnam.* Baltimore: Johns Hopkins University Press, 1986.

———. "How to Win in Iraq." *Foreign Affairs* 84, no. 5 (September/October 2005): 87–104.

Kull, Steven, and I. M. Destler. *Misreading the Public: The Myth of a New Isolationism.* Washington, DC: Brookings Institution, 1999.

Kull, Steven, I. M. Destler, and Clay Ramsay. *The Foreign Policy Gap: How Policymakers Misread the Public.* Washington, DC: Program on International Policy Attitudes, 1997.

Kull, Steven, and Clay Ramsay. "U.S. Public Opinion on Intervention in Bosnia." In *International Public Opinion and the Bosnia Crisis,* edited by Richard Sobel and Eric Shiraev, 69–106. New York: Lexington Books, 2003.

Kurth, James. "Variations on the American Way of War." In *The Long War: A New History of U.S. National Security Policy Since World War II,* edited by Andrew Bacevich, 53–98. New York: Columbia University Press, 2007.

Lacquement, Richard. "The Casualty-Aversion Myth." *Naval War College Review* 57, no. 1 (Winter 2004): 39–57.

LaFeber, Walter. *The Cambridge History of American Foreign Relations: The Search for Opportunity.* Cambridge: Cambridge University Press, 1995.

———. *Inevitable Revolutions: The United States in Central America.* New York: W. W. Norton, 1983.

———. *The New Empire: An Interpretation of American Expansion, 1860–1898.* Ithaca, NY: Cornell University Press, 1967.

Lane, Charles. *The Day Freedom Died: The Colfax Massacre, the Supreme Court, and the Betrayal of Reconstruction.* New York: Henry Holt, 2009.

Langley, Lester D. *The Banana Wars: United States Intervention in the Caribbean, 1898-1934.* Wilmington, DE: SR Books, 2002.

———. *The United States and the Caribbean in the Twentieth Century.* Athens: University of Georgia Press, 1985.

Larson, Eric V. *Casualties and Consensus: The Historical Role of Casualties in Domestic Support for U.S. Military Operations.* Santa Monica, CA: Rand, 1996.

Larson, Eric V., and Bogdan Savych. *American Public Support for U.S. Military Operations from Mogadishu to Baghdad.* Santa Monica, CA: Rand, 2005.

Leigh, Michael. *Mobilizing Consent: Public Opinion and American Foreign Policy, 1937–1947.* Westport, CT: Greenwood, 1976.

Lemann, Nicholas. *Redemption: The Last Battle of the Civil War.* New York: St. Martin's Press, 2007.

Leonard, Thomas C. *Above the Battle: War-Making in America from Appomattox to Versailles.* New York: Oxford University Press, 1978.

LeShan, Lawrence. *The Psychology of War: Comprehending Its Mystique and Its Madness.* Chicago: Noble Press, 1992.

Liberman, Peter. "An Eye for an Eye: Public Support for War Against Evildoers." *International Organization* 60, no. 3 (Summer 2006): 687–722.

———. "Punitiveness and U.S. Elite Support for the 1991 Persian Gulf War." *Journal of Conflict Resolution* 51, no. 1 (February 2007): 3–32.

Liberman, Peter, and Linda J. Skitka. "Just Deserts in Iraq: American Vengeance for 9/11." Paper presented at the American Political Science Association Conference, Boston, 2008.

Lienesch, Michel. *Redeeming America: Piety and Politics in the New Christian Right.* Chapel Hill: University of North Carolina Press, 1993.

Lincoln, Abraham. *Speeches and Writings.* New York: Viking, 1989.

Lincoln, Abraham, et al. *Life and Works of Abraham Lincoln.* 9 vols. New York: Current Literature, 1907.

Linderman, Gerald F. *The Mirror of War: American Society and the Spanish-American War.* Ann Arbor: University of Michigan Press, 1974.

Linenthal, Edward Tabor. *Changing Images of the Warrior Hero in America: A History of Popular Symbolism.* New York: Edwin Mellen Press, 1982.

Linn, Brian M. *The Echo of Battle: The Army's Way of War.* Cambridge: Harvard University Press, 2007.

———. *The Philippine War, 1899–1902.* Lawrence: University Press of Kansas, 2000.

Lipset, Seymour Martin. *American Exceptionalism: A Double-Edged Sword*. New York: W. W. Norton, 1996.

Little, Douglas. "His Finest Hour? Eisenhower, Lebanon, and the 1958 Crisis in the Middle East." *Diplomatic History* 20, no. 1 (Winter 1996): 27–54.

Livermore, Seward W. *Politics Is Adjourned: Woodrow Wilson and the War Congress, 1916–1918*. Middletown, CT: Wesleyan University Press, 1966.

Locke, John. *Two Treatises of Government*. Edited by Peter Laslett. New York: New American Library, 1965.

Logevall, Fredrik. *Choosing War: The Lost Chance for Peace and the Escalation of War in Vietnam*. Berkeley: University of California Press, 1999.

Love, Eric T. *Race over Empire: Racism and U.S. Imperialism, 1865–1900*. Chapel Hill: University of North Carolina Press, 2004.

Löwenheim, Oded, and Gadi Heimann. "Revenge in International Politics." *Security Studies* 17, no. 4 (October 2008): 685–724.

Lowenthal, Abraham F. *The Dominican Intervention*. Cambridge: Harvard University Press, 1972.

Lunch, William L., and Peter W. Sperlich. "Public Opinion and the War in Vietnam." *Western Political Quarterly* 32, no. 1 (March 1979): 21–44.

Lustick, Ian S. *Trapped in the War on Terror*. Philadelphia: University of Pennsylvania Press, 2006.

Macdonald, Douglas J. *Adventures in Chaos: American Intervention for Reform in the Third World*. Cambridge: Harvard University Press, 1992.

Mahnken, Thomas G. "The American Way of War in the Twenty-first Century." In *Democracies and Small Wars*, edited by Efraim Inbar, 73–84. Portland, OR: Frank Cass, 2003.

Mandelbaum, Michael. "Foreign Policy as Social Work." *Foreign Affairs* 75, no. 1 (January/February 1996): 16–32.

Manning, Chandra. *What This Cruel War Was Over: Soldiers, Slavery, and the Civil War*. New York: Knopf, 2007.

Markowitz, Gerald E. *American Anti-imperialism, 1895–1901*. New York: Garland, 1976.

Marsden, Lee. *For God's Sake: The Christian Right and US Foreign Policy*. New York: Zed Books, 2008.

Martel, William C. *Victory in War: Foundations of Modern Military Policy*. Cambridge: Cambridge University Press, 2007.

Martin, Pierre, and Michel Fortmann. "Support for International Involvement in Canadian Public Opinion After the Cold War." *Canadian Military Journal* 2, no. 3 (Autumn 2001): 43–52.

Marty, Martin E. *Righteous Empire: The Protestant Experience in America*. New York, Dial Press, 1970.

Maslowski, Peter. "To the Edge of Greatness: The United States, 1783–1865." In *The Making of Strategy: Rulers, States, and War,* edited by Williamson Murray, MacGregor Knox, and Alvin Bernstein, 205–41. Cambridge: Cambridge University Press, 1994.

May, Ernest R. *American Imperialism: A Speculative Essay*. New York: Atheneum, 1968.

———. *Imperial Democracy: The Emergence of America as a Great Power*. Chicago: Imprint, 1991.

May, Glenn Anthony. *Social Engineering in the Philippines: The Aims, Execution, and Impact of American Colonial Policy, 1900–1913*. Westport, CT: Greenwood, 1980.

———. "Why the United States Won the Philippine-American War, 1899–1902." *Pacific Historical Review* 52, no. 4 (November 1983): 353–77.

Mayers, David. *Dissenting Voices in America's Rise to Power*. Cambridge: Cambridge University Press, 2007.

———. *Wars and Peace: The Future Americans Envisioned, 1861–1991*. New York: Palgrave Macmillan, 1999.

McCaffrey, James M. *Army of Manifest Destiny: The American Soldier in the Mexican War, 1846–1848*. New York: New York University Press, 1992.

McCann, David, and Barry S. Strauss, eds. *War and Democracy: A Comparative Study of the Korean War and the Peloponnesian War*. Armonk, NY: M. E. Sharpe, 2001.

McCartney, Paul T. *Power and Progress: American National Identity, the War of 1898, and the Rise of American Imperialism*. Baton Rouge: Louisiana State University Press, 2006.

McClure, Alexander K., and Charles Morris. *The Authentic Life of William McKinley: Our Third Martyr President*. Washington, DC: W. E. Scull, 1901.

McCullough, David. *Truman*. New York: Simon & Schuster, 2003.

McDougall, Walter A. *Promised Land, Crusader State: The American Encounter with the World Since 1776*. New York: Houghton Mifflin, 1997.

———. *Throes of Democracy: The American Civil War Era, 1829–1877*. New York: HarperCollins, 2009.

McPherson, Alan. "Americanism Against American Empire." In *New Perspectives on the History of an Ideal,* edited by Michael Kazin and Joseph A. McCartin, 169–91. Chapel Hill: University of North Carolina Press, 2006.

McPherson, James M. *Battle Cry of Freedom: The Civil War Era*. New York: Oxford University Press, 2003.

———. *Drawn with the Sword: Reflections on the American Civil War*. New York: Oxford University Press, 1996.

———. *For Cause and Comrades: Why Men Fought in the Civil War*. New York: Oxford University Press, 1998.

———. "From Limited War to Total War in America." In *On the Road to Total War: The American Civil War and the German Wars of Unification, 1861–1871,* edited by Stig Förster and Jörg Nagler, 295–309. Cambridge: Cambridge University Press, 2002.

———. "Lincoln and the Strategy of Unconditional Surrender." In *Lincoln the War President,* edited by Gabor S. Boritt, 29–62. New York: Oxford University Press, 1992.

———. *Ordeal by Fire: The Civil War and Reconstruction.* New York: Knopf, 1982.

———. "Was It More Restrained Than You Think?" *New York Review of Books* 55, no. 2 (February 2008): 42–44.

———. *What They Fought For, 1861–1865.* Baton Rouge: Louisiana State University Press, 1994.

Mead, Gary. *The Doughboys: America and the First World War.* New York: Allen Lane, 2000.

Mead, Walter Russell. *Special Providence: American Foreign Policy and How It Changed the World.* New York: Routledge, 2002.

Meigs, Mark. *Optimism at Armageddon: Voices of American Participants in the First World War.* New York: New York University Press, 1997.

Melville, Herman. "The March into Virginia Ending in the First Manassas." In *The Columbia Anthology of American Poetry,* edited by Jay Parini, 228–29. New York: Columbia University Press, 1995.

Midford, Paul. *Japanese Public Opinion and the War on Terrorism: Implications for Japan's Security Strategy.* Washington, DC: East-West Center, 2006.

Miller, Stuart Creighton. *"Benevolent Assimilation": The American Conquest of the Philippines, 1899–1903.* New Haven, CT: Yale University Press, 1982.

Millett, Allan R. *The Politics of Intervention: The Military Occupation of Cuba, 1906–1909.* Columbus: Ohio State University Press, 1968.

Mirra, Carl. *Soldiers and Citizens: An Oral History of Operation Iraqi Freedom from the Battlefield to the Pentagon.* New York: Palgrave Macmillan, 2008.

Mitchell, Reid. "The Perseverance of the Soldiers." In *Why the Confederacy Lost,* edited by Gabor S. Boritt, 109–32. New York: Oxford University Press, 1993.

Monten, Jonathan. "The Roots of the Bush Doctrine: Power, Nationalism, and Democracy Promotion in U.S. Strategy." *International Security* 29, no. 4 (Spring 2005): 112–56.

Moorehead, James H. *American Apocalypse: Yankee Protestants and the Civil War, 1860–1869.* New Haven, CT: Yale University Press, 1978.

Morgenthau, Hans J. *American Foreign Policy: A Critical Examination of American Foreign Policy.* New York: Knopf, 1951.

Morone, James A. *Hellfire Nation: The Politics of Sin in American History.* New Haven, CT: Yale University Press, 2004.

Morrison, James L. "Educating the Civil War Generals: West Point, 1833–1861." *Military Affairs* 38, no. 3 (October 1974): 108–11.

Mueller, John. "American Public Opinion and the Gulf War." In *The Political Psychology of the Gulf War: Leaders, Publics and the Process of Conflict,* edited by Stanley A. Renshon, 199–226. Pittsburgh: University of Pittsburgh Press, 1993.

———. "The Banality of 'Ethnic War.'" *International Security* 25, no. 1 (Summer 2000): 42–70.

———. "Changes in American Public Attitudes Toward International Involvement." In *The Limits of Military Intervention,* edited by Ellen P. Stern, 323–44. Beverly Hills, CA: Sage, 1977.

————. "Fifteen Propositions About American Foreign Policy and Public Opinion in an Era of Compelling Threats." Paper presented at the International Studies Association Convention, San Diego, 1996.

————. "The Iraq Syndrome." *Foreign Affairs* 84, no. 6 (November/December 2005): 44–54.

————. *Policy and Opinion in the Gulf War.* Chicago: University of Chicago Press, 1994.

————. *The Remnants of War.* Ithaca, NY: Cornell University Press, 2004.

————. *War, Presidents and Public Opinion.* New York: John Wiley, 1973.

Musicant, Ivan. *The Banana Wars: A History of United States Military Intervention in Latin America from the Spanish-American War to the Invasion of Panama.* New York: Macmillan, 1990.

Myrdal, Gunnar. *An American Dilemma: The Negro Problem and Modern Democracy.* New York: McGraw-Hill, 1944.

Neely, Mark E. *The Last Best Hope of Earth: Abraham Lincoln and the Promise of America.* Cambridge: Harvard University Press, 1995.

Nelson, Scott Reynolds, and Carol Sheriff. *A People at War: Civilians and Soldiers in America's Civil War, 1854–1877.* New York: Oxford University Press, 2007.

Ninkovich, Frank. *The United States and Imperialism.* Oxford: Blackwell, 2001.

Nisbett, Richard E. *The Geography of Thought: How Asians and Westerners Think Differently . . . and Why.* New York: Free Press, 2003.

Nisbett, Richard E., and Dov Cohen. *Culture of Honor: The Psychology of Violence in the South.* Boulder, CO: Westview Press, 1996.

Noll, Mark A., and Luke E. Harlow, eds. *Religion and American Politics: From the Colonial Period to the Present.* New York: Oxford University Press, 2007.

Nordholt, Jan Willem Schulte. *Woodrow Wilson: A Life for World Peace.* Berkeley: University of California Press, 1991.

Offner, John L. *An Unwanted War: The Diplomacy of the United States and Spain over Cuba, 1895–1898.* Chapel Hill: University of North Carolina Press, 1992.

O'Hanlon, Michael E. "A Flawed Masterpiece." *Foreign Affairs* 81, no. 3 (May/June 2002): 47–63.

Olcott, Charles S. *The Life of William McKinley.* Vol. 2. New York: Houghton Mifflin, 1916.

Olson, James S., and Randy Roberts. *Where the Domino Fell: America and Vietnam, 1945–1995.* New York: St. Martin's Press, 1996.

Oneal, John R., Brad Lian, and James H. Joyner, Jr. "Are the American People 'Pretty Prudent'? Public Responses to U.S. Uses of Force, 1950–1988." *International Studies Quarterly* 40, no. 2 (June 1996): 261–79.

O'Neill, William L. *A Democracy at War: America's Fight at Home and Abroad in World War II.* New York: Free Press, 1993.

Osgood, Robert E. *Ideals and Self-Interest in America's Foreign Relations.* Chicago: University of Chicago Press, 1953.

Overy, Richard. *Why the Allies Won*. New York: W. W. Norton, 1995.

Owen, Wilfred, and C. Day Lewis. *The Collected Poems of Wilfred Owen*. New York: New Directions, 1964.

Painter, Nell Irvin. *Standing at Armageddon: The United States, 1877–1919*. New York: W. W. Norton, 1987.

Palmer, Bruce, Jr. *Intervention in the Caribbean: The Dominican Crisis of 1965*. Lexington: University Press of Kentucky, 1989.

Paludan, Philip Shaw. *"A People's Contest": The Union and Civil War, 1861–1865*. Lawrence: University Press of Kansas, 1996.

Parish, Peter J. "From Necessary Evil to National Blessing: The Northern Protestant Clergy Interpret the Civil War." In *An Uncommon Time: The Civil War and the Northern Home Front*, edited by Paul A. Cimbala and Randall M. Miller, 61–89. New York: Fordham University Press, 2002.

———. "The War for the Union as a Just War." In *Aspects of War in American History*, edited by David K. Adams and Cornelis A. van Minnen, 81–103. Keele, UK: Keele University Press, 1997.

Pearlman, Michael. *Warmaking and American Democracy: The Struggle over Military Strategy, 1700 to the Present*. Lawrence: University Press of Kansas, 1990.

Peceny, Mark. *Democracy at the Point of Bayonets*. University Park: Pennsylvania State University Press, 1999.

Pérez, Jr., Louis A. "The Meaning of the Maine: Causation and the Historiography of the Spanish-American War." *Pacific Historical Review* 58, no. 3 (August 1989): 293–322.

Perman, Michael. *The Road to Redemption: Southern Politics, 1869–1879*. Chapel Hill: University of North Carolina Press, 1985.

Pike, Fredrick B. *FDR's Good Neighbor Policy: Sixty Years of Generally Gentle Chaos*. Austin: University of Texas Press, 1995.

Pillar, Paul R. "Ending Limited War: The Psychological Dynamics of the Termination Process." In *Psychological Dimensions of War*, edited by Betty Glad, 252–63. Newbury Park, CA: Sage, 1990.

Porter, Patrick. "Good Anthropology, Bad History: The Cultural Turn in Studying War." *Parameters* 37, no. 2 (Summer 2007): 45–58.

Powell, Colin. *My American Journey*. With Joseph Persico. New York: Random House, 1995.

Power, Samantha. *"A Problem from Hell": America and the Age of Genocide*. New York: Perennial, 2003.

Powers, Thomas. *The War at Home: Vietnam and the American People, 1964–1968*. New York: Grossman, 1973.

Pratt, Julius W. *Expansionists of 1898: The Acquisition of Hawaii and the Spanish Islands*. Baltimore: Johns Hopkins University Press, 1936.

Preston, Andrew. "Bridging the Gap Between the Sacred and the Secular in the History of American Foreign Relations." *Diplomatic History* 30, no. 5 (November 2006): 783–812.

Prucha, Francis Paul. *Broadax and Bayonet: The Role of the United States Army in the Development of the Northwest, 1815–1860.* Lincoln: University of Nebraska Press, 1995.

———. *The Sword of the Republic: The United States Army on the Frontier, 1783–1846.* New York: Macmillan, 1969.

Putnam, Carleton. *Theodore Roosevelt: A Biography.* New York: Scribner, 1958.

Quervain, Dominique J.-F. de, et al. "The Neural Basis of Altruistic Punishment." *Science* 305, no. 5688 (August 2004): 1254–58.

Record, Jeffrey. *The Wrong War: Why We Lost in Vietnam.* Annapolis, MD: Naval Institute Press, 1998.

Redkey, Edwin S., ed. *A Grand Army of Black Men: Letters from African-American Soldiers in the Union Army, 1861–1865.* Cambridge: Cambridge University Press, 1992.

Rice, Condoleezza. "Promoting the National Interest." *Foreign Affairs* 79, no. 1 (January/February 2000): 45–62.

Richardson, Heather Cox. *The Death of Reconstruction: Race, Labor, and Politics in the Post–Civil War North, 1865–1901.* Cambridge: Harvard University Press, 2001.

Richler, Mordecai, ed. *Writers on World War II: An Anthology.* New York: Knopf, 1991.

Ricks, Thomas E. *Fiasco: The American Military Adventure in Iraq.* New York: Penguin, 2006.

Roberts, Randy, and James S. Olson. *John Wayne, American.* Lincoln, NE: Bison Books, 1998.

Rochester, Stuart I. *American Liberal Disillusionment in the Wake of World War I.* University Park: Pennsylvania State University Press, 1977.

Roosevelt, Franklin. "Our Foreign Policy: A Democratic View." *Foreign Affairs* 6, no. 4 (July 1928): 573–86.

Rose, Kenneth D. *Myth and the Greatest Generation: A Social History of Americans in World War II.* New York: Routledge, 2008.

Rotberg, Robert I. *Haiti: The Politics of Squalor.* Boston: Houghton Mifflin, 1971.

Rottinghaus, Brandon. "Following the 'Mail Hawks': Alternative Measures of Public Opinion on Vietnam." *Public Opinion Quarterly* 71, no. 3 (Fall 2007): 367–91.

Rourke, John T. *Presidential Wars and American Democracy: Rally 'Round the Chief.* New York: Paragon House, 1993.

Rozell, Mark J. "Media Coverage of the Persian Gulf War." In *The Presidency and the Persian Gulf War,* edited by Marcia Lynn Whicker, James P. Pfiffner, and Raymond A. Moore, 153–75. Westport, CT: Praeger, 1993.

Rubin, Anne Sarah. *A Shattered Nation: The Rise and Fall of the Confederacy, 1861–1868.* Chapel Hill: University of North Carolina Press.

Rumsfeld, Donald H. *The National Defense Strategy of the United States of America.* Washington, DC: U.S. Department of Defense, 2005.

Russell, Richard B., Cal M. Logue, and Dwight L. Freshley. *Voice of Georgia: Speeches of Richard B. Russell, 1928–1969.* Macon, GA: Mercer University Press, 1997.

Rystad, Göran. *Ambiguous Imperialism: American Foreign Policy and Domestic Politics at the Turn of the Century*. Lund, Sweden: Esselte Studium, 1975.

Sadowski, Yahya. *The Myth of Global Chaos*. Washington, DC: Brookings Institution, 1998.

Schaffer, Ronald. *Wings of Judgment: American Bombing in World War II*. New York: Oxford University Press, 1985.

Schama, Simon. *The American Future: A History*. London: Bodley Head, 2008.

Schirmer, Daniel B. *Republic or Empire: American Resistance to the Philippine War*. Cambridge, MA: Schenkman, 1972.

Schmidt, Hans. *The United States Occupation of Haiti, 1915–1934*. New Brunswick, NJ: Rutgers University Press, 1995.

Schmitz, David F. *Henry L. Stimson: The First Wise Man*. Lanham, MD: Rowman & Littlefield, 2001.

————. *Thank God They're on Our Side: The United States and Right-Wing Dictatorships, 1921–1965*. Chapel Hill: University of North Carolina Press, 1999.

Schneider, William. "'Rambo' and Reality: Having It Both Ways." In *Eagle Resurgent? The Reagan Era in American Foreign Policy*, edited by Kenneth A. Oye, Robert J. Lieber, and Donald Rothchild, 41–72. Boston: Little, Brown, 1983.

Schoultz, Lars. *Beneath the United States: A History of U.S. Policy Toward Latin America*. Cambridge: Harvard University Press, 1998.

Schroeder, Paul W. "Alliances, 1815–1945: Weapons of Power and Tools of Management." In *Historical Dimension of National Security Problems*, edited by Klaus Knorr, 227–62. Lawrence, KS: Allen Press, 1976.

Schuman, Howard, and Amy D. Corning. "Comparing Iraq to Vietnam: Recognition, Recall, and the Nature of Cohort Effects." *Public Opinion Quarterly* 70, no. 1 (Spring 2006): 78–87.

Schuman, Howard, and Cheryl Rieger. "Historical Analogies, Generational Effects, and Attitudes Toward War." *American Sociological Review* 57, no. 3 (June 1992): 315–26.

Schuman, Howard, and Jacqueline Scott. "Generations and Collective Memories." *American Sociological Review* 54, no. 3 (June 1989): 359–81.

Schwartz, Barry. "Memory as a Cultural System: Abraham Lincoln in World War II." *American Sociological Review* 61, no. 5 (October 1996): 908–27.

Scott, Jacqueline, and Lilian Zac. "Collective Memories in Britain and the United States." *Public Opinion Quarterly* 57, no. 3 (Fall 1993): 315–31.

Sewall, Sarah B. "Multilateral Peace Operations." In *Multilateralism and U.S. Foreign Policy: Ambivalent Engagement*, edited by Stewart Patrick and Shepard Forman, 191–224. Boulder, CO: Lynne Reiner, 2002.

Seybolt, Taylor B. *Humanitarian Military Intervention: The Conditions for Success and Failure*. Oxford: Oxford University Press, 2007.

Shafer, D. Michael. *Deadly Paradigms: The Failure of U.S. Counterinsurgency Policy*. Princeton, NJ: Princeton University Press, 1988.

Shawcross, William. *Deliver Us from Evil: Peacekeepers, Warlords and a World of Endless Conflict*. New York: Simon & Schuster, 2000.

Sheehan, James J. *Where Have All the Soldiers Gone? The Transformation of Modern Europe.* New York: Houghton Mifflin, 2008.

Sherry, Michael S. *In the Shadow of War: The United States Since the 1930s.* New Haven, CT: Yale University Press, 1995.

Silber, Nina. *Daughters of the Union: Northern Women Fight the Civil War.* Cambridge: Harvard University Press, 2005.

Silbey, David J. *A War of Frontier and Empire.* New York: Hill & Wang, 2007.

Silverstone, Scott A. *Divided Union: The Politics of War in the Early American Republic.* Ithaca, NY: Cornell University Press, 2004.

Simon, John Y. "Grant, Lincoln, and Unconditional Surrender." In *Lincoln's Generals,* edited by Gabor S. Boritt, 161–98. New York: Oxford University Press, 1994.

Simpson, Brooks D. *The Reconstruction Presidents.* Lawrence: University Press of Kansas, 1998.

Simpson, John. *From the House of War: John Simpson in the Gulf.* London: Arrow Books, 1991.

Singer, Peter. *The President of Good and Evil: The Ethics of George W. Bush.* New York: Dutton, 2004.

Singer, Tania, et al. "Empathic Neural Responses Are Modulated by the Perceived Fairness of Others," *Nature* 439, no. 7075 (January 2006): 466–69.

Sittser, Gerald L. *A Cautious Patriotism: The American Churches and the Second World War.* Chapel Hill: University of North Carolina Press, 1997.

Slap, Andrew L. *The Doom of Reconstruction: The Liberal Republicans in the Civil War Era.* New York: Fordham University Press, 2006.

Small, Melvin. *Democracy and Diplomacy: The Impact of Domestic Politics on U.S. Foreign Policy, 1789–1994.* Baltimore: Johns Hopkins University Press, 1996.

Smith, Ephraim K. "William McKinley's Enduring Legacy: The Historiographical Debate on the Taking of the Philippine Islands." In *Crucible of Empire: The Spanish-American War and Its Aftermath,* edited by James C. Bradford, 205–49. Annapolis, MD: Naval Institute Press, 1993.

Smith, Joseph. *The Spanish-American War: Conflict in the Caribbean and the Pacific, 1895–1902.* London: Longman, 1994.

Smith, Tony. *America's Mission: The United States and the Worldwide Struggle for Democracy in the Twentieth Century.* Princeton, NJ: Princeton University Press, 1994.

Snow, Donald M., and Dennis M. Drew. *From Lexington to Desert Storm: War and Politics in the American Experience.* New York: M. E. Sharpe, 1994.

Sobel, Richard. *The Impact of Public Opinion on U.S. Foreign Policy Since Vietnam.* New York: Oxford University Press, 2001.

Sondhaus, Lawrence. *Strategic Culture and Ways of War.* New York: Routledge, 2006.

Stanley, Peter W. *A Nation in the Making: The Philippines and the United States, 1899–1921.* Cambridge: Harvard University Press, 1974.

Steel, Ronald. "An Iraq Syndrome?" *Survival* 49, no. 1 (Spring 2007): 153–62.

Steinbeck, John. *Once There Was a War.* New York: Viking, 1958.

Stephanson, Anders. *Manifest Destiny: American Expansion and the Empire of Right.* New York: Hill & Wang, 1995.

Stewart, James Brewer. *Holy Warriors: The Abolitionists and American Slavery.* New York: Hill & Wang, 1976.

Stouffer, Samuel, et al. *The American Soldier: Combat and Its Aftermath.* Vol. 2. Princeton, NJ: Princeton University Press, 1949.

Stout, Harry S. *Upon the Altar of the Nation: A Moral History of the Civil War.* New York: Penguin, 2006.

Stuart, Reginald C. *The Half-way Pacifist: Thomas Jefferson's View of War.* Toronto: University of Toronto Press, 1978.

————. *War and American Thought: From the Revolution to the Monroe Doctrine.* Kent, OH: Kent State University Press, 1982.

Sullivan, Patricia L. "Sustaining the Fight: A Cross-Sectional Time Series Analysis of Public Support for Ongoing Military Interventions." Paper presented at the American Political Science Association Conference, Philadelphia, 2006.

Summers, Harry G. *On Strategy: A Critical Analysis of the Vietnam War.* Novato, CA: Presidio Press, 1995.

Tate, Michael L. *The Frontier Army in the Settlement of the West.* Norman: University of Oklahoma Press, 2001.

Terkel, Studs. *"The Good War": An Oral History of World War II.* New York: Ballantine, 1990.

Thompson, John A. "Progressive Publicists and the First World War, 1914–1917." *Journal of American History* 58, no. 2 (September 1971): 364–83.

————. *Woodrow Wilson: Profiles in Power.* New York: Longman, 2002.

Tiebout, Frank B. *A History of the 305th Infantry.* Whitefish, MT: Kessinger, 2005.

Tierney, Dominic. "America's Quagmire Mentality." *Survival* 49, no. 4 (Winter 2007/2008): 47–66.

Tierney, John J., Jr. *Chasing Ghosts: Unconventional Warfare in American History.* Washington, DC: Potomac Books, 2006.

Tocqueville, Alexis de. *Democracy in America and Two Essays on America.* New York: Penguin Classics, 2003.

Tompkins, E. Berkeley. *Anti-imperialism in the United States: The Great Debate, 1890–1920.* Philadelphia: University of Pennsylvania Press, 1970.

Totten, Michael J. "The (Really) Moderate Muslims of Kosovo." *City Journal* 18, no. 4 (Autumn 2008), available at http://www.city-journal.org/2008/18_4_kosovo_muslims.html.

Traxel, David. *Crusader Nation: The United States in Peace and the Great War, 1898–1920.* New York: Knopf, 2006.

Trefousse, Hans L. *Carl Schurz.* Knoxville: University of Tennessee Press, 1982.

Turner, Brian. "What Every Soldier Should Know." In *Here, Bullet.* Farmington, ME: Alice James Books, 2005.

Tuveson, Ernest Lee. *Redeemer Nation: The Idea of America's Millennial Role.* Chicago: University of Chicago Press, 1968.

Twain, Mark. *A Connecticut Yankee in King Arthur's Court*. New York: Harper & Brothers, 1917.

Twain, Mark, and David Rachels. *Mark Twain's Civil War*. Lexington: University Press of Kentucky, 2007.

Unger, Nancy C. *Fighting Bob La Follette: The Righteous Reformer*. Chapel Hill: University of North Carolina Press, 2000.

Unnever, James D., and Francis T. Cullen. "Christian Fundamentalism and Support for Capital Punishment." *Journal of Research in Crime and Delinquency* 43, no. 2 (May 2006): 169–97.

U.S. Department of the Army. *The U.S. Army/Marine Corps Counterinsurgency Field Manual*. Chicago: University of Chicago Press, 2007.

U.S. Department of Defense. *Quadrennial Defense Review*. Washington, DC: Department of Defense, February 6, 2006, http://www.defense.gov/qdr/report/Report20060203.pdf.

Valentino, Benjamin, Paul Huth, and Sarah Croco. "Bear Any Burden? How Democracies Minimize the Costs of War." Unpublished manuscript.

Vertzberger, Yaacov Y. I. *The World in Their Minds: Information Processing, Cognition, and Perception in Foreign Policy Decisionmaking*. Stanford, CA: Stanford University Press, 1990.

von Hippel, Karin. *Democracy by Force: US Military Intervention in the Post–Cold War World*. Cambridge: Cambridge University Press, 2000.

Vought, Donald B. "Preparing for the Wrong War." *Military Review* 57, no. 5 (May 1977): 16–34.

Wagoner, Jennings L., Jr., and Christine Coalwell McDonald. "Mr. Jefferson's Academy." In *Thomas Jefferson's Military Academy: Founding West Point,* edited by Robert M. S. McDonald, 118–53. Charlottesville: University of Virginia Press, 2004.

Walker, Dale L. "Last of the Rough Riders." *Montana: The Magazine of Western History* 23, no. 3 (Summer 1973): 40–50.

Walzer, Michael. *Just and Unjust Wars: A Moral Argument with Historical Illustrations*. New York: Basic Books, 2006.

Warren, Robert Penn. *The Legacy of the Civil War*. Lincoln: University of Nebraska Press, 1998.

Weigley, Russell F. *The American Way of War: A History of United States Military Strategy and Policy*. New York: Macmillan, 1973.

Weiss, Thomas G. *Military-Civilian Interactions: Humanitarian Crises and the Responsibility to Protect*. New York: Rowman & Littlefield, 2005.

Welch, Richard E., Jr. *Response to Imperialism: The United States and the Philippine-American War, 1899–1902*. Chapel Hill: University of North Carolina Press, 1979.

Westbrook, Robert B. "Fighting for the American Family: Private Interests and Political Obligation in World War II." In *The Power of Culture: Critical Essays in American History,* edited by Richard Wightman Fox and T. J. Jackson Lears, 195–222. Chicago: University of Chicago Press, 1993.

Wheeler, Nicholas J. *Saving Strangers: Humanitarian Intervention in International Society*. Oxford: Oxford University Press, 2000.

Whitfield, Stephen J. "Korea, the Cold War, and American Democracy." In *War and Democracy: A Comparative Study of the Korean War and the Peloponnesian War*, edited by David McCann and Barry S. Strauss, 216–37. Armonk, NY: M. E. Sharpe, 2001.

Whitman, Walt, and Michael Warner. *The Portable Walt Whitman*. New York: Penguin, 2003.

Widenor, William C. *Henry Cabot Lodge and the Search for an American Foreign Policy*. Berkeley: University of California Press, 1983.

Wilkerson, Marcus M. *Public Opinion and the Spanish-American War: A Study in War Propaganda*. New York: Russell & Russell, 1967.

Willman, Chris. *Rednecks and Bluenecks: The Politics of Country Music*. New York: New Press, 2005.

Wilson, Edmund. *Patriotic Gore*. New York: Oxford University Press, 1962.

Wilson, Woodrow. *President Wilson's State Papers and Addresses*. New York: George H. Doran, 1918.

Wilson, Woodrow, and Arthur S. Link. *The Papers of Woodrow Wilson*. Vol. 41. Princeton, NJ: Princeton University Press, 1994.

Wiltz, John Edward. "The Korean War and American Society." In *The Korean War: A 25-Year Perspective*, edited by Francis H. Heller, 112–58. Lawrence: Regents Press of Kansas, 1977.

Winders, Richard Bruce. *Mr. Polk's Army: The American Military Experience in the Mexican War*. College Station: Texas A&M University Press, 1997.

Wittkopf, Eugene R., Christopher M. Jones, and Charles W. Kegley. *American Foreign Policy: Pattern and Process*. Belmont, CA: Thomson, 2008.

Wood, Bryce. *The Making of the Good Neighbor Policy*. New York: Columbia University Press, 1961.

Woodiwiss, Michael. *Organized Crime and American Power: A History*. Toronto: University of Toronto Press, 2001.

Woods, James L. "U.S. Government Decisionmaking Processes During Humanitarian Operations in Somalia." In *Learning from Somalia: The Lessons of Armed Humanitarian Intervention*, edited by Walter S. Clarke and Jeffrey Ira Herbst, 151–72. Boulder, CO: Westview Press, 1997.

Woods, Randall B. "Dixie's Dove: J. William Fulbright, the Vietnam War, and the American South." In *Vietnam and the American Political Tradition: The Politics of Dissent*, edited by Randall B. Woods, 149–70. Cambridge: Cambridge University Press, 2003.

Woodward, Bob. *Bush at War*. New York: Simon & Schuster, 2003.

———. *Plan of Attack*. New York: Simon & Schuster, 2004.

Woodward, C. Vann. "The Political Legacy of Reconstruction." In *Reconstruction: An Anthology of Revisionist Writings*, edited by Kenneth M. Stampp and Leon F. Litwack, 516–31. Baton Rouge: Louisiana State University Press, 1969.

Woodworth, Steven E. *While God Is Marching On: The Religious World of Civil War Soldiers*. Lawrence: University Press of Kansas, 2001.

Wright, Bradford W. *Comic Book Nation: The Transformation of Youth Culture in America*. Baltimore: Johns Hopkins University Press, 2001.

Zinn, Howard. *A People's History of the United States*. New York: HarperCollins, 1999.

Zuczek, Richard. *State of Rebellion: Reconstruction in South Carolina*. Columbia: University of South Carolina Press, 1996.

INDEX

alternative explanations for, 276n30
changing world and, 8–9
crusade tradition compared with,
52–53, 277n36
as dangerous, 50–51
emergence of, 265
enemy playbook gifted by, 51–52
images of, 35–36
memory skewed by, 52
nation-builders upholding, 49–50
partisanship politics and, 302n98
resolve and, 51
rethinking, 250–67
skepticism regarding, 35–37, 50–52
value of, 267
ways of war and, 10–12, 248–49, 271n8
Quantrill, William T., 64
Quezon, Manuel, 113
Quiet American, The (Greene), 184

Ransier, Alonzo, 74–75, 79
Rather, Dan, 220
Reagan, Ronald, 179, 188, 211
Reconstruction, Southern
accomplishments of, 79–80
black leaders and, 74–75
conservative revival and, 75–76
criticism of, 77–78
deal to end, 88, 281n121
fatigue with, 83–84
Fulbright regarding, 186–87
idealism regarding, 81–82, 83
imperialism and, 86–87
Iraq nation-building compared with, 34
military rule during, 76
Philippines and, 118
Profiles in Courage and, 88–89
redemption and, 87–88
tardiness of, 89–90
terrorism during, 82–83
vengeance and, 80–81
welfarism and, 84–86
religion
Afghanistan War and, 225–27
Civil War and, 68–69, 70–71
Gulf War and, 198
idealism and, 22–23
Iraq War and, 225–27
Spanish-American War and,
100–102

World War I and, 132–35
World War II and, 159–60
Revolutionary War, secession and, 278n32
Rice, Condoleezza, 211, 217–18, 230
Rickenbacker, Edward, 125, 138
Rockwell, Norman, 159
Roosevelt, Franklin, 53, 114
Caribbean interventions and, 143
"Four Freedoms" and, 159
good neighbor policy of, 145–46
Hitler, Patrick, and, 153
idealism of, 158–60
Pearl Harbor and, 163
on policing Western Hemisphere, 140
on responsibility, 160
Roosevelt, Theodore, 102, 106, 135
on difficult steering, 152
idealism and, 132
Philippines and, 110, 112, 116
as Rough Rider, 95–96
World War I and, 122, 127
Ross, Sam, 234–35
Rough Riders, 95–96
Rumsfeld, Donald, 48, 217–18, 230,
242–43, 246, 249
Rusk, Dean, 173
Russell, Richard B., 186
Rwanda, 215

Sam, Vilbrun Guillaume, 139
Samar, 109–10
Sandino, Augusto, 142
Schurz, Carl, 78, 82, 102, 110, 111
Schwarzkopf, H. "Stormin'
Norman," 194
Scott, Winfield, 58
September 11, 2001
images of, 218–19
U.S. resolve regarding, 3–4
vengeance and, 227–28
Sewall, Sarah, 208
Shannon, Robert, 163
Shawcross, William, 209
Sheehan, James, 19
Sherman, William T., 56, 62, 63, 72, 194
Sinanovic, Meho, 206
Smith, Jacob "Hell Roaring Jake," 109,
116, 119
Smith, Moses, 68
Smith, Tony, 24